मी अल्बर्ट एलिस

I am Albert Ellis

Dr. Anjali Joshi

Translated from Marathi by

Meenal Kelkar

Wordizen Books

ISBN 978-93-52019-47-2
© Dr. Anjali Joshi 2016

Cover: Riyaz Merchant, Kitsuné India
Editing: Suchita Vemuri
Layouts: Chandravadan R Shiroorkar, Leadstart Design
Printing: Printed at Repro

First published in India 2017 by
WORDIZEN BOOKS
An imprint of
LEADSTART PUBLISHING PVT LTD
Unit 25-26, Building A/1, Near Wadala RTO,
Wadala (East), Mumbai – 400 037, INDIA
T + 91 22 2404 6887
Wwww.leadstartcorp.com

Dedicated to my mentor

K. M. Phadke,

The pioneer of REBT in India

Preface

D r. Albert Ellis, the eminent American psychologist, is immortal in the history of the subject. He not only revolutionized the field of psychotherapy but also created a new stream of cognitive psychotherapy. Most importantly, he developed REBT (Rational Emotive Behaviour Therapy) in 1955, a psychotherapy that has spread so rapidly in the past sixty years that it finds its application in several areas of life.

It was my mentor, K. M. Phadke, who introduced me to REBT in its true sense.

Phadke has enriched the field of REBT with his concepts and techniques. He has dedicated more than forty years of his life to the study of REBT, while consciously choosing to stay away from fame and acclaim.

Phadke's pioneering journey with REBT began in 1968, when he wrote his first letter to Ellis; who was kind enough to reply promptly. In fact, Dr. Ellis corresponded with him not once but several times, and replied tirelessly to his series of letters. To be precise, this unusual correspondence lasted 36 years.

One may wonder what this correspondence was about. It was a scholarly debate between the ascended master and his stalwart disciple; an exchange of thoughts between two great minds.

It consists of Phadke's innumerable queries and scientific enquiries about REBT and the meticulous answers given by Ellis. This correspondence is the most valuable resource for REBT scholars. It is bound in four volumes and consists of 1,351 pages.

When Phadke wrote his first letter to Ellis, he had no idea that this move would make a notable difference to his life. To spread and promote REBT had become his life goal, and he had eliminated everything else. He kept himself completely away from any source of entertainment. Television, cinema and other cultural programmes ceased to exist in his life thereafter, as they may have distracted him from his study of REBT. Ellis applauds Phadke's contribution with these apt words:

'Of all the followers, I have had, Kishore has surely been one of the most persistent and the very best. I could see from the start that he not only understood my teachings better than any other person in Asia, but was able to think about them and brilliantly add to them on his own and to present them beautifully to both professionals and members of the public. Kishore is indeed one of the most remarkable individuals I have ever met.'

No wonder, Phadke is the first and the only Indian psychologist who enjoys the unique distinction of being a Fellow and Supervisor of the Albert Ellis Institute for REBT, New York.

The Primary and Advanced Courses of REBT conducted by Phadke gave me an in-depth understanding of the subject. I was so impressed by the training that I continued to study this therapy under his guidance, and I still seek it even today.

When I began to study the works of Dr. Ellis from the core, I realised that his thoughts are not limited only to the field of psychology but that they encompass all aspects of life; especially a person's life-philosophy. This motivated me to set my own imprisoned mind free and reorient my thinking. I began to review my own life-philosophy. I had to deal with some fundamental questions about morality-immorality, the role of sexuality in life, the concept of sin, and many such soul-searching questions. As I was trying to find the answers from their roots, my vision became crystal clear. I gave up a few conventional beliefs I was holding on for years, without testing their objectivity. It was a radical transformation for me, for someone who had grown up in a traditional middle-class setting.

And it was during this phase that I came across the unpublished manuscript of 'Albert Ellis: A Rebellious Psychologist', written by Phadke. This script began with an abridged biography of Ellis, followed by the theory of REBT and the description of its fundamental principles and applications. The opening chapter of Ellis' biography caught my attention the most. Dr. Ellis' intellect, his thirst for knowledge and insatiable capacity for reading since childhood, his intensive study of philosophy, his triumph over illnesses, his zest for work till the last breath, his ceaseless and committed efforts to spread rational philosophy in the world — all of it was remarkable and astounding. I was determined to introduce his life to Marathi readers. I obtained Phadke's consent and began to translate his biography. I finished nearly half the work, when something felt amiss. This 'something' was not something I could ignore; it constantly nagged me.

I strongly felt that just describing the incidents of Dr. Ellis's life was inadequate. One would read about his life's journey but not understand his psyche. The theory of REBT states that our behaviour and emotions originate from our beliefs towards events, and not the events themselves. I noticed several gaps when I read the incidents in his life with this perspective. These gaps were related to his thought process, but it was hard to understand this process from simply a description of the events. It felt more important to trace his responses to those incidents rather than the incidents themselves. I strongly felt that while explaining his life-philosophy, it was necessary to lay more emphasis on his thought process. From childhood itself, Dr. Ellis followed a certain philosophy of his own. Even as a child, he unknowingly nurtured the basic principles of REBT in his own life. Somewhere within me, I realised there was an earnest desire to capture the origin of these principles in Ellis' entire life-journey and weave them into a story.

Now the question before me was about choosing the literary genre. I was passionate about writing creatively on Ellis' life. I soon realised that the biography was not the genre I was looking for, and that there was no other alternative to the 'novel'. Until then, I had written narrative non-fiction on topics related to psychology. Although experimenting with a novel was a quantum leap for me, I decided to deep dive into it. I began mapping the mind-journey of his life, a long one. Ellis lived from 1913 to 2007.

I made many new discoveries as I tried to enter Ellis' mind. The first impression the biography gave me was that of a cold and unemotional personality. But as I began thinking deeper, I felt the need to re-examine my view. I had studied his theory of personality. I was acquainted with his in-depth evaluation of emotions and the analysis of empathy he did in REBT. I realised that such evaluation and empathy was not possible unless one had a very high level of sensitivity and the ability to experience intense emotions. Gradually, his sensitivity, which initially seemed non-existent, began to be visible. I also realised that this sensitivity was not vulnerability, but in fact, a never-ending source of his full-blown creativity.

With this new perspective, I began to study his life once again. His love for Karyl in his youth, or the mature love he had for Jane later in his life; neither of this would have been possible without deep emotional involvement. This realization validated my premise about his sensitivity. My derivation that although Dr. Ellis was keen on rational thinking, he was nevertheless quite a compassionate person was confirmed. Now I could see several new dimensions of his personality that proved his compassion but were not outlined in the biography. I searched for this 'compassionate human' in his persona and this novel is the culmination of this search.

Along with uncovering elements of his personality, a study of his thoughts about sex and sexuality was an inevitable part of this search. Dr. Ellis had worked as a sexologist before he entered the field of psychology. His views on sex were received as revolutionary and path-breaking even in a progressive country like America. But these views had all been derived only after scientific research. These views appeared in his essays repeatedly, and he faced severe criticism and opposition for the same. But he showed extraordinary courage and never allowed the criticism to affect his research. His study on the subject of sexology is an important segment of his career and he was duly honoured by several esteemed institutions for it. His views about sex are an inseparable part of his life-philosophy, and have therefore been given their due place in this novel.

Ellis' views on masturbation, sexual desire, sexual freedom, heterosexual and homosexual relationships, the institution of marriage and other perspectives expressed in this book may be open to debate. I have focused solely on Ellis's point of view while writing them. To give justice to his thoughts I have made a sincere effort to place everything before the readers without any reservations.

As I read the biography I realised that the incidents referred in it were very sketchy, brief, and appeared randomly. Some incidents seemed irrelevant. It became necessary to insert fictional fillers in many places without disturbing the original events. These incidents are true but the development or unfolding of Ellis's mind is entirely imaginary.

In the biography, his mother (Hattie), father (Henry), brother (Paul), sister (Janet), friend (Manny), and the women in his life—mainly Karyl, Gertrude, Rhoda, Janet Wolf, Debbie, were all referred to so briefly that it was difficult to describe any of them clearly. To open up Ellis' mental world to the reader, it was extremely necessary to unravel the hidden intricacies of the relationships he had with each of them. I began to study these relationships minutely and as a result, his mental journey began getting clearer. These relationships that enriched his emotional world were not similar in character. Each one was specific, since he experienced each of them at different stages of his life. Each relationship had influenced his life differently but significantly.

To emphasize this aspect, I felt it was necessary to give each person a distinct identity. I began searching for the focal point of each relationship. Once I found that, it became easy to define the position of Ellis in each of these relationships. In this process, along with the main characters, some new side-characters were created quite naturally. As incidents, characters, and circumstances began merging smoothly it became interesting to see various unseen facets of Ellis' personality.

The biographical and theoretical content of this novel is based on the earlier manuscript referred by Phadke. But for all other references about psychology, philosophy, literature, information about New York and other cities, historical and geographical references about America. I have made use of several Marathi and English books and internet websites. I have used original quotes wherever possible.

To my great advantage all those who read the manuscript helped me to improve upon it voluntarily. It made the process of writing a joyful one. This preface would be incomplete if I do not express my gratitude for those who supported me wholeheartedly in this work.

First and foremost, I have to thank my mentor K. M. Phadke. He made available his handwritten English manuscript, the fruit of a ten-year-long study of innumerable essays and articles published in 98 professional journals. He also gave me his consent for adapting it in fictional form, and offered his valuable guidance selflessly from time to time. This extraordinary gesture has definitely elevated my respect for him greatly. He gave me a new vision towards psychology and also towards life. This has helped me not only while writing the novel but also in my professional and personal life.

It is very important for me to thank Dr. Uma Kulkarni and Shri. Virupaksha Kulkarni for their help in the construction of the novel. Their efforts on the manuscript are invaluable. They showed me how to treat writing as a piece of art and gave me elementary lessons in the skill of using dialogues, incidents and language. As a result I began to think about words and language seriously and objectively. All this necessitated a total revision in the script, which I eventually did, albeit under their guidance.

Their involvement in the writing, as if it was their own creation, was very inspiring. They conducted discussions several times on many points, untiringly. It is extremely difficult to express my gratitude for their effort and time (despite their busy schedule) in mere words.

During this period my association with them became deeper and stronger. It was very overwhelming to receive their warm support all the way. Only from them did I learn to improve upon my mistakes without getting discouraged. I also learned how to give positive motivation and how to express views objectively and without insistence. This process of learning was memorable. It has definitely enriched me and I hope to continue this practice in the future as well.

I would also like to thank Nilima Palwankar for the sincere interest she showed in this novel. It was our encouraging discussions that inspired me to continue writing.

Dr. Harishchandra Thorat made a few hard suggestions about the format of the original manuscript. This enabled me to review the manuscript with greater objectivity and awareness. I used his suggestions while rewriting the script. Dr. Milind Malshe and he translated the entire poem, 'Road Not Taken' by Robert Frost, into Marathi and made the selection of precise lines from this work very easy.

I also gave the manuscript to Meenal Kelkar with whom I share a very long and close friendship. Earlier too I have had the privilege of asking her for suggestions for my other works. Once again this time, her remarks and suggestions contributed towards rendering the manuscript complete. Not only did she review the manuscript, she further took on the responsibility of its English translation. With great persistence and arduous efforts, she completed the translation successfully. The entire credit of this script goes to her and I wholeheartedly thank her.

With the same privilege, I requested Mrs.Neelima Mysore to look at the manuscript, and her suggestions were definitely helpful.

Many a time, the experience of writing turns out to be a pleasant process but getting it published can be challenging. Fortunately, for me, it was not so. I am very thankful to Shri Yeshu Patil of Shabd Publication for its Marathi edition.

I also sincerely thank Leadstart Publications for undertaking the publication of this English translation. It is definitely heartening to know that the novel will now reach a wider audience. It's only thanks to their participation that a regional-language novel will receive an opportunity to find its place in the vast arena of English writing.

Lastly, I would like to mention my family, my greatest strength. We often tend to take our near and dear ones for granted. We overlook their sacrifice, their mute cooperation, the inconvenience caused to them; sometimes to such an extent that we consider thanking them a mere formality. I do not want to make this mistake and wish to refer to each of them individually.

My mother-in-law Late Smt. Rohini Joshi, the seniormost member of my family, completed her Masters in Science, but could not put to use her education professionally. Without nursing any regret, however, she took utmost care to ensure that this did not repeat with me. She did not limit her interest in my education alone, but has supported me all along by managing household responsibilities very capably. I could achieve success at every step in my education because of her support. It was only because of her encouragement that writing this novel became easy and hassle-free.

My husband Nikhilesh has always cooperated with my endeavours whole-heartedly. Our professions are entirely diverse; I work in the field of education, whereas he is a businessman. His interest in my field, therefore, holds special value for me. Only when one is mentally at peace one can work with total involvement and enjoy working. I could experience this peace because of Nikhilesh. Words are possibly not enough to describe this kind of support.

The youngest member of my family is Anay, my son. He is too young to understand the novel, but he was a huge help when I was stuck due to technical problems with the computer. Lately, it has become difficult to do any work without his help in this regard.

Directly or indirectly, many have helped me in this work and it is not possible to mention all of them. But it is thanks to all of them that I am able to present this novel before the world. I hope it appeals to the readers.

1st January 2017.   Dr. Anjali Joshi

Translating 'Mee Albert Ellis'

I was not surprised when Anjali gave me the manuscript of her Marathi novel 'Mee Albert Ellis' to read; the writer in her was already in full bloom. I had observed her passion about REBT; she was always busy conducting workshops and counselling. I knew about the meticulous homework she had done for this novel. She was dealing with a personality from a different country, from a bygone era, and most importantly, only a few bare threads of factual information that she had to 'weave', as she says, into a homogeneous fabric. Of course, her efforts made for the perfect woven material.

After reading the book I instantly felt that it had the potential of reaching readers from every social category. Over the years she has received fan mail from Marathi film celebrities, medical practitioners, and even prisoners from Yerawada Jail, Pune. I always felt that the novel had a universal appeal and should be presented before a wider audience, beyond the Marathi readership. The novel was entertaining, but more than that, it compelled the reader to introspect on his own life, his beliefs, and their true worth. The most important quality was the simplicity of narration that made REBT theory easy to understand and apply to one's own life.

It was but natural for me to get involved when the actual translation work began. Anjali and I share a unique friendship; the age difference between us was never a factor. She chose me as one of the first readers for her Marathi work and showed the same trust while giving her consent to translate it into English. Although I had become familiar with REBT, I found the work really challenging. It was akin to a theatre-actor getting into the soul of a character created and envisaged by someone else. The subject of psychology was entirely alien to my engineering background. Because of the difference in the dialects, it was challenging several times to find apt and fitting words in English to match the original expression in Marathi, without affecting the flow of the sentence. I was blogging extensively on various internet platforms and the process of translation was a training exercise in fiction-writing. Anjali had great faith in this latent quality I seemed to possess according to her. We would have long sessions over the intricacies in REBT and serious debates over employment of suitable words, so that there was no deviation or misinterpretation of Ellis' theory. Every language has its own flavour and its roots in the culture of its own land and I have tried my best to retain the original essence that Marathi renders.

Writing had been just a hobby for me so far. I am extremely thankful to Madhavi Purohit and the editorial team of Leadstart Publications for elevating my status to a professional writer. When self-publishing has become the new mantra for today's upcoming writers, I consider it an honour to have my work published and will always remain thankful to Leadstart Publications for giving me this opportunity.

My family, especially my husband Mohan, was my pillar of strength, motivating and supporting every activity I undertake. My children, although thousands of miles away, also lent their support in their own capacity. This kept me going and sustained my spirits during this period.

I am confident that the English novel also achieves the same success as the Marathi one.

1st January 2017   Meenal Kelkar

1

'Bed no. 11?'

'Yes?'

'Name?'

'Albert Ellis.'

'Date of birth?'

'September 27, 1913'.

'Parents?'

'Father, Henry; Mother, Hattie.'

'Disease?'

'Nephritis.'

These questions were asked so often by the doctors on rounds, that I now answered them almost mechanically. This was followed my medical case history. I was truly bored of this routine. It was one of those dull Sundays at the hospital, accompanied by the usual anxiety: Who will come to see me today… Mom or Dad? But it was quite late in the evening, and by now I had no hope of seeing them. This would happen on many Sundays. The time reserved for parents to see their children was between four and six in the evening on Wednesdays and Sundays. Our children's ward had many kids like me and the dreary atmosphere would become very lively with the hustle and bustle of visiting parents on these days. So was it today, except for mine.

The bell rang for the visitors to leave. The doctors had begun their rounds. Now I knew for sure that no one was coming. Nobody had time for me. I looked through the window sadly. The twilight colours had etched the skyline. The West Bronx district was bathed in dazzling neon lights. Inside, there was the clutter of last-minute 'goodbyes' and 'take care' wishes from parents. My heart filled with bitterness. I closed the window shades and tried to forget my disappointment. I was getting accustomed to it these days.

I had spent many such lonely Wednesdays and Sundays. But today, it was my ninth birthday. I longed to see Mom and Dad. I was sure I could not leave the hospital for some more time. I was already depressed. This loneliness was so tormenting. Why am I always so sick? It all started with tonsillitis. Now it is some kidney disease called nephritis. How many times had I been in and out of hospitals since I was five? About eight times. This time I had been bedridden for almost ten months. When will I get rid of this horrible hospital? Mom, please come and take me home. I was desperate to return home.

In the beginning when I was hospitalised, Mom would come to see me very often. Dad would also come sometimes. They would bring many gifts. I would wait for them so eagerly. At times my illness would become very unbearable and these were the few happy moments I longed for during that hospital stay.

But this happiness soon turned out to be short-lived. Lately, neither had Dad visited for a while nor had Mom. What wrong had

I done? Was it my mistake that I was to be hospitalised? Did they not love me anymore? But why? Such questions disturbed me.

Whenever I saw the parents of other children, I would become furious. This familiar scene would make me violent, and it happened today as well. A burst of rage shot through me. I began punching my fists against the side railings of the bed. I even struck my head a few times against the wall. The head nurse came running.

'Albert, I am warning you for the last time today. Every Sunday and Wednesday, you misbehave and create a ruckus. You disturb the peace of this ward. Your tantrums scare the other kids. Can't you see that they have also begun to misbehave because of you? Mind you, if you behave like this again I will give you an injection with the biggest needle I have.'

Her words were terrifying. The image of that burly nurse piercing a thick needle cruelly into my thin frail body just froze me. I immediately became quiet. I had no option but to walk back to my bed and lie down.

But I kept fretting. This was all because of Mom and Dad. Don't they have any feelings for me? Here I am in the hospital lying alone for months together. How could they forget that it is my birthday today? Where has their love vanished? Or was there no love at all? Other children start crying whenever they remember their parents. But I never feel like crying. My parents never showed that much love for me that their absence could make me cry.

I don't know exactly what Dad does for a living. All I know is that he runs some sort of business and that he frequently changes his business. Probably that is why we sometimes have a Cadillac parked outside our house and even a maid to help Mom, and sometimes we don't even have enough food for all of us.

Most of the time, he is out on work. Whenever he is at home, he is busy playing cards. On some days he invites his friends. He hardly enquires about me but he does bid me 'goodbye' everyday when I leave for school. This is all I see of him.

And Mom? She never wakes up before nine in the morning. After finishing some work in the house, she goes to her friend's place to play cards. She likes to play bridge. If not cards, she goes to see operas. Then she returns late in the evening by six. Many a time on her way back, she buys pork sausages and bread or hot dogs for us. Then that becomes our dinner of the day. Sometimes the meat or the beef turns out so stale and dry that it crumbles down even before we can start eating. Sometimes, when Mom is in a good mood, she cooks at home. Usually it is baked potato knish or raw beef pastrami with herbs. These are special Jewish dishes she says, but they taste awful.

I always wonder why all the other children in the hospital eagerly wait for homemade food. Just the thought of it kills my appetite. Many times, Mom returns home very late. Paul, Janet and I get sleepy, waiting for her. Janet is four years younger to me. Without any apparent reason she is always cribbing about something. Paul is one and a half years younger to me. He cannot tolerate Janet's tantrums and often gets into a fight with her. Whenever they start quarrelling I feel confused. I try my best to settle their fight and make peace between them. But it upsets me.

In the story books I read, the parents are so nice and kind. Then why are my Mom and Dad not like them? Don't they feel any love for me? I remember very few times when I felt their affection. Once I was very sick with a splitting headache. I was very uneasy and restless because of the pain. That day Mom sat beside me for a long time, patting me gently. It felt so good. About Dad, I remember only one instance. It was sometime before Janet was born. Dad took all of us on a long drive. We had great fun. We ate blueberry-flavoured ice from a street vendor. I still remember the taste of that cold blueberry syrup dripping from the ice ball. But such memories are very few and I have treasured them deep in my heart.

When I go to see my school friends at their homes, I often see their families chatting together. In our family, we never sit together for a casual chat. Nobody is interested in knowing what the others are doing or what others think about a certain matter. We all live together in one house but separately.

I was four years old when, one day, something unexpected happened. It is still fresh in my memory. Those days we lived in Pittsburgh. Paul and I had a very happy life with lots of friends to play with. Suddenly one day, Mom and Dad packed our clothes and books, vacated the house and pushed us into a train for New York. They told us that we were moving to New York forever. The train was very crowded. Dad stuffed all of us on a small seat. He told us that we were leaving Pittsburgh for goodI would go to a new school and get new friends. I was shattered. I felt as if my life was taking a somersault. New York! So far I had only heard that it was the name of a big city. None of my old friends would be there in New York!. This idea was horrifying. I started crying loudly in the train but nobody paid any attention. I kept on crying till we reached New York. The entire journey was like a nightmare. I still feel uneasy when I remember that day.

Till date, I have never been able to sleep properly. Such was the trauma of that journey!

Mom-and-Dad's behaviour makes me sad. I realise that I have to do something to become happy, but I do not know how and what to do. Once Mr. Johnson, our English teacher, had said to me, 'Albert, you are a born psychologist. Your ability to examine and analyse thoughts is far superior to a grown-up person.' At just eight years of age, I had read all the volumes of the 'Book of Knowledge'. He was very happy about this. He patted me and said, 'Albert, your IQ is probably between 135 and 160. You are not only good in studies but your thinking capability is also very high. One day you will reach great heights in life.'

At that time, I did not know what IQ meant or what 'psychology' was. But whenever I remember his words, I feel good. When I am sad, they lend me support. I feel inspired again.

Today I remember his words. I must examine my thoughts again. Can I choose my parents? Do I have the power to choose the way they should behave? I wanted my parents to treat me with love and affection but I know that however hard I may try, I will never succeed in changing them.

I am still young. I am dependent on them for everything and it will remain so till I grow up. I need to think about what I can do till then and what can be done now. Yes...I can definitely do one thing: If Mom and Dad do not pay any attention to me, 'I' will pay attention to 'myself'.

The confusion in my mind seems to clear now. But what does 'paying attention to oneself' exactly mean?

When I get angry and irritated with Mom's and Dad's behaviour, it is really I who feel the frustration. I wonder if they even know that I am hurt. It is this attitude that makes me angry. This anger then makes the head nurse shout at me. This means my anger and frustration is of no use; it only adds to my anguish. It is better that I stay calm. That is the smartest way to behave and reduce the irritation.

I have also discovered something that is really wonderful. I get upset because of 'my' thoughts and also feel calm and settled only because of 'my' thoughts. And it is only 'I' who decides my thoughts. So, why not choose thoughts that will help me to feel at peace?

I learnt this important lesson on my ninth birthday and I repeated it to myself over and over again.

Although I cannot change my parents, I can change my thoughts about them. I have control over my thoughts, and no one can decide what I should or should not feel or think.

***

The present circumstances are definitely unpleasant, but not dreadful enough for me to lose faith in my efforts. Something good will definitely come out of this.

I planted these optimistic thoughts deep into my mind.

Although I longed to shorten my stay in the hospital, I knew that it was not within my control. Then should I just sit and cry over the situation? Why don't I try to make the best of this stay? Yes, I must do this.

I am learning the magic art of playing with thoughts. We can change the direction of our thoughts whichever way we want. It can be great fun. Like a magician who pulls out a variety of items from his hat, I too have started churning out some novel ideas.

The days in the hospital were quite boring. There were around twenty children in the ward. Every morning, the nurses would bathe us in the common bathroom. Through the entire day they would keep us under strict supervision. We were not allowed to leave our beds without their permission. Even our breakfast and lunch were served in bed. Every two hours, a doctor or a nurse would come to examine us. Throughout the day we were subjected to the torture of various medicines and injections. But at night it was different. The last check would be at ten at night. Then for several hours no one would come to supervise the ward. This was the time we eagerly waited for. We would gather together and play all the possible games we could think of.

During daytime, I would keep thinking of new ideas. Creating new games helped us to forget the boredom. One day, I thought of a new game we could play at night. I shared my idea with the others. In this game, someone had to tell the others about a situation which made him or her unhappy. Even an unhappy situation can be turned to one's advantage and something good can come of it. The others had to think of such advantages hidden in that situation. Whoever found the maximum number of good points would be declared the winner.

All the girls and boys liked the idea and we enjoyed playing this new game. It made our hospital stay somewhat exciting.

I recognised one more advantage of this game. Everybody learnt that any bad situation also had some good in it. It helped calmed down some children who were always grumbling about staying in the hospital.

Because of the diseased kidneys, my stomach, legs and ankles would often swell up. One day, my stomach bloated up so much that the doctors decided to operate upon it immediately. 'Don't worry. We will give you just a small injection. It will make your stomach numb and you will not feel any pain.' The doctors tried to explain to me in simple terms.

But I was scared with the description of the operation. My mouth went dry. I wanted to scream out, 'No, I don't want this surgery.'

But in the next moment I thought: If I get scared and refused to be operated, will my problem disappear? In fact my illness could be aggravated. What if I decide not to be afraid or not to cry? Let me see what happens.

I repeated this to myself again and again as I entered the operation theatre. The operation started. I could see a whitish fluid flowing from my stomach into a glass jar on the table. Very soon, I was engrossed in observing the doctors at work.

And what magic! As I watched, I realised that all my fears had vanished. It was not at all as frightening as I had made it out to be. I felt a tremendous curiosity about what the doctors were doing. In fact, I made a new discovery—that I had created my own fear. I had painted horrible images of the surgery that had scared me so much. This meant that just like I created my fear, similarly, I could also get rid of it. Hadn't I managed this just now? Without feeling scared, I was able to watch the operation in detail. Gradually, my thoughts started getting clearer.

Basically, we create our own fears. Entertaining them or not is entirely in our hands.

A few days after the operation, I was allowed to go home. I had been absent from school for almost thirteen months and had also missed my exams. But it didn't take me very long to make up for the lost time. The school tested me for an upper grade. I passed this test with impressive scores and this allowed me to skip two grades.

Although I was at home for a long period, I was still something of a weakling. So I preferred to stay away from outdoor sports activities.

My kidney disease was cured, but it had left behind one of its symptoms. I would often suffer from severe headaches. They would attack me any time and leave me almost paralysed with pain. No medicine was able to stop these attacks.

Why me? Why do I have to suffer? What did I do to deserve this pain? Such questions would make my headache worse. I desperately wanted to put an end to this pain and suffering.

Then I found that although I could not stop my headaches, I could definitely stop the thoughts that bothered me. These thoughts were not at all helping me manage my pain; in fact, they only made the situation worse. I had two options: To nurse these troublesome thoughts and escalate the pain, or change them and reduce the pain. Of course, I chose the second option.

****

'Paul, why do you fight with Janet? I have warned you so many times. Don't threaten her just because she is younger than you. You made her cry again.'

I could hear Mom shouting upstairs. Paul would often be at the end of such tirades.

'Mom, I haven't done anything. Janet is a big liar. She scatters her toys all over and if I break anything on my way, you scold me. Instead of crying, why can't she keep her things properly?' Paul was arguing back in an equally high-pitched voice.

'Paul, you have become very arrogant nowadays. Janet is too small for all this. Don't you understand? Instead of fighting, you ought to put her things in place like an elder brother. Isn't it?' Mom was almost screaming. She was probably late for some party and Paul's behaviour had only added to her delay.

As expected, she frantically called me. 'Albert, I am getting late. Come here at once and clear this mess. I am so fed up with these daily fights.''

By the time I rushed downstairs, Mom had already left in such a hurry that she even forgot to shut the door. I watched her passing the gate as I closed it. Feeling utterly helpless I tried to restore the situation. Janet had strewn her toys all over the living room. She was crying in an intolerably shrill voice and Paul was also shouting at her in retaliation.

This happens very often. Paul and Janet have a fight. Then Mom tells me to manage the situation and coolly leaves for her appointment. Janet is very cranky; she breaks into tears for no reason and keeps yelling for Mom. She knows that Mom will always scold Paul. This is exactly what provokes Paul. The moment he comes across Janet, he gets irritated. But Paul is also to be blamed. He is not the simpleton he appears to be. He gets some wicked pleasure in harassing Janet.

'Mom ....sssss'

Janet's shriek broke into my thoughts. Paul was attacking Janet with her toys. One of them had hit Janet on her forehead and she was bleeding. Now she began howling so loud that Paul just stood there, stunned by the result of his action.

For a moment I too stood numb. Then I rushed towards her. 'Paul, run. Bring the first-aid box.' I shouted. He obeyed without a word. I cleaned her wound, applied a medicinal cream, and covered it with a bandage. I did whatever I could think of at that moment.

No amount of scolding will improve Paul, I realised. On the contrary, he only gets more violent. He is mischievous not only with Janet but also with other boys from our neighbourhood. He often injures them while fighting. Then he calls me to settle the matter. Even in school he behaves arrogantly with his teachers. He never finishes his homework. But because I am his elder brother, the teachers complain to me about his misbehaviour. I am really confused. I do not know how to get through to him.

But there is something good about Paul as well. He never disobeys me. We both share the same bedroom but we never fight, nor do we argue over anything. Paul is genuinely a nice boy but it is really intriguing to see how upset he gets the moment he sees Janet.

Whenever I observe Paul, I feel I should study the emotion of anger further. Does anger get aroused naturally? How is anger or any other emotion created in our minds? It is not clear to me how emotions actually develop, but I certainly know that Mom and I do not get angry when we see Janet. Then why does Paul?

The true reason, according to me, is that nobody is interested in understanding what the three of us feel. I am the eldest. So I have to take care of Paul and Janet. Janet is the youngest, so she is pampered by Mom. Paul is more sensitive than I, so he suffers more than me. I know he craves for Mom's love, so I try to sympathise with him. I always treat him gently. He is also aware of my affections and listens to all that I say.

But Mom and Dad never display such affections. Mom is always busy in her own world of cards, friends, entertainment, and parties.

Once, when she had opened her cupboard, I saw some of her old photographs. How beautiful she looked. I just couldn't believe that the gorgeous lady in fancy costumes was my Mom. Only when I pestered her a lot, did she tell me that she had been an amateur stage artist when she was young. She had also won many prizes for her work in those days. I was astonished to learn about Mom's talent. But I do not see anything of her talent now. I had never seen Mom acting on stage. How can our inborn talents just disappear?

Why didn't she make any effort to pursue her talent? Mom does everything half-heartedly. She is never passionate about anything. To follow something zealously is not in her nature. She is content with her small-time pleasures. How can I expect love and attention from her? Why should I get affected by her behaviour?

And in Dad's case, such a situation does not arise at all. He is hardly home. So his behaviour hardly matters to us. Our house is quite large. The living room, kitchen and the guestroom are on the ground floor and all the bedrooms are upstairs. I am not sure why, but Dad stays like a guest in the guestroom, so Mom and Janet share the master bedroom.

But one thing is certain. Dad's personality is very impressive. I loiter around him when he talks with his friends, especially Aunt Rosy. Dad is very witty. Their conversations are so cheerful. I love listening to their lively chats.

This is how my parents are. They both enjoy their lives to the fullest, but in their own individual ways. There seems to be no place for the three of us in their lives. Sometimes, I feel as if we were picked up from some orphanage.

This thought depresses me a lot.

But I am not like them. I do not like such a life. And if I do not want such a life, I need to change my thoughts, which keep circling around one feeling because of their behaviour: utter disappointment.

I have decided to accept everything in life without grudges. But this decision requires some real hard effort. I must ignore the way Mom and Dad behave with us and not let their attitude affect me. My behaviour should not depend on theirs. I must think seriously on these issues.

***

These days, Mom seems to have sobered down. There were fewer occasions on which she lost her temper. All three of us—Paul, Janet and I—were terrified of our mother's volatile temper and her punishments, and no one ever had the courage to disobey her or protest against her orders. Any opposition was futile. We had no option but to obey.

I vividly remember one incident, which happened while I was at the hospital. We were all busy playing the game I had invented. This time, I started the game by placing my own case as the 'difficult situation' for which the others had to find positive solutions: A family in which the parents do not pay any attention to their children.

Everybody seemed to be confused with the problem.

'There is nothing good about this situation,' said Jacob.

'Nobody will like such a situation,' remarked Erin.

'Let's all think together. No situation is entirely bad. Some good always comes out of it. Let's see if anybody can find it,' I said.

'I have something to say,' Daniel raised his hand.

Daniel was the youngest of us all. We looked at him curiously, wondering what this little fellow had to say.

'When someone's parents are not paying any attention to their children, then the children are free to behave as they wish. When they pay too much attention, constantly keep a tab, and instruct their children on things to do, and so on, then the children cannot do what they want. So it's always good to have no attention paid to you. It's great fun to be able to do things on our own. Isn't this also a great advantage?'

Everybody clapped in approval as Daniel finished. Of course, he was the winner of the day.

Daniel's words were deeply engraved in my mind. I had never thought of this. I realised that there was also a positive side to Mom-and-Dad's neglect. Unexpectedly, it granted me the freedom to behave as I wished.

I was very excited with this new revelation and decided to make good use of this freedom. I began training myself to become independent. Although I was not earning, I was old enough to do some small household chores. Why should I depend on Mom for small things? It is always better to do things yourself than to depend on somebody. Far easy and less troublesome this way. After deciding this, I felt at ease. I started helping Mom wholeheartedly in her daily work and even in her shopping. Mom was, of course, very happy. 'Albert, you are the apple of my eye,' she would often say.

As a part of this training, I took control over many things. I bought an alarm clock for myself and began getting up early. It felt like a punishment to wake up when it buzzed every morning, but I trained myself to overcome the inertia and get up right away. To encourage this habit, I would constantly keep going over the work planned for that day. I fixed a daily routine which involved preparing a breakfast of egg rolls, omelettes, or pancakes, after I woke up. After watching me for a few days, Paul too began waking up early and getting ready for school. But getting Janet ready proved to be difficult. On waking up, she would start crying for no reason. I would either ignore her or give her favourite pretzel sticks to make her stop. Then, while chewing those sweet and salty sticks, she would slowly get ready for school. Just before Mom was up, I would be all set to go to school with Paul and Janet.

I learnt to cook. After returning from school, I would prepare dinner for everybody. I learnt to make simple dishes like rice, vegetable stew, mashed potatoes, roast chicken or lamb, and a few other easy recipes. After that, it was not necessary for us to wait for Mom any more. Paul and Janet started getting their dinner at proper times. As such, I had decided to look after them on my own as much as possible.

I was convinced that things only seem difficult till you master them. Once you learn, the same appears easy. We unnecessarily blow issues out of proportion and make them appear more complicated than they are.

I gradually started teaching myself to simplify the things that I found difficult, such as, going to school. Our house in Andrew's Apartments was on the 183rd Street of Bronx County. On the way to school, we had to cross this main street with its usual morning-traffic rush. With Paul and Janet in tow, I would feel scared about negotiating with the speeding cars, and we would often request some passers-by to help us cross. But, many a time, there would be very few people on the road, and most of them would refuse, being in a hurry themselves.

Paul and I studied at St. Peter's, which was an all-boys school. Janet's school, St. Victoria Girls' School, was on a street behind ours. We usually first dropped Janet and then walked back to our school. The longer we took to cross the main street, the more we would get delayed for school. Meanwhile, the supervisor, Mr. Lopez, would be waiting at the gate to punish latecomers. He would hit the students really hard on their palms. I dreaded getting late. We were often subjected to beatings from him.

Finally, one day, I decided to stop asking for help while crossing. I had to be independent if I didn't want any punishment from Mr. Lopez. Why should we depend on others for help just because of our inexplicable fears? I gave this problem some serious thought. If we followed traffic rules properly, there was no reason to be afraid while crossing. Then why was I scared?

I realised that just before we crossed, I would murmur exclamations like 'Oh, gosh. Horrible,' to myself and generally be in a terrified state of mind. I would imagine one horrifying accident or the other, where some vehicle crushed all three of us to death. No doubt, crossing was dangerous, but my imagination had made it many times more dangerous than it actually was. The mere thought of crossing made me nervous.

I kept reminding myself that just as I choose to scare myself, I can also choose not to be afraid; or else, I will have to always depend on others for help. If I continue this way, I will suffer from a total lack of self-confidence.

I made up my mind. I taught Paul and Janet all the traffic rules. Then, one day, I held both their hands, mustered up all my courage, and crossed the street cautiously. Oh yes, it was so easy to cross. I was overjoyed. I felt as if I had conquered the world. I had foolishly created a mountain out of a molehill. In fact, there was great happiness to be found in overcoming hurdles and moving ahead. I had learnt the meaning of courage by actually experiencing it.

I had learnt that courage is not 'absence' of fear, but that it means 'mastering' fear.

This approach helped me in my schoolwork too. Now everything seemed easy. I started enjoying competing with the other boys in my class and taking up challenges. I could grasp all the subjects faster and was overjoyed when I could answer the difficult questions asked by teachers in the class. I started finishing my homework in time.

There was, however, one thing that I still lacked confidence in, and that was completing a recitation in front of the class. Even though I knew the poem by heart, when I was asked to recite it before the class, my heart would start beating fast, and I would tremble with fear. My mouth would go dry and I would feel thirsty.

I decided to tackle this problem as well. I realised that I had created fear even before I actually crossed the road—simply because I was worried about making errors while speaking in public. I would think: What if I forget? What if I don't recite properly? My fears were about all that could possibly go wrong. These 'what ifs' were the actual cause of my fear. To overcome this, I started rehearsing at home in front of the mirror. I would tell myself emphatically that even if I did mess it up, what would not be the end of my life. For the next three months I consistently practised talking in front of my friends, and whenever I got the opportunity, I would give a small speech in front of a group.

One day, to everybody's surprise, I signed up for an elocution competition in the school. Till that point, I had never felt this courage. Did it mean, then, that our feelings depended on what we thought? Yes. I was convinced of this. I could secure only a consolation prize in the competition, but the praise and the kudos I got from Mr. Johnson were far more valuable to me.

I realised that anything which appears difficult in the beginning can become simpler after some effort.

***

Summer activities usually started in June, when the weather turns warm. As always, Mom told us to put away our winter-wear.

'Now we will need these only in October.' I said to Paul.

Summer was the season of outdoor games like football, baseball, and thus, the season of unpacking sports material. Quite a number of Irish, German, and other Europeans lived in our neighbourhood. The atmosphere would be lively with the sounds of cheering and hooting children playing everywhere.

Football tournaments resumed on our school grounds, too. I was not permitted to play because of my weak health. It could even prove fatal if I disobeyed the doctors. So, although I was fond of these games, I could not participate in any outdoor sport. I had even accepted that even if I desperately wished to play like the others, it was wrong to expect that every wish of mine should be fulfilled. But in spite of this, I would feel disturbed.

Then, one day, I realised that even though I could not participate, I could watch others playing. Was that not enough to enjoy the game? Why should I miss that joy?

I began to watch the football matches held on school grounds regularly. I was the only student who attended every game played in our school that year. As a result, I became an expert on the game simply by following the matches earnestly.

Gradually, many of my friends began following my advice before playing. We would not only discuss the game, but also have lively debates over various other topics like books and school activities. This made me realise that to master a subject, one should have deep knowledge and understanding about it. This could be achieved by reading as much as possible on that subject.

Once, Mr. Johnson read out some excerpts from Henry Thoreau's book, *Walden*.

'How many a man has dated a new era in his life from the reading of a book.'

This sentence kept haunting me. I repeated the thought in my head and pondered over it. It occurred to me that nobody, not even the doctors, had forbidden me from reading books. I started reading every book I came across. I was convinced that to have in-depth knowledge, I had to read a lot more than just textbooks.

Like other boys my age, I was also fond of popular books like the Frank Merriwell series by Gilbert Patten and Horatio Alger's *Ragged Dick*. But I soon realised that all this fell under shallow reading. I needed something more serious, which could cultivate new thoughts in my mind. Eventually, I lost interest in popular fiction. I wanted to read something that could inspire me, enlighten me.

Since early childhood, my eyes have been sensitive to bright light, and I have had to wear special protective glasses. But even with these glasses on, I was unable to read continuously for hours. My eyes would burn and start watering. This would later lead to severe headaches. How horribly painful it was. To make all this agony bearable, I had to put in eye-drops every two hours.

After applying the medicine, I would close my eyes and lie down to rest, but my mind would writhe in anguish. 'As it is, my poor health does not permit me to play, but I love reading so much. Then why am I deprived of the joy of reading too? Why do I have to suffer like this?'

When such thoughts disturbed me, I found a clever solution of driving them away. It was to cross-examine them the moment they popped up.

While trying this method I realised that I did not have answers to such questions. But even if I did have the answers, were they capable of improving my eyesight? I had only one option. I had to take care of my eyes as instructed by the doctors so that they did not worsen. No amount of frustration would help me in curing them. Instead, I must focus only on finding some solution to the present situation. There was a limitation on my reading capability, but not on my thinking. I was free to ruminate in the resting period between two reading sessions. This could be the best use of that idle time.

I immediately put this thought into action and a truth dawned upon me. Mere reading was not adequate. I should evaluate and analyse what I read. I should use my own intelligence. I was totally convinced of a tip an eminent person had given about reading. He had said, 'A page digested is better than a volume hurriedly read.'

I followed this quote sincerely. I decided to delve deep into every subject and try to understand the author's mindset. This helped me understand how much I agreed with his o her ideas. Only deep reflection and contemplation could make this possible.

Only then could I claim that I had read the book.

***

Once, in the language class, Mr. Johnson asked us to write an essay on our 'best friends'. I wrote:

'I play with many, but I do not have any close friends. I do not belong to any group and I do not enjoy belonging to any group either. I have no interest in chatting or goofing around. For me this is not important in life. I prefer friendship only with a few like-minded persons.

'Amongst these friends, the one truly close to me is my younger brother, Paul. Although he is younger to me, I can always share my feelings freely with him. Most of the times, it is I who does all the talking. I talk to him about the books I read, about my conclusions, or about the decisions I make after reading. I generally have some distinct opinions, to which he listens patiently. I really do not know how much he understands or agrees with them. But he listens to them very attentively and with great affection, and this is very important for me.

'One common factor that binds both of us is music. For us music can express feelings better than words. We often talk to each other through the language of music. When we are alone, we like to listen to Beethoven and Mozart symphonies. When soulful soft melodies float in the air, it becomes difficult for us to control our emotions. Our feelings pour out and merge with the tunes. Soon, we both get lost in the magical world of music. Such is my bond with Paul. It is indescribable in words.

'My other close friend is Manny Birnbaum. We became friends when I was six. He is Paul's friend too. Manny lives on 181st Street, just behind our apartment building. We have cut a hole in the wall common to our buildings. So whenever we want to see each other, we do not have to walk all around the street; we simply squeeze ourselves through this hole.

'I like Manny. He is not inquisitive like others. He often comes to our place. Most of the time Dad is away, but Manny has neither tried to probe about this, nor does he express any pity about our plight. I feel very comfortable in his company. His dad is also away many a time; probably, that is why he is able to understand our situation. Such empathy is very important in true friendship, I feel.

'I don't remember ever quarrelling with him, except on one occasion, when he beat me during our fight. I am thin and Manny is heavy-built. Mom first scolded him, and then, not being satisfied just at this, she marched to Manny's place and reported the whole incident to his mother. She also told her several times to warn Manny about his misbehaviour.

'But Manny is large-hearted and has never held any grudge against me for this or hurt me again. He is also a very good friend to Paul. I hope this friendship among the three of us stays solid like a rock forever.'

My essay was chosen as the best essay by Mr. Johnson. He remark was: 'Albert's thoughts are very mature for his age.'

So many memories came alive. I was lost in nostalgia again.

The three of us have great fun together. Our favourite activity is taking a long stroll. We love the Bronx Botanical Garden on 200th Street very much. Although a bit far, we walk the distance to this garden. It is spread out over a large area; so large that it accommodates almost twenty-seven small and big gardens, such as the Rose Garden, Orchid Garden, Herb Garden, Rock Garden, and many others. There is also an Adventure Park for children to play in. But my favourite is Forest Land. One can see the real beauty of nature in this garden, where there are have preserved trees, fruits, and flowers in their natural state. We all like to take a walk in this 'land'.

Sometimes, Paul and Manny go to play in the play area and I stay back to enjoy the beauty of nature in the garden. My mind is rejuvenated with fresh thoughts in the pleasant.

On Sundays, the garden remains closed, so we go to Van Cortlandt Park on 240th Street. This park is to the northwest of the Bronx and farther than the botanical garden. So we take a short ride on the bus and walk the rest of the way very leisurely. This is the third largest park in New York. Paul and Manny like it because it is much bigger and there are more things to play with. I simply take long walks and think over the books I am reading.

But we get to enjoy such walking tours only during summer. The cold sets in from October and all the summer activities come to a halt.

I still cannot forget last year's winter, when I saw a game of ice-hockey for the first time. Till then I had only heard about this sport. It was difficult to get tickets for the Madison Square Garden's ice-hockey tournaments. But Manny somehow managed three tickets for us. The experience of watching ice-hockey in the chilly December weather was really awesome.

This winter we decided to do something different. We planned a trip to the Wolman Ice Skating Rink in Central Park. There was a huge Christmas tree adorned with colourful lights in the middle of the rink. The white floor was shimmering with the reflection of the lights. I knew how to skate, but my fragile health did not allow me to do much skating. Nevertheless, I enjoyed watching the graceful movements of Paul, Manny, and the other skaters on the bright silvery surface of the rink.

But at the same time, I was also watching something else.

Most of the children came along with their parents. The fathers were pampering them with chocolates and candies, and the mothers were feeding them lovingly. All the parents showered so much love and care on their children. I watched the scene, somewhat jealously. How lucky these children were. Will I be ever blessed with such love from Mom and Dad?

Immediately, I stopped myself from such self-pitifying thoughts. I had learnt to drive away such negative feelings by now. I said to myself: Only because I am deprived of the love the other children enjoy, I am able to think differently, and it is this ability that makes me a special person.

The three of us had saved a few cents from the pocket money we got. It was from these that we were able to pay for the bus fare, tickets to the hockey rink, food, and other such small expenses. Whenever we saved a bigger amount, we would reserve it for a movie show. The long summer vacation would begin in June. That was when the theatres played our favourite movies. This was mainly why we would anxiously wait for the holidays. The Webster Theatre was at a walking distance on 167th Street. During the summer vacation, children got a special concession in the ticket fare. We took full advantage of this discount and splurged all our extra savings on movies. We saw several movies like *Pony Express, Dick Turpin, Merry-go-round, The Vanishing American, Pampered Youth,* and others during this vacation. We may not have understood the movies, but we thoroughly enjoyed the cinematic experience of the big screen.

At times we also played cards, or board games like chess, at home. Mostly, we played at Manny's place. His house is smaller but cosier than ours. He has no siblings and his mother goes to work. Sometimes, when she is at home, she chats with us and also gives us food to eat. How nice we feel in Manny's home!

Why don't we feel so in our house? Why do we prefer to stay out rather than be home? We are always more relaxed and happy when we are away. I wonder if Manny also feels likes us in our home.

Manny rarely comes to our place, and whenever he did, he always seems to be in a hurry to leave.

'Albert, shall we go out and play,' or 'let's go to my place,' he keeps insisting.

In the beginning, I thought he was scared of Mom. But even in her absence he would do this.

Whenever Manny came, the scene in our house would be the same: Mom away from home and Janet screaming over something. 'Now will you stop crying, or I will beat you. Go away. We want to play here,' Paul would keep shouting at her.

That would make her cry even louder. Paul would then get violent. He would push her with force, pinch her hard, and make the situation worse. In Mom's absence, I felt it was my responsibility to make peace between them. But even if they fought in her presence, Mom would stay closeted in her room and just ignore them. She never let herself be affected by this commotion. It was only when Janet screamed intolerably loudly, that she would emerge in fury. Then Paul and I would just run out of the house to escape her beating. I do not know why, but it was Paul who often got spanked even when he was not at fault.

I do not have much affection for Janet. As a brother I feel close to Paul but not to her; maybe because I am fed up with her daily tantrums. Sometimes I too beat her, because she is never happy with anything we do for her. She is the most pampered one in our family, yet she finds some new reason every day to cry. My nature is just the opposite. I am afraid of becoming a whiner like Janet, so I try my best to stay away from her.

But, sometimes, I feel that Paul and I treat Janet very badly. Quite often we do not allow her into our room and keep the door closed to avoid her. One day, Manny asked us, 'Why do you behave so rudely with Janet? She is younger to you. How can you ignore her when she cries?'

'Manny, you say this because you don't live with her. She is irritating. Try to spend a whole day with her and you will know,' I defended.

I also remember telling Paul and Manny: 'All girls are whiners like Janet. If we speak to them, we might become whiners too. It is better to stay away from girls.'

Since then, we look upon all girls as our enemies. Not only did we stop making friends with girls, but we also stopped playing or talking with them. All three of us had agreed not to talk about Janet or any other girl among us henceforth.

***

'Hattie, Hattie, calm down. If you lose your mind, who will take care of your children?' Aunt Fanny was trying to console Mom in a gentle voice.

Mom kept on sobbing and crying.

Just a week back Aunt Fanny had come to stay with us. She is Mom's elder sister from California. Whenever Mom was in trouble, she would call her. I knew that Mom also obeyed her.

I could sense from the situation that again something was amiss. I tried to find the reason but both of them ignored me. As usual, Aunt Fanny occupied Janet's room, so Janet was moved to ours. Paul and Janet were neither aware of the happenings and nor could they understand anything. I suspected a serious problem. Mom had not stepped out of the house the whole week. Aunt Fanny and she would just sit in her room for hours talking in hushed tones. I wondered several times: what they could possibly be talking about?

Once, at midnight, I woke up feeling thirsty. To my surprise, there was a light on in Mom's room and the door was ajar. I was curious. I stealthily hid myself behind the door. It was dark outside but I could hear them clearly. Mom was sobbing.

'Why did Henry leave me? What have I done? What does Rose have that I don't? What made him leave me and start a new family with her? Fanny, they were having this affair for the past six months and I had no knowledge. I never thought that Rose would do this to me. How could she destroy her best friend's marriage?'

The moment I heard the word 'Rose', several incidents flashed in my mind. Aunt Rose was one of Mom's closest friends. Mom would always talk of her very lovingly. She had come a few times to our place. Aunt Rose was strikingly attractive. She would dress immaculately and could draw one's attention immediately. I noted that although she would come to see Mom, whenever she visited, Dad would stay back; even if he was all dressed up to go out. He would become his talkative-self again and the dull atmosphere of our house would instantly transform into a lively, cheerful one, full of fun and mischief. Dad would crack jokes and Aunt Rose would respond, saying, 'Oh, Henry, you are so funny.'

But she had not shown up for a while now. Oh! Dad too had been away for many days off late. He is generally never at home, so his absence had not struck me.

'Fanny, what should I do now?' Mom was asking desperately.

'Is there anything we can do? Now listen. Just sign those divorce papers and send them back to Henry. It is not wise to resist. Henry will also not wait any longer. Remember, he has left the responsibility of all the three children entirely to you. They are so young. Albert is eleven, Paul, nine, and Janet is just seven. They have to complete their education. Now, you must not forget practical issues. Why should you alone bear the burden of raising them? Henry should also share the expenses. Hattie, have courage. Demand a proper alimony. Ask him for the ownership of this house.' Aunt Fanny was talking in a firm voice.

Mom stopped crying. She seemed to have collected herself a little. She appeared calmer after the advice.

Divorce? I questioned myself as I dragged myself to my bedroom. Why does this word sound so terrible? Am I shocked to learn that Mom and Dad are getting a divorce? To be honest, no. But what does divorce really mean? Just to stay separately? That is not much different from the present situation. As it is, we hardly get to see Dad. As for Mom, her presence or absence, neither makes a difference to us. Then why did they have to discuss this so secretly?

A couple of years ago, Dan's parents were divorced. Dan was my classmate. I had heard only a few whispers about it in class. Dan's mamma had demanded alimony from his dad. That was when I first heard the word. I even searched in the dictionary for its exact meaning. Alimony means 'a fixed amount a husband had to give his wife for household expenses after a divorce'. Later, Dan left our school and moved elsewhere.

I was suddenly reminded of Dan again. How sad his face was in those days. I missed him and felt unhappy as I thought of him then. I feel uneasy whenever I remember him. My heart sincerely longs to see him.

We do not meet Dad nowadays. It is as if he has severed all relations with us. Why did he ask for a divorce? So he could not get along with Mom, but was that our mistake? How could he forget all of us? Why did he never think of us when he made this decision? I missed him a lot. Even though he was rarely at home, we would feel so secure when he was. Those warm goodbyes he wished us when we left for school.... I felt like I would cry as I remembered his loving hugs. Didn't he remember anything of this when he left us? Does he remember us when he eats our favourite cheesecake? How could he forget these moments? Why did he not feel like seeing us even for a final goodbye? So many questions but no answers! I was in turmoil.

I was numb with sadness, remembering our happy moments together; even though they were few. I cried silently in bed. The whole night I tossed sleeplessly. With great effort, I controlled my tears. My head was reeling with many unanswered questions. Is our attachment, even in such close relationships, so shallow, so superficial? Are all bonds so fragile that they break forever, because of a simple divorce? That means those whom I consider close, are really not close. Paul and Manny are so dear to me. Will they also leave me some day? Are all relationships so short-lived? What is the truth? Is it that every person in this world is actually lonely?

I felt devastated. What was true? What was untrue? At night, Dad, Aunt Rosy, Mom, Aunt Fanny, Paul, and Janet kept appearing randomly in my dreams. I felt dizzy with conflicting thoughts running wild. I could rein them in only after seriously understanding my sorrow.

Only 'I' could gain control over my mind. I warned myself that I should not harbour false hopes of a happy ending like in storybooks and movies. I should stop wishfully thinking that Mom and Dad would get together again or that some miracle would reverse the situation to what it was earlier. As such, I never approved of sweet endings in films and stories. They do not teach us to face the hardships we face in real life.

'Mom and Dad are getting a divorce—that is the reality, although bitter. I have to accept it, however strongly I may hate it.' I repeated to myself.

I shut my eyes tight. I could see everything I had read in books. Thoughts of great writers which that were deeply set in my mind began rising up.

I had read in books about how great persons had faced several challenges in their lives. From them, I had learned that when we are upset, we should first examine if we are able to change the situation. If we can, we should try to change it as far as possible, fully or partially. But if we cannot, we should accept reality.

I started asking myself certain questions. I knew I felt uneasy about the subject of divorce. Was this uneasiness going to reverse the situation? The answer was 'No'. Neither had anyone talked to me about divorce nor do I have any role in taking the decision or preventing it. It will only make me feel worse if I continue brooding over it.

Dad was already settled happily with Aunt Rose. Soon, Mom too will be busy in her routine. Paul and Janet are least worried about the divorce. They are too young to understand its implications. But I may destroy my life if I kept grieving.

The sky was lit with the orange hues of a new dawn. Fatigued with thinking, but feeling calmer, I made a decision.

Henceforth I would not make place for any such thoughts in my mind. If they still follow me, I will question whether they are of any use to me. If they persist, I will overpower them with positive thoughts. I will free myself from their hold and try to compromise with the circumstances as much as possible'.

Aunt Fanny called me over to talk before she left.

'Albert, your Mom and Dad are now divorced. You can see your Dad only once in a year. As Hattie is not working, you will have to manage your expenses with whatever money Henry sends. You are the eldest, and also the most sensible. So you have to take care of Paul and Janet.' Her eyes welled up as she spoke.

I had no other option other than to nod in acceptance. I had no tears like her. Rather, I would not allow any. I was a grown-up, I was strong, and now the responsibility of my family was on me.

***

Mom slowly returned to her former routine. It was difficult for her to stay away from old habits for long. She got busy with her friends and outings once again.

The days she received the money from Dad, would be days of celebration. At dinner we would have a special dish and our favourite cheesecake as dessert. Mom would spend generously.

She gave me 50 dollars every month as pocket money.

'Albert, this is all I can afford to give for all three of you together. You have to manage your expenses, as well as Paul's and Janet's, in this amount. You are now old enough to learn how this can be done.'

I was extremely curious about how much money Dad gave her every month and how much she could save from that. But I did not dare ask her this question. I knew she would get annoyed. I was afraid that she might even stop giving me this money.

But I would constantly be under tremendous pressure thinking of the remaining days of the month. Life had become very tough. We were facing a severe financial crunch. We began to understand the value of every single penny. I was obsessed with finding different ways to cut down expenditure.

'No muffins or cookies for breakfast?' Paul would complain. Janet would cry for her favourite pretzel sticks. If Mom bought those for her, Paul would fret and fume.

At last, one night, I could no longer keep the secret about our condition from Paul. When he was about to go to bed, I told him all that had happened so far, about the divorce, about our poor condition, about the money Dad sent, and about our thrifty living. I bared my heart out. Paul was silent. I could not guess if he understood the gravity of the situation.

'So what are we supposed to do now?' He asked me quite naively.

'We have to spend less. We should not insist on muffins and cookies. When we go out we will walk as much as we can before taking the bus. If the place is really very far, we will take the Greyhound.'

I saw a question on his face.

'The Greyhounds are those blue buses recently started. They are cheaper to travel in.'

He stared at me for a while, his expressions changing rapidly. 'Does this mean that Dad will not even come to say goodbye?'

I did not answer; I did not have the courage to answer.

Suddenly, Paul burst into tears. I was confused and, more so, surprised. I had never seen him crying in this manner before. Whenever Mom beat him, he would suffer the pain silently. He never allowed any tears. I had seen Janet and others cry, but Paul? It was unbearable to see him cry so loudly.

I was disturbed. I did not know how to pacify him. Did I make a mistake by confiding in him? For a moment I regretted my action, and patted him gently.

I sat in despair, suffocating with my pent-up anguish. I had no one to look up to for support. Paul was at least able to cry; but I could not, even if I wanted to.

***

December was coming to an end. That day, we had our supper a little late. Mom called out to me from her room. Janet was fast asleep.

'Albert, since three months your Dad has not sent me any money. I do not know the reason for this. I have sent him many messages, but there is neither any reply nor any money. I do not know if, as usual, he has incurred a loss in his new business.

Henry has a bad habit. You may not know about it. Even if he has plenty of money, he will not part with it. I have no idea what has really happened, but the truth is we have not got any money.'

'But, Mom, according to the court's order, he has to pay the decided amount, isn't it?' I asked impatiently.

'Yes, that's true. But to make him pay in time, I will have to sue him in court, which needs a lot of money. I cannot afford to pay the lawyers. Even if we try him in court, there is no guarantee that Henry will pay. But it is a fact that we did not get any money from him in the past three months '.

'So what can we do now?' I was really shaken.

'I am confused as well. I do not see any way. I had been giving you money from my savings so far. But now even my savings are slowly being drained. I have no hopes of Henry sending me any money next month either. Whatever is left with me is just enough for food and a few essentials. We have to do something urgently. Our condition is quite bad.'

By the time Mom was finished I had turned into a statue. It was shocking. Somehow I had always carried a fear of this day ever since Aunt Fanny had first talked to me about divorce. Unfortunately, my fears had come true. Discussing or arguing with Mom was of no use. She was equally crestfallen.

'Don't worry, Mom; I will take care of this.' I said on the spur of the moment. I do not know what prompted me to give this assurance to Mom. I had not at all thought about how I was going to fulfil this promise.

It was dark outside. The windows were shut, but a chilly draught was leaking through the cracks. Winter was setting in fast. The temperature had already plummeted below zero. Although I had assured Mom that I would take care of the situation, I had no idea what one could do in that freezing weather.

My mind was crowded with thoughts as I came back to my room. What had made me say this? Of course, my words were definitely motivated by some thinking set deep in my subconscious mind. I would have to stay calm to find an answer.

Do our thoughts and actions depend on the weather outside? If it were so, all people would remain indoors during winter and not to work. This means that our thoughts are independent of external conditions. They are always in our control. We can decide up to what extent we can let these external conditions influence our decisions. We can change our decisions the way we want and also reverse them.

I was already sharing household work. Why couldn't I also share the duty of earning money? Why should I feel shy about working? The sooner I start earning and become self-reliant, the earlier I will become independent. I decided to start hunting for work from the next day itself.

Mr. Johnson had read us an essay on 'Self-Reliance' written by the great philosopher Ralph Waldorf Emerson. I had noted down some of the important thoughts expressed in this essay in my diary. He had written:

'Trust thyself. A man is to carry himself in the presence of all opposition, as if everything were titular and ephemeral but the great man is he who in the midst of the crowd keeps with perfect sweetness the independence of solitude.'

I wanted to earn and help Mom as much as possible. As soon as I came back from school, I would hurriedly get ready, put on winter-wear and go out in search of work. It was possible to find work with small shopkeepers after school in accounting or sales. So I started meeting shopkeepers of the West Bronx area where we lived. I combed the area so well that soon I knew every detail about every street, from numbers 160 to 200. But I was finding it very difficult to get a job fit in the time-slot I could offer after school. One day, a stationery shopkeeper told me to check with The Frost Agencies on 171st Street. Their helper boy had just left and they were urgently in need of a replacement. But he warned that I should meet him early morning, not later than six.

I was so happy that I even forgot to ask what work was expected of me. I was prepared for anything; I desperately needed a job.

That night, I could not sleep due to anxiety. I woke up early. It had snowed all night. From the window I saw that the trees and houses were covered with thick snow. It was white everywhere. I had already cleaned my old snow-shoes from last year and kept them ready. But, alas! They would not fit me at all. I had grown taller during the year! I searched the entire house. At last, I found a pair of old shoes discarded by Dad in the basement. They were big for me and worn out too. But I did not mind. I was happy that at least I had something to wear in the snow. These would do for the time being. I got ready in a hurry and headed for The Frost

Agencies. It was very cold and the street was empty. Only some snow-ploughs were to be seen clearing the streets. Although I was wearing a thick overcoat, I kept shivering from the cold.

I knew 171st Street very well. I could easily find The Frost Agencies. It was a small newspaper stall. Heaps of newspapers were stacked and kept in order, so, it was also a newspaper distribution agency. Two persons were noting something down while talking with each other. I could not see their faces clearly as they were covered with scarves. One of them was tall, the other was fat.

'Excuse me gentlemen, I am here to see Mr. Frost,' I said.

'Yes?' The fatso turned towards me and asked.

I told him why I was there. He observed me closely.

'Your name?'

'Albert. Albert Ellis.'

'Age?'

'Twelve.'

'Twelve? You look younger. Your shoes weigh more than you probably.' He remarked. 'Where do you live?' He was still observing me keenly.

'On 183rdStreet, Andrews Apartments.'

'Albert, have you worked anywhere earlier?'

I shook my head to say 'No'.

'Do you know what the work here is?'

I again nodded in the negative.

Mr. Frost pointed out the stacks. 'You can see these newspapers. All of these are delivered in the morning. So I need some help. The main job is done by Mort,' he said pointing towards the tall man standing next to him.

'We have a van for delivery, which Mort drives. You will go with him. Most of the apartments where we deliver are on Park Avenue. One cannot park vehicles on this street. Mort will drive you up to the apartment buildings and you will drop the newspaper in the mailbox of every apartment. Then your job is over. But you will have to finish this as fast as you can, because we cannot keep the van for a long time on the street. Can you manage this?' he asked.

'Yes, I can.' I was more excited about finding a job than knowing the nature of work.

'Will you be able to carry the pile of newspapers?'

'I will try,' I said.

'Okay, then. You have to report here every morning by 5.30 sharp. You will work nearly for two hours. First, you must remember the name of the newspaper to be dropped for each customer. If you make a mistake, you will get a complaint from the customer. After you finish, you will tally the number of newspapers you have distributed with the number of customers. If you misplace any issue any time, you will have to pay for it from your wages. I will not tolerate any excuses like 'it rained today' or 'it was too cold' or 'I have work at home' or that 'I have exams today' or anything of this sort. If you miss even a single day, I will cut your pay. I will pay you five dollars a week. Do you agree?'

It was possible to work here without disturbing school. I agreed instantly. Mort explained my job to me and I began working from that morning itself.

We soon became friends. Mort was silent by nature but amicable. He was five or six years older than I. Like me, he was also working while studying, but had missed two years of school. Now he was studying in second year at college.

After watching me work, Paul said that he wanted to help, so could he join me too? I asked Mr. Frost if Paul could come along with me. He made his terms clear immediately.

'You may bring him but I will not pay him.'

This was alright with me. Paul could be of great help to me even if we got no extra money. With great enthusiasm, Paul began coming with me daily. My workload became much lighter because of his help. Paul would count the number of newspapers and then put them in order of apartment numbers. After some days he even started putting them into the mailboxes along with me.

Paul had a funny habit of talking in his sleep. I would often wake up at midnight because of this. Curious to know what he was chattering about, I would listen closely. He would murmur something like 'Number 123, New York Times. Number 126, Daily Post. Number 129, New York Post.' Paul seemed to work even in his sleep.

Mr. Frost was happy with us and he raised my wages within just a few months. He also hired Paul. Together we earned enough to pay for our sundry expenses. We would forget all our hardships when we counted our self-earned money. It gave us the confidence that we could overcome every difficulty in life with determination.

'I have a snow-suit. Even I want to join you.' In the beginning Manny kept nagging us. He thought it was all fun, that we set out for some adventure every morning.

'You can go out because your Dad is always away. But even my dad is away from home many times. I also want to come with you.' He would persist.

I had to lie to Manny that I was not permitted to bring along so many others with me. I gave him various excuses. But he was not convinced. Finally one day I had to say a firm 'No' when he insisted on meeting Mr. Frost himself.

Manny was visibly dejected. I felt guilty about his disappointment and sincerely wanted to let him know of this. But somehow I could never bring myself to do it.

I only kept talking to him in my mind.

'Manny, this is not fun at all. We are almost half asleep when we leave early in the morning in the biting cold. It is warm inside our homes, but outside we have to battle harsh, chilly winds. It is difficult to manage piles of newspapers while wearing heavy winter jackets. We have to rush to deliver the newspapers in time without missing the order of the apartment numbers. Above all, we have to face admonitions from Mr. Frost for every small mistake. There is really no fun. You will never understand why we have to do this. Your Dad goes away only sometimes, but our Dad has gone away forever. There is a vast difference between the two, Manny.'

***

2

I have become obsessed with reading these days. All through the day, I keep thinking about books — while working or before sleeping, even while eating. I eagerly look for intervals of spare time to read. I like the world of books and prefer books over people. People keep changing their attitudes very often. Those we consider dear today may not remain so in future. But books are like faithful friends. They are always available to guide us. They are a permanent source of support in every crisis. They give us new thoughts and help us to face life.

Over the years, my range of subjects and authors has grown wider. I read literary works by reputed authors as well as books by great philosophers. It gives me immense pleasure! I read in whatever spare time I get. I am convinced that leisure is not easily found, one has to strive to get it. In school, I read during the recess break or in between two classes. At home, I read even while toasting bread or roasting chicken. Paul and Manny tease me and call me a bookworm. But I have become so fond of reading that nothing disturbs me. I just ignore them. Nowadays, I prefer reading over playing with Paul and Manny or other friends.

In the school library, I sought out *Walden* by Henry Thoreau. His thoughts haunted me as I came back. Why does this happen with me whenever I read any book? I got the answer to this question today when I read

'If a man does not keep pace with his companions, perhaps it is because he hears a different drummer. Let him step to the music which he hears, however measured and far away.'

Soon, I had the opportunity of experiencing the meaning of his message.

Mort had planned his birthday party for the second of April. He had invited only a few of his friends, including me. He did not invite Paul as he was too young to fit into this group. Although I had bought a gift for Mort, I was in two minds about attending the party. The friends he had invited were from his college and I thought that perhaps I might feel isolated amongst them. But I had no other important work that day. Moreover, Mort had persuaded me to come with such great love and affection that I could not refuse. Finally, I decided to attend his party.

As expected, his friends were much older than me. All the girls and boys were enjoying music and dancing. A sumptuous spread of food was laid by the side. The atmosphere was riotous with laughter, jokes and pranks. This was my first experience of such a party. I was unable to understand even their jokes or codes. I could not mingle with the crowd.

I stood perplexed. I sat on a chair and watched the ongoings. There was a small crowd on my right busy in serious discussion. A smart-looking boy was saying something and the others were attentively listening to him. He was speaking very confidently. I became curious. I joined the crowd.

'What is philosophy? It is love of wisdom. What is the aim of philosophy? Its aim is to make one think. Philosophy is the most suitable subject for those who are seekers of knowledge, for those who like to gain knowledge.'

'But Sid, of what use is philosophy?' Somebody queried.

'So, his name is Sid.' I thought.

'Philosophy teaches you to see the world in a larger perspective. Other subjects educate you for a job or for some business. But philosophy teaches you to live a meaningful life. It can reach the core of everything. That is why it is said: "All sciences are born in the womb of Philosophy".' Sid said animatedly.

'What do you plan to do if you major in philosophy?' Someone enquired.

'I will be a Professor of Philosophy. Then I shall be able to study all the world-famous philosophers, right from Aristotle to Kant, Nietzsche and Schopenhauer.' He replied with confidence.

I was impressed. From his words, very unexpectedly, I found what I was searching for. I realised what I wanted to do in life. I was thirsty for knowledge. I wanted to do a deep and serious study of life. Only philosophy could satisfy this urge. My mind was filled with various thoughts.

There are so many different subjects in the world. Each one has its own merits. But only philosophy suited my interests. Mr. Johnson always said that I was much ahead of others my age in reading. I used to feel very proud whenever he said this. But, now, I was somewhat ashamed of myself. How totally unaware I was about the subject of philosophy. I had not read any of the great philosophers Sid mentioned. I was now determined to study philosophy and to become a professor, like Sid.

I also discovered that you get true joy in doing things about which you are confident and passionate. I plunged deep into my study of philosophy. I was eager to read what Epictetus, Spinoza, Kant and Bertrand Russell wrote. The school library did not have many books on philosophy. Through Mort, I got in touch with Sid, who introduced me to The New York Public Library. 'This is a very good place for those who are interested in fundamental research,' he said.

This iconic library on 42ndStreet was truly the best for researchers. It had a vast collection of books and journals made easily available to readers. Besides, the library was free of charge. I was extremely happy. This library was able to fulfill my insatiable desire to get more and more knowledge.

As I stepped inside, I remembered what Benjamin Franklin had said in his autobiography: 'The library afforded me the means of improvement by constant study, for which I set apart an hour or two each day.... Reading was the only amusement I allowed myself. I spent no time in taverns, games or frolics of any kind and my industry in my business continued as indefatigable as it was necessary.'

This soliloquy made a great impact on my mind. I, too, wanted become as great and as famous as him. I was ready to work, however hard it was necessary, to achieve this greatness. Nothing can deter me from this, I told myself.

I reorganised my routine for the summer. After my morning job at Mr. Frost's, I would finish my work at home and go to school with Paul and Janet. I would do all the schoolwork during recess break or during the play class. After dropping Paul and Janet home, I would straight head for the New York Public Library. Late in the evening, after a stroll in Bryant Park, I would return home. During exams, I would study late into the night. I made use of every minute I had at my disposal very carefully.

Bryant Park was just opposite the library. I loved taking a walk there but it was not as well-maintained as the other parks in the city, and mostly visited by drug-addicts and drunkards. This park was created in memory of Mr. William Cullen Bryant. He was a famous poet who had also been the editor of *New York Evening Post*. In the centre of the park was a huge statue of Mr. Bryant. Whenever my mind was agitated with clamouring thoughts, I would often sit on the lawns in front of the statue.

'Albert, please stop visiting this park. It is dangerous,' Mort said to me, when he heard about my daily visit to the park from Sid.

'This park is notorious for criminals; well-bred, respectable people do not frequent it.' He was persistent in his warnings. Although I stopped going to the park, a number of questions started pestering me.

What is decency or indecency? What is meant by well-bred or ill-bred? Are drunkards and drug-addicts always indecent, and are non-addicts always decent? One may agree that the habit of drinking or drug-addiction is bad, but how can we declare them to be 'totally indecent' people?

When I was unable to find answers to such questions, I would visit the library. I had no one to guide or help me in deciding what was right and wrong, and what was good or bad. I, myself, had to make these judgements and only books could help me in making this discretion.

I started reading voraciously. I read the works of philosophers like Socrates, Plato, Aristotle, Epicurus and Marcus Aurelius. I also studied the work of great thinkers like H. G. Wells, Upton Sinclair and William James. I was not always able to understand what I read, but I would contemplate and try to comprehend the meaning carefully.

All these writers were definitely illuminating, but can we say that whatever they propound is the absolute truth? I found it difficult to accept their hypotheses naively because my analytical mind was always active. It was against my nature to accept anything without critical evaluation. I did not accept any idea until I was totally convinced. After reading every book, I ruminated upon it and then formed my opinion. I do not know if my opinions were right or wrong, but I was satisfied that they were formed only after thorough critical analysis. A book titled *Philosophical Essays* by Bertrand Russell appealed to me very much. I felt as if it was written only for me. His thoughts would linger in my mind for a long time.

I was often reminded of what Mr. Johnson said: 'Only reading is not sufficient to grow intellectually. It should be coupled with writing. You should write down your thoughts. Such writing helps in giving clarity to your thoughts, and in making them specific and logical.'

I began keeping a record of all ideas, irrespective of whether I agreed with them or not. At the end of every week, I would make notes from this record, and conclude with my opinion. These opinions were my own, not accepted blindly or borrowed from anybody. These opinions were the result of intensive reading and study.

I discovered one advantage to this method. One may feel that he has understood a thought or a concept but the real test of this conviction is when you start writing on it. Writing is far more difficult than reading. You can claim that you have understood a subject only if you can write with clarity and precision. The practice of writing leaves a lasting impression in your mind. So, to master a subject one must learn to express it in precise words.

***

'There is a Summer Film Festival starting from this Monday in Central Park. The preparations are on in such a grand scale. They have erected a huge screen, 20 x 50 feet, and they will be showing all classic films.' Manny was panting as he had jumped over the fence to give us this news as fast as he could. Paul began dancing in excitement.

'But, Manny, what about tickets?' I asked worriedly. This was very important.

'Oh! The biggest surprise is that it is free for students. Isn't that great news? We just have to show our school identity cards, that's all. But we will have to go there very early to reserve our seats. The show will start at 7 pm but we will have to reach by five in the evening.'

'This whole week will be so much fun!' Paul was almost screaming.

Lately, I was losing interest in the movies. But this was a real treat, and above all, it was free. I was excited to. Armed with a water bottle, snack-box, and a light blanket, we would march to the park in the late afternoon. It was almost like a daily picnic. The movie would get done by 10 at night. Watching films on the lawns of Central Park below a starry night was a unique experience.

'How lucky are those who live nearby! They can attend every film-festival held here.' I would say to myself.

The week went by very fast. The last movie was on Saturday and called 'Saturday Afternoon'. Its storyline in brief was something like this: A man named Peter could not get along with his wife, Jessica. They fought all the time. Finally they divorced and Jessica got custody of their two children. But Peter hated Jessica so much that he hired a goon to kill her and get back the custody of his children.

There was not much substance in the story, but Paul and Manny were impressed with Peter's character. He was a brave person, they said.

'The end was very good. Peter taught Jessica a good lesson.' Manny remarked as we returned.

'Jessica was harassing Peter too much. She got the right punishment.' Paul seemed to agree with Manny.

I made no comment.

'Albert, didn't you like the movie?' Manny asked.

'What is the matter? Why are you so quiet?' Paul was also curious.

'No, nothing serious.' I bluffed.

It was beyond their capacity to understand what I felt. Conflicting thoughts were troubling my mind.

The movie depicted that Peter solved his problem by killing Jessica. But was this action right? Can you get rid of a problem that way? After learning about the cold-blooded murder of their mother, won't the two kids face new problems? Wouldn't it be a shock to Jessica's parents? Most importantly, would Peter ever get rid of the contempt he had for Jessica, after killing her? Or would he still seethe in anger whenever she was mentioned? What exactly did he achieve by killing her?

Suppose, one even agreed that it was Jessica who was entirely at fault. But one cannot forget that she was human, and so, likely to make mistakes. We all err sometime in our lives. Perhaps she would have corrected her mistakes later. But to kill her, by presuming that she will never improve, is entirely wrong. When he did not know what could happen in the future, why should he take this extreme step?

Isn't it dangerous to take somebody's life just because one does not approve of a certain behaviour in the other person? It is unjust to kill somebody and take away their right to live. We come across many people with whom we disagree or whose behaviour displeases us. But nobody will feel safe if everyone decides to follow Peter in such situations. Such a mindset will spread the feeling of hatred. We have to stop glorifying such actions and attitudes, or else it would encourage violence and aggression in society.

I returned home with these thoughts in my mind. I was compelled to think more seriously.

Basically, to what extent is another person responsible when we experience an emotion? Peter was convinced that Jessica was solely responsible for his anger and hatred. But had it been so, all others around her would have felt similar hatred and anger towards her. Her parents and children seemed to love her and they did not carry such hard feelings.

As I went to bed, it occurred to me that it must be Peter himself and not Jessica, who was responsible for his feelings. He had cultivated a wrong attitude towards her, believing that she was mean and quarrelsome, that she deserved harsh punishment, and that that punishment was to take her life itself. Due to this attitude, he must have wasted considerable time in fretting and cursing her.

By nursing this resentment, he had lost his capacity for tolerance too. In such a weak state of mind, some incident must have fuelled his anger and provoked him to commit a heinous act like murder. Without his knowledge, his attitude had made him so uneasy that he lost control over himself.

There is definitely something wrong in the attitude adopted by Peter. It was incorrect to label Jessica as a 'totally bad' person just because he did not approve of certain traits of her behaviour. One may not be able to tolerate some specific behaviour. But this does not justify Jessica's denigration; she cannot be declared as a totally dishonourable person. Jessica was wrong at times, and did behave badly. This facet of her behaviour was only a part of her personality. But to decide that she was unworthy of staying alive was wrong. Everybody makes mistakes in life, but we cannot mark all people as bad and kill them. We may punish a person for his intolerable behaviour, or even help him improve; but to end that person's existence is entirely wrong. Peter would not have resorted to a beastly act like murder, had someone convinced him of this.

Gradually, things began getting clearer. I was also following the same path with Janet. Because I did not approve of Janet's behaviour, I had started hating her as a person on the whole. I had even stopped talking to her. The anger I felt was only because of the bitter attitude I held against her, and not because of her behaviour. Now things started unfolding before me. Only if I change this attitude, will I be able to change my feelings towards her.

Yes; henceforth even if I am not able to bear with her, I was not going to humiliate her any more, or hate her as a person.

I felt relieved. I was able to untangle my thoughts to some extent. The truth had dawned upon me: if we are able to distinguish between a person's specific behaviour and his personality, we can eliminate enmity among people. I wanted to put this thought into practice immediately.

As soon as I saw Janet the next morning, I wished her. I said, 'Janet, I want to say something very important. I want to apologise to you. I have been treating you very badly and meanly. But now I have decided to change myself. I make this promise to you right now. If I ever forget about it and behave as before, do remind me. I honestly want to change myself. Please be frank. Tell me what you feel.'

Janet was too surprised for words. She was not able to understand what had caused this change. The answer was only known to me.

While trying to change myself, I also found that when a person examines and critically evaluates one's own attitude, irrespective of the cause, only then is change possible.

I knew that I had not changed because of the movie. *Saturday Afternoon* was just coincidental. The movie alone was not instrumental in changing me. It was not that influential. Had it been so, even Paul and Manny would have changed their thinking. It was only my contemplation after the movie that motivated me to change. It was because of this that I could replace my earlier attitude with a new one, and this new attitude was the reason for the change in me.

I started making serious efforts to change my behaviour towards Janet. To my happiness, after a few days, my efforts began showing results. Janet was extremely touched by the sincerity of my feelings. She too began mending her ways. Slowly, we forgot the animosity between us. I got rid of the simmering anger I carried against her. The relationship as a loving brother got revived once again.

I tried to explain this to Paul, but in vain.

'Does it mean that even if Janet is at fault, it is only I who has to change and forgive her? This is not fair. You know she lies and sheds crocodile tears… just to make Mom beat me. She gets pleasure when Mom scolds me. And yet it is me whom you ask to be patient and change. This is impossible.' He was furious.

Paul was not in a state of mind to understand my plea. I tried to convince him that Janet too had changed when I changed.

'No, Albert. I am sure Janet can never change. Right now she is just pretending to be nice to you. Just wait; soon she will be her old self again.' Paul was adamant.

Even after consistently trying to persuade him, I was unsuccessful in changing Paul's opinion about Janet. It is important and also necessary that one should feel the urge to change, before attempting to change. If not, then all the efforts made by others will be futile.

I noted this observation in my diary.

***

'Reading maketh a full man; conference a ready man; and writing an exact man.'

This observation by Sir Francis Bacon, the great British philosopher-thinker, is apt. When we learn to imbibe knowledge, to express it in precise words, only then is our speech effective.

Reading has become my life. Consequently, I have also become more confident about my writing abilities. Last year, *New York World*, a reputed magazine, had announced an essay competition with the title 'An Outstanding News Event.' Mr. Johnson encouraged me to participate. It was a pleasant surprise to learn that I had secured the first prize.

But, although I was progressing in my reading and writing skills, I was lagging behind in oratory. I was brave enough to talk in front of my schoolmates, but even a few strangers in the audience made me nervous. I needed to make an extra effort in elocution.

At this thought, I stopped and made a determined ation decision to improve speech-giving in the coming summer.

It was our custom to visit the Botanical Garden daily, every summer. That year, a new tennis court was opened for children in the garden. As soon as we reached, Paul and Manny would rush to the tennis court, and I would be left alone. I began thinking about how I could use this solitude to improve my oration. While walking in the garden, I would experience a strong urge to share my thoughts with somebody.

An idea struck me. There were many children who would spend time only chatting on the lawns. I decided to convert them into my audience. I began sitting with them on the grass. I would discuss the books I read. Gradually, I became friends with them. I soon realised that I was good at speaking and that everybody seemed quite impressed with my talks. I, too, began enjoying the experience of my small discourses.

Each day at the garden then became a challenge. I pondered over further improvement in speaking. Soon, I came up with a plan. First, I would decide the topics to be discussed the next day. I allotted each topic a certain amount of time. Then I would revise the points I could discuss within that time-frame.

After some days, I reviewed my technique. To gauge the impact of my talk, it was necessary to see how much of my speech the listeners remembered. Here, I found that they remembered only my passion and enthusiasm and not the content. Sometimes I would stray away from the main subject and keep ranting. One cannot convince others simply by talking aggressively. I was wasting my energy unnecessarily. I could put forth the same views in a controlled but firm tone. It was important to be logical and precise.

I made some improvisations in my method with this in mind. We do not have to struggle for words when we are convinced, and I had realised this. I started visualizing the sessions the way I wanted them to be. This helped me while speaking. I trained myself to concentrate on the main thought, without getting emotional.

My talk would generally start with an introduction: 'Friends, today I will speak to you on … "such and such" … for …"X" length of time.' I learnt that briefing them in this manner and adhering to the time-limit was also important. Then I would follow up with— 'We will discuss "such and such" points within this time period. So let us start with "X".'

When all the points are reviewed prior to speaking, speech becomes fluid and effective. Talking should not be overcrowded with too many views. I took care of this aspect, too. After finishing a point, I would summarize it and announce that it was over, before moving on to the next. Finally, before ending my speech, I would once again cover all the points in brief.

I read a research report on 'memory' that said we tend to forget 80 percent of what we hear on the first day itself. So, revising all the points again at the end can help retain them, even if briefly. I would prepare my speech only after thorough study, and present it in a precise manner.

The response I received from the children in the garden was encouraging. I was successful in carrying out my plans as I had decided. The summer break was utilised properly.

Something else became clear that summer. The more my reading habit grew, the more I was drifting away from Paul and Manny.

Instead of playing with them, I found more joy in reading Darwin, Kant, Spencer, and John Stuart Mill. Manny and Paul had grown closer to each other and I was getting more and more left out. Of course I did not regret this. I was determined to do something spectacular in life even though I was totally ignorant about what to do or how to achieve it. One thing was certain—this would be possible only with power of knowledge.

I felt as if I belonged only to the world of books. But, sometimes, I would feel very lonely. Music would soothe my mind during such moments. I have felt connected with music since childhood. I remember when I was very small, while working around in the house, Mom would always be humming sweetly. I would try singing those same lyrics in a different tune. Music would cast a magical spell on me those days.

I have grown up now, yet I long to hear Mom's voice. I learnt many compositions because of her. Sometimes she would sing so soulfully that I would stop working and become all ears. Like Manny, I did not enjoy fast or peppy music. I was more drawn towards classical music like Mom.

Mom would never miss a single opera in the city. She had a friend working in the Grand Opera House in Manhattan who would often manage free passes for Mom. Whenever Mom was in a good mood, I would tag along with her. Paul, too, was fond of music but he liked playing more; so most of the time, it was I who got the chance of accompanying Mom to the operas.

The first opera I saw with her was *Rose-Marie* by Friml. It was on a huge, magnificent stage, with expert musicians, dazzling sets and enchanting music. I lost myself as I saw it unfold. I was not a good singer, but during the show I sang, albeit silently, along with the orchestra. I realised that every singer is a good listener, but every good listener is also a silent singer.

In our house, there was an old radio bought by Dad. In the morning, some of my favourite tunes, like 'You are in my love, 'High Jinx', or 'Broadway, would be played. I would forget all my stress while listening to these songs. This radio-set barely worked and needed repairs. Many-a-time Paul would slap it to get it to start. But even though the cost of its repair was meagre, it was very difficult to spare any money for it.

Since childhood, I had planned to buy a gramophone when I grow up. There was a shop of musical instruments on my way to school. I would look at the gramophone everyday while passing this shop. It was priced $150. But, these days, I would rather buy books instead of the gramophone. I would also have a wide range of books to select from those which were about my favourite compositions, as well as those which tell us about the inspiration behind such masterpieces.

Earlier, I would be content with only listening. But, eventually, I felt like exploring why the medium of music was so effective. There was far too much curiosity in me about the composers of great musicals. I would try to listen to Rudolf Friml, Victor Hubert, Richard Strauss and other great composers on radio as much as possible. I slowly began to understand why I was getting not just carried away, but more and more obsessed with music.

When we listen, we get engrossed not only in the musical notes of a composition but also in its lyrics. So it is obvious that while listening, we also think. It is this thinking that gives rise to certain feelings in the listener's mind. Music strengthens these feelings, which touch our heart. Our mind is then roused with emotions. When we respond to good music, we clap, we exclaim, 'Oh, so beautiful!' or other similar such expressions. This means that along with thinking and emoting, we also act. We get totally involved in music only when thoughts, emotions and action, all three are initiated simultaneously. Music has the power and capacity to influence our minds. Therefore, it is able to reach our hearts.

There is definitely a joy in experiencing things that touch your heart, but more joyful is the revelation of *how* it touches your heart. This process of learning and understanding was so delightful.

***

It was the 31st of October. There was excitement everywhere because of Halloween. For all of the past week, Paul and Manny had been busy in preparations for the day. Manny had already made the Jack-o-lantern and left it to dry. He was proficient at making beautiful carvings on dried pumpkin. He does it so exquisitely that it exactly resembles a human face. Paul is busy collecting old dresses for the Halloween costume. Mom has already brought candies and chocolates to give away.

Right next to 183rdStreet is 182ndStreet. All the children and our friends from these streets gather together. We hide our faces in black-and-orange coloured Halloween costumes and go on a rampage shouting 'Trick or Treat'. It's great fun. We demand goodies when somebody fails to recognise our faces correctly, and when we return home we are loaded with them. We do not have dinner at home that night; instead, we eat together around a bonfire, scaring each other with horror stories. This is the way we celebrate Halloween night every year.

But this year, I don't feel any excitement. I am unable to enjoy myself as I have done all these years. For the past few days I am feeling very uneasy. It started from the day I got a book on physical geography from the library.

'Albert, please suggest some new ideas for the costume,' Paul had begged of me so often that week. But I was not able to think. I was not at all at peace to think of any.

'Albert, you have to join us at least for the bonfire. What fun we had last year playing the game of ghosts you invented. Please find a new game this year, too.' Paul and Manny were pleading.

To satisfy them I played for some time and came back. I was not interested. There was some kind of churning within me. All this began happening with me since the day I read the book on 'Physical Geography'. Since evening, I have locked myself in my room. I just want to lie down and think peacefully over what I read in the book.

I have not slept well the entire week…I strongly feel the need to examine the ideas and assumptions I have nurtured so far. After reading the volume, my world had turned upside down. My mind was battling a storm within after learning about how this universe, humans, and life came into existence on this earth.

I asked myself: Why should one believe in an idea? Should there be a logical reason to believe or should we accept an idea just because we are told so?

I wanted to evaluate the concept I held about god. I wanted to examine how sound the concept was.

I now know how human or animal life originated on this earth. All the life we see on earth today is the result of evolution over several million years. It was not created in one single stroke, as depicted in religious scriptures. This proves that the scriptures are false and deceitful. If they are based on falsehood, how can one believe in the god mentioned in these scriptures?

When I go to the synagogue, I am told by the rabbi to have faith in god because *he* helps us in times of need and saves us. But then I asked myself, did *he* come to help me when I was in need? How much I prayed when I suffered that killing headache. Nothing could stop that pain. Mom, Dad and I, all of us would regularly visit the synagogue and pray. Then why were we left with this fate? Why didn't *he* rush to help us? Why couldn't *he* stop Mom and Dad's divorce? Why couldn't *he* improve our miserable conditions? It was definitely a breach of faith that god is kind and never hurts anybody.

Even though I had prayed earnestly, god had never come to my rescue and I was quite sure that *he* never would. So I had to learn to be strong and not depend upon god anymore.

I really found it hard to believe that just by keeping my faith in god I would be saved from a calamity. However pitiful and damaging our experience may be, saying that 'our trust in god will ultimately prove to be beneficial' proves that we are turning a blind eye to the truth.

Then what is the truth? The truth is that the incidents in our life and our prayers are not related to each other at all. When it is so, no amount of praying is going to affect our life. In fact, there is no specific cause behind the happenings in one's life.

The books on philosophy also revealed one more truth—that the concept of justice is man-made and that it has not come into existence per se. Then why should we carry a false presumption that the god who created this world is a just and impartial entity?

If god was truly just, then he would award us suitable justice befitting our deeds. Why should we then offer special prayers for justice? In fact, we do not seek justice from god when we pray. On the contrary, we keep beseeching god to fulfil our wishes. We not only stop at this, but also try different methods to please him and get his blessings.

The rabbis say that god is very kind and that you can overcome all difficulties if you surrender to him unconditionally. But nobody has so far been able to prove this decisively. These unanswered questions give rise to more questions. None of the rabbi's answers have convinced me. Should I trust them blindly only because they are the religious heads? Should I forget that I am intelligent enough to think independently?

The rabbis tell us about different ways of surrendering to god, and I know of many who follow them. But to surrender in this manner appears like we are begging for mercy by belittling ourselves. It means we have to praise god in different ways to please him. It means to plead with god to shower us with blessings. Can we then regard this god, who is greedy for praise and adoration, who gets impressed with prayers, to be omnipotent and almighty? Then he is not very different from an egotistic person who easily gets influenced with flattery. To worship such a god is an indication of the loss of one's self-respect.

'This universe is god's creation,' says the rabbi.

I was not satisfied with this answer because the next question immediately in my mind was: 'Who created god?' Unable to remain silent, I did ask him.

'Nobody needs to create god, he is self-existent.' He replied.

Instantly, the next question that cropped up in my mind was, 'Like god, can't the world also be self-existent?'

But I kept quiet because the rabbi had warned us of god's curse if anybody raised insulting questions about 'him'. I saw that many were scared after this warning, but I was not. It depends upon us whether to get afraid or not . Of course, I chose the latter.

In the synagogue, we were also told that we can find peace by praying to god. I tested this and was disappointed. If one has great faith in something, he can get peace by praying even to Satan, not only god.

As I explored further and deeper, I found that such beliefs might harm us. A faithful follower might feel shattered on realising that this kind-hearted, almighty god has failed to help him. Chances that he will become sad rather than happy are more. It may even lead him to depression. His trust in god will harm him, instead of being an advantage. It might also lead him to accept that all that happens is only for his betterment. Although this is a wrong and shallow approach, he will accept it because such an acceptance is going to help him retain his faith in god.

Instead of adopting this explanation, it is more helpful to admit that our knowledge and strengths have their own limitations. Whatever Herculean efforts you may undertake, nothing is capable of preventing a catastrophe in life. The only way is to stay firm and find a solution.

There is no need to think intelligently when you believe in something. It does not necessitate testing the truth behind it. Also, it does not call for any efforts. But critical evaluation of a subject requires hard work. It demands maximum use of our intelligence and that makes it very difficult. That is why we try to avoid critical evaluation and tend to resort to blind faith. Ultimately, we form a habit of believing, without thinking, or discovering if soothe belief is realistic. This habit of avoiding hard work is harmful because it makes us lazy and dependent on god.

We become mentally weak because of the habit of passing our burden to the 'omnipotent god'. This habit of avoiding a burden or responsibility is then not limited to god alone. We apply it to other circumstances, too. In times of crisis, we try to take refuge not only in god, but anyone can become our saviour. Not only god, but his self-proclaimed favourite disciples also become entitled to worship; and we worship them without even questioning the rationality behind it.

'Should I accept something just out of faith?' was the question dogging me these days. After fully evaluating the matter, I arrived at a firm 'NO'. Accepting it prima facie will mean avoiding the effort of examining its veracity. I am capable of examining opinions critically and I do not want to accept something on the basis of faith alone.

When I look around me, I observe that atmosphere seems to encourage such unaware believers. This tendency is so widespread and has penetrated so deep into our lives, that it trains us to become fatalistic right from our childhood. How this happens is perfectly explained by the famous sociologist La Barre. He says, 'In our society, a child perforce becomes a Right Thinker before he learns to think at all.'

How true this observation is.

So naively we imbibe ideas and principles about morality and behaviour from our parents, teachers and all those around us, right from our childhood itself. Of course, as children we do not have the capacity to evaluate these and We have to depend on others for our basic needs and also for love and care. But we become such slaves to this habit of dependency that, even when we grow up, we do not exercise our ability for independent thinking. We continue to accept things unquestioningly. We keep on depending on others, and it becomes an utmost necessity to pass our responsibility to a stronger person.

I have also been brought up in this culture but I also have the freedom to accept or reject. One can teach oneself to check the worthiness of a belief. So from today I decided that I was going to defy the concept of god that I have carried so far. To disbelieve in god is regarded as haughty or shallow. But I have taken this decision after careful thinking and I will make a sincere attempt to adhere to it.

But this poses another question. So far no one has been able to prove that god exists, but it may be possible in the future. So, on what basis can one challenge this possibility today? To say that one can never prove god's existence is an obstinate and irrational attitude. It is more appropriate to say that the existence of god is still unknown. This agnostic approach appears logical. To be technically correct, one may also say that the probability of god's existence is very low, say 0.000000001 percent. Therefore, I would prefer agnosticism to atheism.

I am a fallible human being, so I am imperfect. But I will use my intellect to become independent. I believe in my strengths, and to achieve what I want in life, I will go ahead without waiting for some godly help.

The agitation in my mind subsided. I was feeling better. I had been able to streamline my thoughts to a considerable extent.

I could hear the sounds of the Halloween party celebrations outside. But I was neither getting disturbed nor did I feel like joining them. I had just made a very important decision in my life.

From my window, I could see the golden flames of the Halloween bonfire. The glass panes were reflecting its light and it filled my room with soft yellow brightness.

As if that light was showing me a path to the future.

***

3

It was the first week of March. The library was crowded as it would usually be in the first week of every month. I was in queue to return my books. A girl was standing in front of me. I thought I had seen her somewhere while passing through the streets. Maybe she lived in our neighbourhood.

Her dark brown hair was tied with a hair-clip but a few strands were still loose, caressing her face. She looked so comely when she tried to brush them back. She wore a light pink skirt and a matching blouse. The colour of her dress enhanced her beauty. The complexion of her rosy cheeks was complemented by the colour of her dress. I covertly kept staring at her.

Suddenly, she looked at me and smiled.

My heart began beating faster. I somehow managed to smile back.

'Do you stay in the Bronx?' She asked, her blue eyes looking straight into mine.

My pulse raced and I trembled with nervousness. 'Yes.' I muttered.

'Which street?'

'183rd Street, Andrew's Apartment.' I stammered.

'We were living on 180th Street sometime back, in Steve's Apartment. But it was on lease. Since January, we have moved to Queens. Now our apartment is owned by us; it is not a rented one.' She spoke quite casually.

I was mostly speechless. Although I was glad we were speaking, I did not know what to say to keep it going.

'Why are you here? Is it for some school project?' She asked. Perhaps she took pity on my awkwardness.

'Yes.' I was too stupefied to speak in more than monosyllables.

'I have come for a school project too, on the topic of "Exploring Libraries". We have to visit all the prominent libraries of the city and gather information. I may have to come here for one more week.' She spoke spiritedly.

Her number was called at the counter and in the next moment, she disappeared.

I stood gobsmacked. This was my first experience of talking to an unknown girl. I went to my table, but could no longer concentrate on reading. Soon, I left the library.

The sudden encounter and brief chat with a beautiful girl gave me a heady feeling. I started walking. Wherever I looked she kept appearing before me. In that mood, I kept roaming around, her voice echoing in my ears. Had she been living in the Bronx, I would perhaps have had a better chance of meeting her again. So far, I had not ventured much beyond Bronx. I only knew that

Queens County was somewhere near the airport. It was very difficult to trace her in such a large area.

I knew neither her name nor that of her school or which class she was in. I had not asked her for any details. As I repented my stupidity, I realised that I had reached 180th Street. I had never noticed Steve's Apartment earlier. Today, I saw it properly. The apartment was locked. Its new occupants had probably not arrived yet. I returned home but could not forget that girl. I kept imagining her sitting at the balcony of Steve's Apartment or strolling lazily around on the lawns or seated in a car and waving at me. That night I dreamt only about her.

I eagerly wanted to go to back the library the very next day and get the details of her whereabouts. But I was also worried about the impression I had left upon her. I was hardly able to speak. I felt ashamed. I finally decided it was better to skip the library and avoid further embarrassment.

I spent the following week, restlessly, at home. I lost interest in studying or reading. My mind kept imagining situations in which she was in danger, and, when I rescued her like a braveheart, she looked at me in great admiration. I painted similar incidents in my mind all through the week and whiled away the time happily, day-dreaming.

There has been some change in me off late. I found it very difficult to emerge from my world of fantasy. I thought about other girls too, besides the one I met in the library; girls I came across on the streets or in the neighbourhood. When I remember their attractive, shapely bodies I feel a certain kind of excitement.

I get goosebumps, there's a flush of energy, and my thoughts begin to run amok.

I have felt a strange new awakening in my body. As my body transforms internally and externally, my mind runs fickle and wild. I didn't have the courage to speak with any girl, but even images of my encounters with them satisfied me. In my imagination, there was no fear of rejection from anyone. How could they reject me? They were my creation.

Our school, St. Peters, is an all-boys school, so there is no possibility of encountering girls. Yet, most of the boys have girlfriends. When I go to pick up Janet from her school, I see more boys than girls at the gate. A majority of these boys are from my school. I, too, would love to have a girlfriend like them but I do not know how to get one.

I do not know how to recognise if a girl is interested in me or not. Even if I can somehow guess their feelings, I have no clue about how to take things forward. These questions pester me and I do not have the answers. Even making eye-contact with a girl embarrasses me. So dating someone is a very remote possibility.

At Janet's school, I stare at the girls from a distance. I imagine of falling in love with different girls. But these 'love affairs' are secret and private. I like getting lost in dreaming of these affairs. Paul and even Manny are unaware of my dreams. Although we had decided never to talk about girls among ourselves, there's no denying that now I just cannot ignore girls! On the contrary, that is the uppermost topic in my mind.

As I think back, I realise that I may have had this attraction right from my childhood. When I was hospitalised for my kidney disease, I remember being very happy whenever a beautiful nurse was appointed to our children's ward. It used to be satisfying, watching her body and her movements; a bonus if she had the duty of bathing us. Those were among the few happy days in that boring hospital. Whenever she stooped, I would skilfully try to   touch or see her body beneath her dress. Now, I understand that I had a strong attraction towards female nudity even at that young age.

In the ward, the nurse would carry two children at a time for their bath, and she would not differentiate between boys and girls. Meanwhile, I was extremely curious about the differences between a boy and a girl. With great interest I would observe the body of the girl bathing alongside me. There was not much difference except for the genitals. From a distance I could see her body only partly. I really wanted to touch and explore further, but of course, I couldn't do that in the presence of the nurse. I had to be content with what I could see from a distance.

All these memories unfolded in my mind like beads from a broken chain.

One of the games I devised during that stay was to correctly differentiate between a boy and a girl, in the dark. When the bell rang at 10 in the night, the head nurse would put off the lights and return to the main lobby. Then we would all gather together in the centre of the ward in pitch darkness. One of us would hold a torch and the one whose turn it was had to name the person on whom he threw the torch-light. We all had to wear identical night gowns in bed, and so it was a tricky thing to name a child correctly in that dim light.

Whenever it was my turn, I would deliberately lose to get another chance. In reality, due to my lengthy stay, I knew every child perfectly well. I would purposely aim the torch only at girls, trying to sneak a peek at the uncovered part of their bodies. Sometimes we got so rowdy that the head nurse would come running and warn us to stay quiet. We tried to remain vigilant, and get right back to bed at the slightest sound of her footsteps.

Luckily, no one found out about the game, or else the hospital authorities would have confiscated the torch — the most important player in our game!

I still remember Gloria, whose bed was next to mine, very clearly. I liked her very much, and one day, with great courage, I confessed this to her. To my surprise, she said she liked me too. We promised to meet every day, even after leaving the hospital. Of course, this promise was never fulfilled. After leaving the hospital, we neither met nor could I trace her anywhere. She had vanished. I have to stretch my imagination quite a bit now to picture how she might look today. None of my imaginary romantic adventures with her materialised, but they definitely had a special place in my memories.

My first crush was actually someone whom I met before Gloria. Her name was Mary. We met when we were both around six or seven years old. Blue eyes and blond hair, she looked just like a doll, and lived on 182nd Street, very close to us.

We would play together quite often. Many a time we would chat for long hours in my room. In those days, there was a maid in our house to help Mom, and she would keep an eye on both of us whilst doing her work. I do not quite remember what we chatted about for so long but I cannot forget our last evening together. It was a Sunday, although I cannot recollect the exact date.

Mom, Dad, and Mary's family had gone out together that evening. Our maid, too, was on her weekly off. Mary and I were chatting as usual, all alone in the house. Suddenly I had an idea.

'Shall we behave like the elders today?' I asked Mary.

'What does that mean?' She was confused.

'Mary, elders hug and kiss each other. We will also do this so that we know why they behave in this manner.' I explained to her.

In the beginning, she hesitated. She was afraid, she said. After considerable amount of pleading, she agreed. I embraced her tightly, and without any inhibition, kissed her a number of times. This was my first experience of a female touch. Mary also seemed to enjoy it. She was giggling the whole time.

Suddenly, an idea flashed in my head. I had suppressed my curiosity about female genitals for so long, but on that day, it surfaced again with great force. We were all alone. Yes… This was the right opportunity and the right time.

I summoned courage and began undressing her. Mary, too, was anxiously watching my actions. Finally, I had a successful look at the female private part, the vagina. It was extremely different from a penis, which lies outside the male body and, therefore, was quite noticeable. But not so with the vagina. I got hold of a torch to observe more closely and got ready to probe further.

But, alas! It turned to be the most horrifying moment of my life. Our parents dashed in right then and all four of them began hurling a volley of abuses at us. Our mothers went so wild with anger that they were just a step away from kicking our faces in.

'Aren't you ashamed? How dare you misbehave in this way at this age?' They screamed in unison as our fathers tried to pacify them. Mary started crying and I began begging earnestly for forgiveness. There was utter chaos.

'You little scoundrel. Do you want to become a whore?' Mary's mom shouted as she dragged her out of the room. She began beating Mary furiously.

At this, I lost all courage and began crying loudly. I suspect this was more because I had to give away my opportunity at the last moment, rather than that Mary got beaten up because of me.

I did apologise out of fear of getting beaten. But I am still not sure of the exact reason behind my apology; because even as I was crying, there were many questions flocking to my mind. In school, we were taught to search answers to satisfy every curiosity. I was just doing the same. Was it not applicable to my inquisitiveness about female private parts? Are there separate rules for this query? Is this to be done secretively and stealthily? And when such an action is discovered, why is it termed as a 'misbehaviour'? Why are our genitals treated specially, and why should we feel ashamed to see those parts closely? I never got answers to these questions. Did Mary have such questions too, I wondered. I would never know because, soon after, their family moved away and we never met again.

Mary had left behind fond memories. That incident had easily been one of the most thrilling experiences of my life. But it was also laced with the sorrow of parting, which I cannot forget. Are all our relationships so short-lived? As soon as we develop an attachment with someone, a mishap seems to destroy it and leave behind only memories. But these memories are so poignant that even a slight trigger can create a spectrum of visuals. The touch of her soft velvety body is still alive in my mind and it continues to arouse me even today.

Nowadays, I am always in a disturbed state of mind. Why does this happen? My thoughts run wild these days; I had lost control over them. My mind is consistently preoccupied with girls; their bodies and my imaginary love-making to them. While I think over many other subjects, the topic of girls always remains at the centre; a topic that not only keeps me busy, but of late, has also become my favourite.

Memories of the girl I met in the library, of Gloria, Mary, and some others, were always alive in my mind, but I never found them as interesting as I find them today. But they were also a distraction to my studies. I could not discuss this with Paul and Manny and break my own rule; I could depend only upon books for help.

After searching for several days, I found a volume written by William Leyer on the physical and psychological changes that occur during adolescence. The book opened a wonderful world of psychological transformation before me. He wrote: 'The development of human being is an ongoing process from birth to death. Physical development starts from birth. It becomes rapid at adolescence and ends at adulthood. Physical changes are visually noticeable but psychological changes can be only guessed from a person's behaviour. Although we can see physical changes starting at adolescence, psychological changes actually begin much before and are very intense. The most important psychological change is a strong mutual attraction between two sexes.'

I marked this page, closed the book, and contemplated.

The book clearly indicated that the upheaval going on in my mind was a common psychological change observed during adolescence, and very natural. Everyone undergoes this change to some extent.

I guessed that the psychological changes in me started from childhood. But then these psychological changes were not accompanied by any physical change. As a result, they did not become too intense. The attraction I had for girls since childhood was an indicator of the psychological transformation that had started within me. Perhaps this had started much earlier, even before the phase of physical change was over. My interest in girls, my attempts to impress them, to flirt with them, to remain close to them, had developed long ago. But during this period I was not aware of the dimension of sex. I was quite ignorant of sexual acts; satisfaction of curiosity was the only intention behind those actions. Besides knowing to differentiate between a girl and a boy at that age, I also had tremendous curiosity about the actual difference between them.

I opened the book to read more about the process of psychological changes.

'The major change during adolescence is the active imagery of the mind. Although this starts much before, its intensity and frequency increases considerably after adolescence. Love-making with one's favourite friend, adventurous events, winning awards, felicitations or incidents of bravery are some the most common subjects of these imaginary visuals.

'At this age, one tries to create a special place for one's 'self' in the society. One experiences a strong urge to prove himself to be extraordinary. This urge cannot be expressed openly. So it gets manifested in such imagery. But this 'self' is so strong that it does not get satisfied simply by imagining only once; like a movie, one creates a chain of episodes in his mind.

'The origin of this imagery is in the mutual attraction between the two sexes. One may think this imagery as his or her secret but in reality it is so delectable that it is relished almost by every person on this universe.'

I finished reading and returned home, with a whirlwind of thoughts. I had arrived at one conclusion: This imagery which starts from our adolescence, probably remains with us throughout our life. We spend considerable time in this activity because this experience is more thrilling and exciting than real life. We have no control over incidents in real life but it is not so with our imagination. It is this difference that makes us want it more and more.

This was perhaps the reason I enjoyed my imaginings with a girl, be it Mary, Gloria, or the girl from the library. The romantic escapades I had in my fantasy were definitely far more interesting and enchanting.

***

It happens very often. If I notice, even slightly, any woman, young or old, her entire body appears in my mind. Her unintentional touch or even the texture of her dress excites me. These women, in reality, may not have a beautiful body, but in my imagination, they are very attractive and buxom. Their bosoms, their buttocks, their thighs, take the size and shape I want and these keep varying. Strangely, I am more attracted towards women who are older than me; the only exception being Mom.

None of the women I come into contact with, like my school teachers or those whom I see on the streets, or the mothers of my friends, have escaped my observation. I am not conscious of the relationship I hold with them when I see them; only their femininity becomes significant to me. There's a riot in my mind when I imagine them nude, in an undressed state, or when I visualise their actions sexually.

I become ecstatic at such moments. I sense my penis becoming stiff and I desperately crave human touch. Unknowingly, I touch my penis again and again, wanting to rub vigorously. This urge is mortifying, and I have to suppress it when I am in the school or on the street. I have to take great care so that the puff in my pants is noticed by no one. I somehow manage to control myself but I cannot get rid of these suppressed desires. I desperately make my way home to some privacy, rushing to the washroom as soon as I reach. The stiff penis in my hand and as I shake it vigorously, I feel invigorated, intoxicated with pleasure. All the women become alive before me and as I continue, a strange sensation spreads across my entire body. Like an overflowing river that finds an outlet, I feel something releasing from my penis. So, this is the 'orgasm', the climax of intense sexual pleasure. As the white sticky fluid oozes out of my body, I slowly awaken from my delirium.

The next thing I find is that I'm ashamed of myself, greatly ashamed. The women whom I imagine during my release are all have had a noble relationship with me. This reality is very harsh and bitter too. Each one of them is related to me—they're my teachers, aunts, neighbours. My persistent erotic fantasies regarding them make me feel very guilty and this guilt haunts me all the time.

I know that what I am doing is called masturbation, and the fluid secreted is semen. But this knowledge alone does not stop my uneasiness. I cannot share it with anyone and all this is very suffocating. It had been hammered into me that masturbation was bad and immoral; a sin. The guilt I feel in my alleged bad and immoral action keeps pricking at me and seriously interferes with my life.

'A drop of semen carries thousands of sperms. One may ejaculate only for the sole purpose of reproduction. If one masturbates to eject it out, one loses his potency many more times. Such a loss of semen later results in illness. One suffers from various diseases, finally leading to death.' Mort had said this to me one day while chatting.

Did that mean that my potency would diminish in the proportion of the frequency of masturbation? Was I going to turn into an impotent, diseased person? I was really scared and insecure. It was alright as long as it was limited to my imagination only, but this physical discomfort which comes along with it, was not at all welcome.

I had to change the direction of my thoughts. I decided to control myself and stop masturbating.

Making this decision helped me feel calmer and I started gathering information to make its implementation easy. Coincidentally, I came across an article in the Sunday edition of *The New York Times*.

It said: 'Food and masturbation are closely related to each other. Spicy food makes one masturbate more. If one eats more boiled vegetables, wheat bread and fruits, one can reduce his sexual urges.'

I followed this advice. I had warned myself that however strong the urge, I must not masturbate. But I could adhere to this rule only during the day. At night I would feel like setting myself loose. My pent-up desires would make me desperate, but my determination would prevent any further action. Instead, I would resort to reading till my eyes shut with extreme fatigue. Despite everything , I was not able to drive away erotic thoughts about women and the subsequent stimulation of my organ. In the end, I would be compelled to masturbate and ejaculate.

I was unable to identify what was going wrong. I was behaving exactly as I had decided. I had changed my diet too. But none of this had helped drive away my thoughts about women. The more I reminded myself about my decision, the more forcefully they would return.

I pondered over the situation with a peaceful mind and discovered my mistake. I had followed Mort and the advice given in the article with complete faith, without evaluating it. Without verifying if diet could really influence one's mind, I had blindly put it into practice. It had never occurred to me that the two may not be related.

Why did I do this? I was so afraid and worried about the consequences of my behaviour that I had lost discretion. I had accepted everything I came across, without using my intellect. I had sought no scientifically-tested answer to my query of why one should not touch certain parts of the body. I decided to analyse and evaluate this question once again.

My very first objective was to discover the roots of the process of masturbation. I went through books that provided scientific analyses of sexuality. I read all three volumes of *Studies in Psychology and Sex* by Havelock Ellis, books on marriage written by Dickinson and Beam, *Encyclopaedia of Sexual Behaviour* and *Sex, Love and Morality* by William Robinson, *Concerning Specific Forms of Masturbation* by Wilhelm Reich, and other books on this topic. I discovered an invaluable treasure-trove of knowledge in these volumes and realised that so far, I had very little and very unscientific information about masturbation.

Masturbation is the action by which one plays with one's own sex organ in a way that it normally satisfies sexual desire. This word has its origin in a Greek word. Normally one uses their hand, but one may also use other methods.

Masturbation is also called autoeroticism, which means self-stimulation. More than 90 percent of the people satisfy their sexual desires by masturbation. But since it is regarded as a secret act, to be performed in privacy, one does not always have access to correct information. It is also observed that in many species, both sexes practise masturbation. Our genital organ is capable of giving bodily pleasure and it is very natural to seek pleasure by touching it. This is why we see even infants touching their sexual organs. But since semen is not created by the body at this age, there is no ejaculation. Sex hormones begin to secrete from adolescence only. When one develops a strong sexual desire, these are passed out of the body. Masturbation does not harm one's body in any way.

The formation of semen is a continuous process and it continues to form as long as sex hormones are generated in the body. This process does not stop after masturbation. Just as formation of semen is a function of sex hormones, elimination of the stored semen is also a function of these hormones. And just as our body creates semen, our mind creates sexual desire to facilitate its release. The mind and body, both are involved in this process.

I eventually realised that the idea of masturbation being immoral or sinful is very deep-rooted in most people. This feeling of guilt is not limited only to the idea of masturbation, it also affects sexual desire. When it is perfectly natural to have sexual desire, why should one feel guilty about it?

I decided to go to the root of this guilt.

We feel guilty only when we commit a sin or act immorally. I decided to examine thoroughly what exactly was immoral in the act of masturbation.

My action can be immoral if I break the rules of morality. But what does one mean by 'morality' in the first place? According to philosophy, morality implies that every individual should follow certain norms to maintain discipline in the society. This indicated that morality is linked to social behaviour and not to an individual's private behaviour. Consequently, masturbation cannot be termed as 'immoral.' I was not breaking any rules of morality.

Hypothetically, if a person is living alone on an island, then none of his actions can be labelled as moral or immoral. We cannot regard actions in terms of morality as long as they do not affect others directly or indirectly. A person who masturbates does no harm to others, so the issue of morality does not arise. But a person may harm one's own self if masturbates in excess. This habit can then become self-destructive. But even in such a case, there is no basis for calling him 'immoral'.

I had one more question related to sexuality. Can we consider ourselves immoral for our mental actions? As long as we do not convert such 'immoral' thoughts into actions, it is not appropriate to apply the criterion of morality. For example, if a person decides to make a donation to charity only in his mind, but not in practice, we cannot call him a philanthropist. In the same way, we cannot call a person 'immoral' when he only 'thinks' immorally.

By the same rule, sexual desire is not the same as a sexual act. There is a difference between having a desire and acting on it. I dream lustfully of women older to me, but only in my imagination. I do not act upon these desires or cause them any harm in real life. Why should I then consider myself guilty of a crime? Instead, if I disregard my desire, or falsely refute my fantasies and suppress my feelings, would that not mean that I am betraying 'myself'?

I made the important decision to accept wholeheartedly all my thoughts about sex, irrespective of whether they were considered right or wrong.

I repeatedly told myself: 'I am human. I too possess the natural instinct of sexuality, like all human beings. I will not deny this instinct.

But being human, I have inherited intelligence also. Therefore, before taking any action, I will use all available knowledge and my own wisdom to judge if my actions are right or wrong.'

As I liberated myself from this guilt, my mind began to breathe freely once again. I began to think afresh about masturbation. I soon discovered that one did not need their hand or any other external means to release semen. It could be achieved simply by using the imagination. After this, while masturbating, I would let go of my imagination as freely as I wished. By creating a variety of imaginary visuals, I began enjoying masturbation to the fullest.

If you masturbate day after day in the same way, at the same place, it is likely to get boring. To enhance the experience, I tried out different techniques. I searched for new isolated places other than the washroom. I would try using my left hand sometimes instead of the right, or sometimes I would change the pressure or the speed of fondling. I decided that it was natural to masturbate twice a day, without any reservations and guilt, and followed this routine regularly.

I had read several books by experts to know that masturbation did not damage our bodies in any way. Hence, impotency was impossible. On the contrary, thanks to the experiments I carried on myself, I discovered that masturbation actually has some advantages. The first was, of course, the fulfilment of one's sexual desire. The second was that one was able to forget the stress of routine life.

But to avail both these advantages, one must be rid of the guilt of masturbation.

***

4

It was my first day at college—the City College of New York. I was to study Business Administration, although the university was famous for many other courses too. Prof. Fredrick Robinson, the president of the college, was about to address the students gathered in the magnificent but packed Harris Hall.

I was sitting near a window. The college was built on the scenic Manhattan hill. As I glanced out, buildings, roads, people, all looked like very tiny toys. Amidst this crowd, the county of Harlem was distinctly noticeable. Harlem was a borough in Manhattan, lined by the blue Hudson River which flows from east to west. It was fast developing as the cultural and business hub of the Afro-American community. As I took in the scene outside, my mind began reviewing the past few years of my life.

By the time I entered high school, I had lost interest in textbooks. Success obtained by rote learning was of little significance to me. So, as soon I understood a lesson, I would start thinking independently on the topic. I considered it far more important to write in my own individual style, instead of repeating what was in textbooks. The conventional method of learning bored me. But I knew I had no other choice but to follow the old method, if I had to go ahead in life. Despite my alternative learning style, I graduated from high school with honours. I had even ranked seventh in school.

Suddenly, a hush fell over the hall. Prof. Robinson had arrived. After greeting everyone, he welcomed the students and began his address:

'The City College of New York has a great historical tradition. When Mr. Harris founded this college in 1847 as the Free Academy, he had only one aim in mind. He wanted to make education easily accessible to people from every stratum, irrespective of one's cultural, religious, or economic background. "Open the door to all" is the motto of this college. We are ranked as one of the country's best educational institutions. I am proud to say that six of our alumni have won the prestigious Nobel Prize so far.'

There was big round of applause in the hall.

'The current year of 1930 will be a revolutionary one in the history of our college. From this year we will be admitting girls in the college as well. I hope we get an encouraging response from them in future.'

Suddenly, I realised what this beautiful campus was lacking. There were only boys everywhere; girls were scarcely seen, although admission was now open to them. I could not locate a single girl in the within the thick crowd that had gathered.

I was disappointed. This would be a lot less fun without girls, I thought.

Another big round of applause brought me back to the hall.

'Now, young men, the responsibility of carrying forward this great tradition rests with you all, and you have my best wishes and blessings for this work. I am confident that one of you sitting here will bring more international accolades and keep this tradition alive.' Prof. Robinson had finished. His speech was followed by a few votes of thanks. My mind strayed again.

Sid had told me about City College. He had studied here.

'It is definitely better than other colleges. Do not try for admission anywhere else. They have seats reserved for Protestant students and you will find it very difficult to get in. The church has strict rules of attendance, whereas in City College the authorities are very lenient. After he was made president, Sir John Finlay adopted a liberal, egalitarian policy in administration, and the same continues till date.

'There is another special feature at this college. Your entire tuition fees are waived if you are a resident of New York. If you study hard and rank in the merit list, you will be also awarded a scholarship. I won this scholarship consecutively for all four years,' Sid told me.

I found this information very useful. I was in dire need of the scholarship. Dad had stopped paying us and we were in a very poor state of affairs. Expenses were increasing day by day and some form of action was urgently necessary. After giving serious thought to our financial problem, I decided to start a business. I began with a small business of pant-matching, as it was possible to manage this alongside my college studies. Often, the pants of a suit wear out faster than the coat. So, it considerably reduces the cost if one is able to replace only the pants, but only if they perfectly match the old one. I would get such pants stitched by a tailor and supply it to the customer. I involved Paul in this business as a help.

In the beginning, I tried buying pants from original makers and selling them on my own. But this turned out to be a failure. After some days, I met a guy called Matthew, a trader. He would buy our entire lot. Once this venture stabilized a little, we stopped distributing newspapers. But although we were making a profit out of this enterprise and it made out burden somewhat lighter, we were still falling short of money.

The programme was over. It was the first day of college and we had no lectures. I collected the time-table from my department and started back home.

I would now have to get accustomed to the subway train. I gathered information about the sub-way. It was the fastest and cheapest mode of commuting in the city, and very safe, too. The terminal closest to the college was at 137th Street. It was a large terminal. I had purchased a metro-card a few days ago. The date of purchase did not matter; it would be activated only from the date of travel. I could also use it for the bus service.

I spread out a map of the Manhattan subway system. After Dyckman Street were 181st Street, then 168th Street, 157th, 145th, and finally 137th Street. I repeated the route several times as I boarded the train. Thoughts about my future also began running alongside the train, perhaps a bit faster too.

I wanted to be a writer. My mind was full of thoughts and ideas and I would not rest easy until I penned them down. As a writer, I would have the freedom to write without any constraints.

But to pursue writing as a full-time profession is not easy. First, I have to be self-sufficient. So, my primary aim should be to become financially independent; and for this I have to work or own a business.

In the past few years, due to considerable development in trade and industry in the city, one could see several commercial centres mushrooming everywhere. There was greater demand for accountants and managers as compared to other positions. Therefore, I had opted for the Business Administration course. Although I have no liking for it, I have chosen to major in Accountancy because it can help me in my future prospects, and possibly fetch me a good job. I will have the financial stability necessary for an independent writer.

***

The first semester commenced. Apart from my major in Accountancy, I had chosen English Literature as an elective. I had become fond of this subject because of Prof. Johnson, who had taught us with great interest at school. I would be easily absorbed in my study of literature. Shakespeare's classics, poems by Wordsworth, Browning, Shelley, and Tennyson, would transport me to some other world. Prof. Johnson had introduced us to many of them in school, and I had read most of them before. But I discovered new meanings when I read them over again. I also found that my emotions were stirred intensely while reading. My real life was not so colourful or exciting, and so I would get carried away with the literary expressions of different emotions. I admired the authors, the prowess with which they expressed different sentiments. I would read with awe the various shades of love, sorrow, grief or despair, put into powerful words by these great litterateurs. What a great contribution literature has made to humanity, by reaching the core of the human mind. What a great capacity literature has, to bring forth different nuances of human emotions.

With spring, the second semester began. The college campus turned green. It was a large campus, sprawling over 35 acres, from the 130th Street up to the 141st Street. During spring, the entire campus wore a fresh green colour. Bright yellow daffodils, light pink tulips, lavender-hued orchids, white and yellow crab-apples, and the lush greenery of the lawns took over the entire landscape. It was a visual treat. Even the different greens of the small creepers adorning the walls or pathways would enhance the beauty of this natural palette.

Spring made our drab college lives refreshing and Wordsworth's poetry come alive: 'Poetry is the spontaneous overflow of powerful feelings; it takes its origin from emotions recollected in tranquillity.' Poetry is created when powerful feelings gush spontaneously. Poems are born after recollecting emotions with a peaceful mind. I felt as if every piece of literature said something about life; it only required interpretation and understanding.

This semester, I had one more subject in my course— Psychology. It included General Psychology and Applied Psychology as subsidiary subjects. Prof. Alexander Mintz was our professor for both. He had a special affection for me and there was a reason for this. All those who had opted for Psychology had to pass an intelligence test and I had secured the first position.

Success in this test was indicative of a high level of intellect.

'You are gifted with an extraordinary intellect. I hope you use this for fundamental research in Psychology,' he would often tell me.

'What does it mean to be highly intelligent? It means one possesses a natural ability to do things better than others. But even if one has intelligence, it may not be apparent many a time. It needs the support of hard work and sincere efforts. One has to learn the skill of using this ability. It requires dedication and persistent effort, or else one cannot make progress in life.'

I would always remember his words. In the beginning of the second semester, I began the process of self-examination. I soon found that although I obtained good grades at school and in the first semester of the college, I had the potential of doing even better. I had not utilised my potential fully. The main reason for this under-performance was my laziness and my habit of procrastination. Now I felt I must study discover under whichwhat circumstances I had developed this habit! I also found the school curriculum very dull and boring. So I would put off my study and get low grades because of this habit.

I remembered that I had this habit since the beginning of my school years. In high school, I never completed my studies according to schedule. I would study late into the night before every exam. This would obviously result in poor marks. In fact, I was so lethargic about studies, that I never even brought home the books I kept in my locker. This continued into college. To put an end to this habit, I examined my attitude to the conventional method of studying. I always looked down on my school work believing it to be complicated and also dull. There is no urgency to study today, I would tell myself. It can be completed later at leisure. It never occurred to me that I should check to see if this was the right attitude to carry around. It was a fact that studies were uninteresting and uninspiring. But I had adopted an irrational approach that one should only prioritize that which is interesting and postpone the rest.

Why did I think so? Because it was to my convenience. Such procrastination provides only temporary relief, but ultimately it does no good. One has to face the real situation some day. Besides, you also carry a feeling of guilt. When I said that I was not worried about grades, I was, in fact, deceiving myself. It was a lame attempt to hide my laziness. In fact, to achieve something in life, you have to be serious about your performance. If you are not, you tend to aim small and under-utilise your potential. I wanted to grow big in life; I wanted to go ahead in life! I will sincerely try to change my habits!

I began to bring this change in me immediately. One of the ways to get over your inertia of doing some disinteresting work is to start that work first! I found that I would feel boredom from the start of the study itself and then I would postpone it. So I planned to get rid of this 'start' itself. To begin with, when I got ready to study, I began reminding myself again and again that I had to study only for a few minutes, after which I had the liberty to decide whether to continue or not. The first few minutes were my acid test. Once you overcome this stage by pushing yourself, it becomes easy to continue. This initial period is very difficult to conquer. Once you start, the realisation that you are actually studying reinforces your will to keep going.

Prof. Mintz had emphasised the importance of such

'reinforcement', which was crucial for sustaining change. Gradually, I was able to increase this from five minutes to fifteen minutes. Finally, after a few days, I got rid of my habit of procrastinating. I named this method, 'the five-minute plan'.

This effort resulted in a remarkable change in my performance.

At the end of every semester, we were required to submit four papers of a self-study report on a topic selected from our course. During the first semester, I had submitted these papers late, almost at the fag end; due to my old habit of procrastination. But by the second, I had improved considerably.

The college library would be less crowded at the beginning of a semester. I chose my topics right at the start and this gave me ample time to prepare. I submitted them much before the scheduled date, at the beginning of the semester itself. The professors were surprised, and I found one more benefit. I had more time at my disposal for the final exams; so I could fully focus on them. Of course, my performance was much better in the second semester. I was fond of Literature, Philosophy and Psychology; but I made special efforts for Accountancy too, a subject which I somewhat hated. As a result of my hard work, I obtained good grades as well as the scholarship for the second year of college.

I had definitely learnt a lot from my new practice. Procrastination gives short-term relief but is harmful in the long run. I was convinced that it was useful to think of the future gain rather than present relief.

Only when I reconditioned my mind with this attitude, was I able to free myself of old ingrained habits. This would not have been possible merely by talking about its disadvantages.

***

It is impossible to forget that Friday evening. Generally, I would return home from college by six in the evening. Most of the offices would close between five and half-past five. The 137th Street terminal would be overcrowded. When the train arrived, along with the crowd, I was also pushed inside where there was barely space to stand. Passengers squeezed themselves around me from all sides. In front of me, there stood a young girl.

As the train picked up speed, her butt began brushing against the lower part of my body. I tried to shrink into myself. But it continued to happen. Initially I thought it was due to the speed of the train. Soon, I realised it was not so. It was a deliberate action to stimulate my organ. I was unable to see her face but her action had aroused me enough. My penis hardened, sensitive to the touch of her buttocks. I was so excited that I ejaculated in the train itself. Everything happened so fast. It took me some time to regain normalcy from that state.

I approached the door of the compartment near my station and secretly glanced at her. She was not attractive but appeared to be very skilful in this action. I was ashamed of my wet trousers, and walked home in embarrassment, careful to conceal the patch. But the unexpected yet titilating incident lingered in my mind. Suddenly, I had found a new way of satisfying my sexual urge. I barely saw a girl in college and being intimate with those from my neighbourhood was next to impossible. I did not have courage to speak with any of them. Till then I had only two options, either to masturbate or to enjoy my fantasies. This new method was very convenient. I was not required to talk to any woman or to plead with her or, as suggested by my friends, to undress her. Without all of this, I was able to gratify myself, at least partially, if not fully. Moreover, it was difficult for anyone to identify me in the crowd. That night, I dreamt only about the train, the crowd, the girl, and those pleasurable moments.

Gradually, I grew well-versed in this technique. The main terminal of Van Cortlandt Park, the Marble Hill Junction, Dyckman Street, 207th Street, 168th Street, and the city bus stops … I surveyed these and many other crowded places, and noted the times when they were crowded. Then I started frequenting these places as much as possible.

The most surprising part was how successful I was every time in finding someone willing to be a partner in this game. I could recognise the mute compliance of the woman from her smallest gestures. I did follow one rule though. Even if I had a slight doubt that the woman was reluctant, or if she shrunk her body, I would instantly withdraw. I was against forcing myself on somebody. After some days I became such an expert, that I began wearing a condom to keep my trousers dry. I lost count of the number of women with whom I enjoyed these adventures.

I do remember one woman very distinctly. She seemed to be around 35 years of age. She would wait, like me, at the Dyckman Street subway station every morning. We would deliberately wait for the platform to get overcrowded and then start our secret affair. I was soon addicted to our morning association. One day, in the evening, I was surprised to see her in the same compartment of the train while returning from college. Although the train was not crowded, she sat very snugly next to me. I almost lost my mind. There was no communication between us, but with every jerk of the speeding train, different parts of her body kept touching mine. I began feeling dizzy.

When she got down at her station, I followed her. I was almost inebriated with excitement. We reached her apartment. I took the elevator after her and stood at the door of her flat.

'Please do not enter. I am married and I have two kids,' she sternly whispered in a hushed tone and hurriedly slammed the door in my face.

That woke me from my delirium. While following her, I had not realised that I had reached the 215th Street. After this incident, I never followed her or any other woman. But it did not affect our daily morning affair and we continued our routine for quite a number of days without any problem. One day, she disappeared altogether. Possibly, she had changed her job.

Once, in the train, I saw a woman catching a man by his collar and thrashing him furiously for nearly ten minutes. As I saw this scene, my heart began pounding. I began sweating profusely. I was already ridden by a feeling of guilt that my behaviour was wrong. Until this incident, I had been successful in suppressing this guilt deep down, below my outburst of lust. But now, it was poking at me. What was this process going on in my mind and body? I began searching hectically for more information.

I learnt that this type of behaviour, where one seeks pleasure by rubbing one's body against that of someone else in a crowd, is called frotteurism, and the person who does this is called a frotteur. Frotteurism is defined as sex-play without intercourse. Instead of an actual sex act, a person fulfils his sexual desires by this way. Such an act can be treated as offensive if performed without the consent of the partner, and the person can be also tried in court for this crime.

A new chain of thoughts began.

Being under the influence of strong sexual demands, I had never given my behaviour serious thought. I had presumed that I was doing no harm by following frotteurism. Also, I chose only those women who were willing. I would tell myself: It is not wrong if the act is consensual and if it satisfies both the partners. But now I reviewed this stance seriously. I remembered the expressions on the face of that unknown woman, when she shut the door before me. Shockingly, it revealed one more aspect of my behaviour. I had carelessly assumed that she approved all of it. But the truth was that she approved of this frotteurism only as long as it was done secretively. She had shut the door out of fear of exposure. Obviously, she too carried a feeling of guilt like me. This act was not only affecting both of us, but also her husband, who was a complete stranger to me. Her consent, which I had presumed, was a deceitful one. She was deceiving her husband and, although indirectly, I was also party to it. My participation in this deception was not right.

I could also not forget the angry woman who lambasted a frotteur by catching him by his collar. It was very clear that this woman did not approve of frotteurism. But in this, one did presume the consent of a stranger at the start of the act. Even if I withdraw after knowing her reluctance, I definitely offended her during the initial moments, however brief they may be, when I forced myself upon her against her will. So whether the frotteur is a man or a woman, they are wrong. Frotteurism is practised in crowded places and generally with strangers. In such circumstances, it is not possible to have prior knowledge of consent of the other partner. So there is all likelihood of offending someone. Therefore, the fury of the woman who caught the man by his collar was quite justified.

I regretted that for so long I had behaved improperly. But I kept myself from feeling guilty about it. There is a difference between feeling guilty and feeling regret. In regret, we accept our mistake; we take responsibility for that action, and try not to repeat the mistake. We also make efforts to improve ourselves. But when we consider ourselves guilty, besides accepting our mistake, we also criticise ourselves and subsequently condemn ourselves. Thus, we also denigrate our 'total personality' as a human. We presume that in the future, too, we are likely to commit the same mistake. Consequently, we become incapable of changing our behaviour.

I admitted that I behaved incorrectly, but I did not think that I was worthless. I forgave myself and accepted my mistakes. I did not condemn myself in totality. But I was determined not to let this happen again. This made it easy to focus on the important issue of finding ways to improve.

I longed for female companionship. But I decided not to satisfy this need by secret or furtive methods. I was not able to communicate with women, but I prevented myself from concluding that I would never be able to communicate in the future as well.

Instead of avoiding confrontation with a problem, it is advantageous to battle it out. I felt ready to tackle the next problem in life.

***

As I stood before the mirror, I remembered what the doctor had said the day before.

Our college had arranged a medical camp for the students and he was the chief doctor. Like everyone else, I also underwent all the prescribed tests; but I was asked to see him personally, after the test reports were ready.

I could see my reports lying on his table.

'Albert, from these reports, I see that you seem to have diabetes,' he started.

I was shocked. I looked at him blankly.

'You are suffering from "Renal Glycosuria". It means sugar has been detected in your urine, although not in your blood,' he explained.

He began giving me more information but I had gone numb. His words fell on deaf ears. He patted me and I came back to my senses.

'Don't be afraid. This disease is not fatal. You can control it with a proper diet. From now on, you have to eliminate all sweet and sugary items like cake, ice-cream and chocolates from your food. To maintain good health you have to follow only this restriction.' The doctor tried to console me.

This was truly disastrous. My health problems started first with tonsils, followed by kidney malfunction, then headaches, weak eyes, and now diabetes. The problem with my eyes was life-long. Now this added disease meant several restrictions on my eating habits. And I was so fond of sweet things!

I told myself repeatedly that unpleasant things are inevitable in life. I had no other option than to accept this reality. It was up to me to accept it either gracefully or grudgingly. I opted for the first. I decided to carry on with this new disease without complaining and without self-pity. Yet, it took quite some time to come to terms with it.

Although I had accepted the new development with a rational mind, eEvery time I stood before a mirror, I would remember my ailments, the doctors and their warnings, the hospital days, and the different advice given by different doctors. How miserable life had become. I would hate my diseased reflection in the mirror, the thick spectacles. Several thoughts would keep nibbling at my mind.

'Oh shit, how weak and thin I look! These ugly glasses have totally spoilt my personality. Which girl could be attracted to such a boy? I will never be able to satisfy a woman. I do not look smart. I cannot impress anyone. I am just a bookworm. I am worthless.'

To impress a girl one should have a rugged personality, a sturdy body like Samuel, my classmate. He is not proficient in academics but he is so macho. He is always dating some girl or the other. 'They follow me willingly,' he boasts, and I have to admit that it was true.

I was jealous of Samuel. I look down upon myself. I was still not able to chat freely with a girl. How could I ever expect someone to date me? I always feared that girls would look down on me. I have courage to speak only with Paul, Manny, and a few close friends.

I had such self-talk a number of times! This continued for a while. One evening, while observing myself in the mirror, I realised that 'I' had not accepted 'myself'. I did not love myself, and considered myself a worthless person. How then could I expect others to love me? When I was deploring myself, how could the opinion of other people matter? If I do not respect myself, then who else in this world will respect me? I cannot force others to accept me, but to accept myself wholeheartedly was definitely within my capacity.

I decided to examine to what extent the statement—'I am worthless'—was true.

I lacked good looks because of my ailments. Did I look down upon myself because of that? It was my belief that not being attractive made me good for nothing, and inferior to others. I decided to examine this inferiority complex.

Every person lacks some quality all the other. Do all people in world then bear an inferiority complex? Even handsome people are affected by complexes. Similarly, many unattractive, plain-looking persons can display confidence in their behaviour.

This showed me that my 'good-for-nothing' assumption was wrong.

I was unable to speak to women because of the fear that they would despise me or reject me. I was worried that their reaction might prove that I was worthless.

How can the negative opinion of another person decide my worth? In reality, if a girl did consider me worthless, the logical conclusion should be that I did not live up to her expectations. But how does that make me unworthy? With the same logic, if someone praises me, do I become a person of high stature? Was I going to change my opinion about myself according to that of others?

The truth is that every person has some shortcoming. But when he evaluates himself on basis of this shortcoming and concludes that he is totally unworthy as a person, an inferiority complex sets in. It prevents him from accepting his own 'self' unconditionally. I was also labelling myself as an entirely useless person on the basis of a single attribute.

The difference between the statements: 'The colour of my pants is black' and 'My colour is black' is the same as that between the statements: 'I am despicable because I do not look manly' and 'I am despicable as a person'. Treating myself as a meritless person was the main reason behind my inferiority complex.

I remembered an example given by a psychologist. Suppose, some of the fruits kept in a basket are very ripe, some are juicy, some are raw and yet to ripen, and some are rotten, then can we describe all the fruits by a single adjective? Of course not.

An individual's personality is similar to the fruit basket. It consists of different characteristics and categorizing it singularly as good or bad, or of high or low status, or by a single general quality is difficult.

This clearly meant that, like some of the fruits in the basket, I did possess some good qualities as well as a few deterring aspects like my illnesses; but it was inappropriate to regard myself as totally undeserving or deserving, because of them. So I stopped attributing these adjectives to my personality. Instantly, I felt relieved. All the suffocation disappeared. Now, with a cool mind, I thought over the difficulties I faced while talking to a girl. I found that I was mainly worried about the possibility of insult or rejection.

I decided to study this worry. I prepared a list of some questions I could ask myself. I had read about this technique in the biography of Socrates. This method of disputation was very useful in understanding a subject. Zeno, the Greek philosopher, had used this methodology even before Socrates. I decided to give it a shot.

I asked myself: What is so disastrous if I talk to a girl and get rejected?

The answer: This experience is definitely painful, but not so acute to be considered disastrous. I am unnecessarily exaggerating the intensity of my pain.

My second question was: How far is it right to presume that I would be rejected by all girls, just because a few of them could possibly reject me?

To this, my answer was: No. It is not realistic to believe so. There is also a possibility of getting positive responses from some.

It was obvious that my unrealistic thinking made me hesitant in talking to a girl.

My next question: If I fail to communicate with a girl today, why should I assume that I will always fail in future?'

My answer: It only means that I have failed today. It is baseless to predict that I will fail in all future adventures also. It is because of such unreasonable predictions that I cannot progress.

My last question was important: If all the girls reject me, do I become worthless?'

My answer was a firm NO. My worth did not depend on the opinion of the girls. They may not find me deserving but I was definitely worthwhile and deserving to myself.

The advantage of this dialogue method was that I was able to eradicate all the incorrect assumptions that were the base of my worry. I had been making illogical and exaggerated statements so casually. I never thought of examining these statements before.

I decided to put these new thoughts into action. I thought of a plan. Just changing my foolish thinking was not sufficient; I had to consistently practise talking to girls. One cannot learn to swim merely by reading books about swimming or listening to a trainer talk. One must take the plunge and test the waters. So my next action was to make an actual attempt to talk to girls.

I surveyed the Bronx Botanical Garden where we three— Paul, Manny and I—would go every evening. In the centre of the garden was a beautiful oval-shaped platform with several benches. One could relax on these benches and enjoy a panoramic view of the entire forty-acre garden complex. A small waterfall and the Bronx River were on the right. Thick, colourful bunches of flowers from the rose and orchid gardens lined the left side. In front, a little away, one could catch a glimpse of the Children's Adventure Park. The chirping and frolicking of children made the atmosphere lively and cheerful.

I noted that most of the girls visited the garden in the evenings, between six and seven. So I began scouting the benches on the platform to see if any girl was sitting alone anywhere. I had instructed myself to start a dialogue within a minute of the encounter. I was afraid that if I allowed myself more time, my old misapprehensions would overpower me. To initiate dialogue, I had selected some topics, like the weather, the garden, or events happening around us.

Nature is an easy subject. So, I would start with: 'How beautiful is this garden.'

Or, sometimes, 'What a beautiful scene,' while looking at the Rose and Orchid gardens.

Or, at times, glancing at the Bronx River, I would say, 'Oh, the drops from the waterfall can be felt even here.'

Girls are also usually fond of children. If I noticed a girl watching the children playing around, I would say, 'How cute are these kids!'

If a girl did not pay attention to such statements, I would switch to, 'What fine weather.'

I got a variety of responses through this experiment.

Some stayed mum.

A few got irritated. 'Shut up,' they would retort.

Some girls would just frown and leave.

A few displayed expressions of annoyance.

But some responded politely. They did not talk much, but they answered my questions.

And some turned out to be so talkative that they bored me with their chatter.

From this experience, I was convinced that rejection by a girl just meant that she did not like my specific behaviour, not me entirely. Keeping this in mind, I continued trying my technique on different girls.

I followed this routine for almost a month. Every day, after returning home, I would make a note of this experience in my diary. After a month or so I reviewed the diary.

In one month, I had introduced myself to almost 130 girls. Out of these, 30 girls had left the scene before I could start any dialogue and the remaining ones had responded to some extent.

Out of the 100 who responded, one case was most interesting. Although it was a singular experience, one girl had actually shown interest in meeting me. She asked me out on a date, and we decided to meet the next day at the main gate of the Brooklyn Bridge at six in the evening. Dressed in my finest clothes, I reached the appointed place at five sharp. But when she did not show up even as late as eight, I decided to turn back.

This incident did not upset me. On the contrary, I strolled on the bridge and enjoyed the scenic view of Manhattan before returning home.

I saw one more advantage to this experiment.

I had learnt to overcome the disappointment of such occasions, apart from being able to conquer the hurdle of speaking with a girl. Henceforth, I was not going to hesitate before asking out a girl I liked.

***

I had decided to transform myself. I undertook a new task. I was going to get rid of the insomnia, which had become chronic. I suffered from chronic insomnia since childhood. I would sleep barely for a few hours at night, and this little sleep was never sound.

When I tried to find out more about the causes of insomnia, I discovered that it was not only a physiological disease but also a psychological one. The first cause, in my case, was physical: I had a very low level of thyroid hormones and was already being medicated for this deficiency. The second reason was more serious than the first: It was the worry I had about my sleeplessness.

I began examining what exactly my worry was.

I would keep brooding over every unpleasant incident that happened during the day. This brooding would continue even at night, which would be uneasy and restless. It was the beginning of insomnia. My agitated mind would not calm down easily. A nagging thought—that I had wasted the whole night brooding—

would keep harassing me. This feeling would further hamper my sleep. After some time, the thought that all my efforts to sleep were ineffective would further add to my anxiety. In this fashion, I would keep on piling layers of anxiety. Without getting disturbed there was a need to remove these layers one by one.

I reviewed my sleeping habits. I was not able to sleep even by 2 a.m. Logically, by this hour, one should at least feel sleepy. So, the reason was not only physical. In reality, my mind would be full of various thoughts surrounding my insomnia. These thoughts would not let me sleep during the remaining bit of the night.

The thought mainly culpable for my sleeplessness was: 'I should not have had this illness.' I decided to deal with this by asking some logical questions to myself: Who am I to decide this? Is it realistic that I should not suffer from any ailment in life? Do I consider myself the greatest and the mightiest of all to think so?

While analysing these questions, it became clear that it was not in my control to choose a disease or to decide whether a particular disease could afflict me or not. I do not have the power to make such decisions. I am not at all extraordinary, or the greatest or mightiest person on this earth. It is alright to say that 'I would have been happy but for this sleeplessness'; but it is entirely illogical and baseless to say that 'I should never suffer from sleeplessness'. The trauma arising out of my irrational thinking was aggravating my problem. I definitely could not escape the suffering, but I could at least stop the problem from becoming more serious. Only after clearing these causative factors one by one, was I able to concentrate on the physical cause of my insomnia.

After consistent efforts, I was successful in overcoming my insomnia. After that, I turned my attention towards the basic problem of getting good sleep. To manage sound sleep, I began focusing my attention on the pendulum of the wall-clock as soon as I lay down. Its rhythmic movement would sometimes induce sleep.

I did not become anxious if this didn't work. I had already learnt to prevent anxiety. I would try the imagery technique whereby I would solve puzzles, think about the books I read, or court girls. After some days, I mastered this technique too. At last, after relentless efforts, I was liberated from this stubborn illness.

Prof. Johnson had, one day, told us about a quote by the Roman philosopher Seneca, which proved right in my case: 'We suffer more often in imagination than from reality.'

How accurate was his observation of the human mind.

I was gradually learning the mental process behind restlessness. Whenever we face a problem, we are disturbed. Later, by asking ourselves not to get disturbed, we add to this disturbance. This leads to one getting more and more engulfed by the problem. I have named this state, 'disturbance about disturbance.' The first priority should be to free oneself from 'Second order disturbance.'

***

The brightly-lit entrance of 'Yummy Donuts' was quite prominent. This was a cafe very close to our college and popular for its fast-food. Before entering, one had to take a card or a 'ticket' at the entrance. This ticket was free. The list of the items one ordered and the bill would get recorded on this ticket. At the exit, they would check if the bill was paid. One could leave the cafe only after payment. My friends had told me about this procedure in the first semester.

As soon as we entered the café, everybody placed an order. These were all moneyed guys.

'Albert, why don't you have something?' Everybody insisted.

On the table arrived the potato wedges, fries, sandwiches, and pastries that they had ordered.

'Albert, you can have coffee at least.' They knew about my diabetes and diet restrictions.

I secretly searched my pockets. Ten cents. I did not wish to spend those precious ten cents unnecessarily. I hesitated, but after a while it became difficult to refuse all of them. Finally, I had to yield. I ordered coffee.

But the actual reason was something else.

I was afraid that the cashier and even my friends might look down upon me if I did not order anything. Although I was not hungry, although I needed those 10 cents for some other purpose, only because I was worried about the opinion of others, I spent them on a cup of coffee. With great reluctance I gulped down the bland, sugarless coffee. I could not enjoy even a single drop. The feeling that I had spent money wrongly made the coffee bitterer than it was.

I could not forget this incident even after coming home that evening. This happened very frequently. I would spend money carelessly and then repent it later.

I decided to put an end to this habit. I examined my behaviour. Why did I spend carelessly so often? The true reason was that I was always worried about the opinion of other people—the cashier, my friends. This anxiety was deeply set in my mind. I had to uproot it.

Was it absolutely essential to earn praise and admiration in life? It was definitely not worth worrying all the time about the opinion of other people.

And while I cared about others, I had forgotten about my own likes and dislikes. I was ignoring myself, my needs, my priorities. Were those opinions and comments, for which I was paying a price, consistent? Could I be sure that every single action of mine, even if it had a good purpose, would not be criticised by my friends? I had noticed that people always have two different opinions on every issue.

I was realizsing my mistake. It was not wrong to try and impress others or to make some special effort to gain their goodwill. But to insist that they should always speak well of me is irrational. While making this effort, I had shut the doors of my mind to my own self. I was paying a heavy price in the process, by suppressing my desires. I was trying to prove to others that I was different from who I was, and while doing so I was being dishonest with myself.

With an open mind, I subjected this incident to my disputation method: 'How should I behave in order to please everyone?' 'Can any one kind of behaviour universally please each and everybody?' 'Is it absolutely essential for us to earn admiration from one and all?' 'Is it possible to please everyone?' 'Is it right to force myself to fulfil this unrealistic demand?'

While searching for answers to these questions, I realised that no such behaviour which satisfies everyone, exists in this world; nor can it be defined. There is no such rule—which tells us that we should always seek the approval of others—because this is not possible in practice. It was my pig-headed obstinacy to presume so.

What if one of my drawbacks gets revealed before others? Does it make me an unworthy person? It will only indicate that my action was unsatisfactory in one out of several occasions. So, to treat me as totally unworthy or useless, on this basis, is definitely an exaggeration.

After this brain-storming, I determined to check if others approved of me, but I promised to not get disturbed if they did not.

I did implement my decision when we visited 'Yummy Donuts' the next time. While leaving the café, I was not ashamed of my blank ticket. The matter that I had considered so serious was actually very insignificant to my friends. No one noticed my blank ticket, no one ridiculed me, nor did the cashier at the exit sneer at me. I felt like a free bird. The real cause of my worry was me. My unrealistic thinking had aggravated my problem. How much easier it was in reality.

But my mind was still bogged by more questions. Would I have still been so strong had someone actually ridiculed my blank ticket?

I began evaluating myself. I should be ashamed if I did something which should not be done publicly. I would damn myself. This meant that the feeling of shame is self-damning. I had to stop feeling shamedful. I convinced myself that henceforth I had to evaluate a particular behaviour of a person specifically and not his entire personality. I would feel ashamed; but I could also refuse to feel ashamed. I had that choice. I avoided things of which I was ashamed. To stop this tendency, I decided to fight it out. But this required some risk and guts.

I thought of an adventurous plan.

I decided to deliberately do things that made me feel shameful. I was not going to avoid them. I would face them directly. I was going to train myself to avoid feeling ashamed, even if it resulted in embarrassment. The first step was to find things that I regarded as shameful. I chose a situation which commonly occurred.

While walking on the streets, if I felt the need to relieve myself, I would search for cafés that had a restroom outside, so that no one would know that I had used it. But it was generally very difficult to locate such cafés and it would be very uncomfortable to control the urge. Most of the cafés on my way to the college had toilets located inside. So I was compelled to take a ticket and enter the café. If I only used the restroom without buying any food, it meant showing a blank ticket while leaving. I was ashamed of this, and would avoid such cafés.

I hit upon a plan. I selected a few cafés on my way that had restrooms inside. I would use these even if I was not in urgent need and show the blank ticket at the exit.

Many a times, the cashier displayed no expression.

Sometimes, the guy would just raise his eyebrows.

A few even returned a sarcastic smile.

'Free ride, ha!' one cashier had remarked.

They all were reacting to my behaviour and not to me as a person, I reminded myself.

This experience encouraged me to undertake more such daring experiments. I would purposely behave like an idiot. I learnt to tolerate negative reactions. I told myself to bear with rejection, snide remarks, and the criticism people hurled at me.

But I followed certain principles while behaving in this fashion. The first one was never to violate public rules and regulations. The second one was never to offend or insult anybody. These experiments had to be harmless.

I selected three places for such experiments. All of them were far away from my house and in crowded localities, where nobody would recognise me.

The first place was the newly-built Rockefeller Centre. It was a very big business centre, spread across 21 acres from 48th Street to 50th Street. Many high-profile businessmen would frequent this complex of 18 buildings. I selected one at the centre.

It was November, but the weather was still warm. Offices in this complex would have a lunch-break at one. I had worn my best suit. A well-dressed man came out of the building. I quickly followed him and said, 'Please excuse me.'

He turned back with a questioning look.

Very politely, I began, 'I have just been released from the mental hospital. Could you please tell me what the current month is?'

His expressions changed instantly. His eyes widened. He started walking away fast, without uttering a single word. But he turned back a few times to look at me even as he kept walking ahead.

I marched to another building in the complex. I spotted a man who was walking leisurely, lost in his own thoughts. 'Please excuse me,' I said.

He stopped at my words. I put the same question as before. 'November,' he curtly replied and left in a hurry.

My next target was a man near the Channel Garden. On hearing my question, he examined me from top to bottom and said mockingly, 'You idiot, you need the address of the mental hospital, not the month,' and turned away.

Although these responses were negative in character, they did not seem so dreadful to me. Gradually, I taught myself to remain calm in such situations.

The newly-built Empire State Building on Fifth Avenue was the next place for my experiment. It was the tallest building in the world, with 102 floors. There were observation decks on the 86th and 102nd floors. It was a favourite tourist attraction and, hence, would be extremely crowded most of the time. Although I had never been on these decks, I was more interested in my experiment than observing the city from the top. I entered the building and carefully studied the lobby.

The evening was getting cold. A chilly wind was blowing, although there was no forecast of snowfall. I put on my woollens and reached the lobby.

Three men were emerging from it. I stopped them. 'Please excuse, I have been released from the mental hospital just now…,' I repeated my earlier question..

One of them stared at me with a bewildered expression. The second person escaped, murmuring, 'I don't know.'

The third simply ran away in fright. I observed his expressions as he ran. He seemed to perspire even in the cold.

The Grand Central Terminal was my third venue. There is usually heavy traffic here throughout the day. The entrance of the terminal and the interior was decorated with beautiful chandeliers and marble statues. Many people would visit just to see this grand interior. There were seats for people to rest, and overlooking these seats was a huge shiny brass clock suspended from the wall above. This clock was visible from every spot in Grand Central.

I reached the terminal at ten minutes to six. I had worn a wrist watch, too. When the clock was chiming six, in a loud voice, I asked an old man sitting there, 'Sir, what time is it, please?'

He looked surprised. With a frown on his face, he pointed towards the clock above. I repeated my question, this time in a much louder voice. This drew the attention of some people around us. I noted their expressions.

Some persons found me funny.

A few passed remarks laughingly.

Some, I felt, were actually sympathetic.

And some wanted to mock at me.

While I was leaving, I heard someone say, 'Oh, poor guy. So young. Looks to be from a good family. What a pity.'

This experiment taught me to face any experience without shame. My behaviour was ridiculous and idiotic. But it was just 'a specific' behaviour; it did not make me an idiot, or a mad person. I imbibed this conviction within me. There was no reason to feel ashamed of myself. I learnt the skill of isolating 'myself' even when I received adverse comments from others.

I benefitted from this newly-acquired skill in my routine life as well. It was especially useful in dealing with Matthew. He would buy pants from us, but also often blast us on some minor issues, like colour or texture, and create a ruckus. Many a time, he would shout, abuse, insult, and belittle us. It was terrifying to talk to him and I would push Paul to handle him. I conveniently considered that negotiating with Matthew, pleading with him, or convincing him was not my job.

Now, I no longer felt tensed while dealing with Matthew. I had been avoiding this experience. I realised that I would never progress if I continued with this attitude. So later I began contacting him personally instead of asking Paul.

I was now convinced that I did not become unworthy if Matthew said so. This gave me more confidence while dealing with other clients.

I named this method my 'Shame-Attacking Exercise'.

These were a tough test for me. But I learnt to take risk and overcome hurdles. I also brought out my hidden persona. If I had not undertaken these exercises, some facets of my personality would have remained unexplored forever.

The Shame-Attacking Exercise had definitely enriched my life.

***

There was a cafeteria at the basement of Sheppard Hall in college, and a corner of this cafeteria was the meeting place for a group of boys who called themselves the 'Panther Gang'. Members of this group were from different continents, and came from different religions and cultures. Some were local residents and others were migrants. Each one had to share something with others and this was the common factor that brought them together. I joined this group. One could get a good deal of information from the discussions held within the group. I liked these discussions more than the college lectures. Very often, there would be debates on political issues. Everyone spoke with great fervour on current hot topics, expressed opinions freely, and argued enthusiastically. A favourite topic on which hectic debates were often held was: Whose ideology was superior, Leon Trotsky's Marxism or Stalin's Marxism? This debate would almost bring the opposing teams to blows. My ideas began growing new offshoots and I, too, started expressing them vehemently on this new platform.

Some of the friends from this gang introduced me to a new organisation called Young America & New America, which I joined.

It had been started by a local music teacher with the aim of reforming the economy of the country. Its promoters believed in utilising only natural resources for economic reforms; they were not interested in associating with any foreign organisation. They did not support the ideology behind Marxism. In fact, this organisation was a strong critic of Marxist principles. Its members did not believe just in following ideologies but in more practical and feasible ways of reform.

I was quite impressed by this concept of self-compliance. I soon became an active member and started working as a salaried organiser of one of its revolutionary wings. In this capacity, I was very often required to make speeches. The Shame-Attacking Exercises helped me even here. I had improved in elocution but I was still scared of talking before a new audience. I was scared of getting mocked if my talk was ineffective or if I made some mistake.

I wanted to eliminate this worry. It was eclipsing my talent as a good orator. I adopted the motto of 'Sticks and stones might break my bones, but words can never hurt me'. I had the choice of not getting hurt by what people said. I had to use this while addressing the public.

Unfortunately, the revolutionary wing was weak and died a natural death. But I was grateful that it gave me the opportunity to overcome my fear of bitter reactions or mockery.

The Panther Gang published a weekly called *Campus,* mainly for the student community. I began writing articles, poems, and songs for *Campus,* for which I received favourable responses from the students. Soon, I became its chief columnist and poet. I would express my revolutionary ideas and thoughts without inhibition. *Sexual desires in college students* was one such article which became extremely popular within a short time. During that week, almost every student was seen carrying that issue of *Campus*. I was on cloud nine.

But I was rudely brought back to earth within a few days.

I received a notice from the college officials which read: 'You have written objectionable articles in the *Campus* weekly. We will shortly inform you of the action that will be taken by college authorities.'

It was difficult for them to ignore my brazenness. A meeting was held to discuss the issue. I was also called to attend this meeting.

However, without allowing me to speak, the committee declared its verdict:

'You are accused of writing erotic and inflammatory articles. Our institution is known for its good students. You are spoiling the students with your writing. Henceforth you are not allowed to write in this weekly. As a punishment for this offence, you are barred from entering the college for two weeks starting tomorrow.'

I was not allowed to defend myself. It was a unilateral decision by the college authorities. I walked out of the meeting extremely disturbed.

One may not accept a thought if one does not like it or agree with it. But it is strange to restrict someone from even expressing it.

A thought should be debated with another thought. It is a misuse of power, to force people to accept only what one party thinks. It is also unjust. I write only about truth in sexuality. I genuinely do not consider it to be indecent. They are afraid because it exposes their hypocrisy. They are afraid to acknowledge their own true feelings.

In reality, it is a peculiar situation for most college students like me. In conservative societies, one is not allowed to have physical relationships until they marry. But sexual desires are awakened from the stage of adolescence. The period between adolescence and marriage is considerably long. Orthodox cultures do not guide us to find ways to gratify our sexual desires. On the contrary, we are asked to suppress such natural desires till marriage and practise self-control. Why should we torture our minds and bodies by staying celibate? Why does nature make this change from adolescence? One cannot find answers to these questions in religious scripture. What should a person like me, who has reached sexual maturity, do to satisfy his sexual urge?

In my article, I had written: 'It is natural to have sexual desires. It is more harmful, psychologically, if we fail to recognise the existence of such desires and suppress them. Try to look for proper ways to fulfil your sexual urge. There are only two options for unmarried college students like us. These are masturbation and surreptitious physical relationships. Apart from the danger of contracting diseases, there are other risks involved in having secretive affairs. Hence, masturbation is the preferable option. We can get gratification without involving someone else. Till you become eligible to have a real sexual experience, this is one way to make yourself happy. In fact, people practise masturbation even though it is prohibited. But it is not approved by society. This pressure of disapproval makes us feel guilty about it. One expects happiness in the fulfilment of sexual desires, but guilt mars this happiness. So friends, throw away this guilt and shame and experience the joy of masturbation without inhibition.'

I regard my suggestion of masturbation as an alternative to surreptitious relations as an act of decent behaviour. I do not mislead anybody by my writings, nor do I lie when I express my thoughts. I prefer to attack real issues point blank. When I do not want to treat a woman as my sister or mother, I do not hide my feelings hypocritically, by calling her so. If a woman arouses me sexually I admit it truthfully, because I am true to myself. I have openly accepted my sexuality without inhibitions. But I am aware that this is very difficult for most people.

However, accepting one's sexuality does not grant you absolute freedom to behave as you wish. I observe all social norms and will follow them in the future too. Till date, I have not knowingly crossed any limit of decency. In spite of this, I was accused of spoiling students. I considered this charge as totally baseless.

Denying expression of independent thought amounts to prevention of independent thinking. Instead of banning such expression in the college magazine, students should be allowed to write freely. They should be encouraged to open their minds and voice their feelings. They should be able to share their sensitivities truthfully. Calling their writing objectionable, and not allowing them an opportunity to defend themselves, indicates that their freedom of expression is not being recognised.

I form my own opinions. My opinions are different from others. ItI understood that it would be difficult to get my opinions about sexual freedom approved by society, as long as sexuality is treated as a sin. Till then, if I try to put forth these opinions, I will definitely invite criticism. I have to prepare myself to face severe opposition and preserve my independent thoughts, of which I am totally convinced.

Even if others try to demoralise me, it is entirely within my control to not get demoralised, and this decision is exclusively mine.

***

5

The recession, which started in 1929, has reached its peak in 1934. The country has not yet managed to recover from the "Great Depression". The nation's economy is in a shambles. About 13 to 15 million Americans are jobless. The unemployment index has risen by 24.9 percent. The salaried class is facing a six percent cut in wages. Thousands have been rendered homeless as they are unable to repay their home loan. Around two and a quarter million people are wandering in search of food, shelter and employment. Every sector is gripped by recession. In January last year, there was a job-cut to the tune of two million and seven thousand and 45,000 were laid off in the retail sector. Development in industry and finance is almost dead. But we are hopeful that President Roosevelt will save the country from disaster during his presidential term by taking some emergency measures.

I was disturbed after reading this article in *The New York Times*.

All the newspapers were full of news and reports expressing similar sentiments. Recession has created havoc in the entire country. What great dreams I had when I joined college. I had chosen the Business Administration course with the hope of securing a good job. I had no aptitude for this subject. Now I had acquired the degree, but could see no prospect of employment. All that was happening around was totally against my expectations!

I could have earned some money in the pant-matching business. But like others, even Matthew suffered heavy losses and shut shop, and so did we. I had to start my hectic search for a job. But the economic situation was so bad that all I heard from my friends were about people losing their jobs. If someone was lucky enough to find work, he would be paid only on a weekly basis. Above all, there was no guarantee of the job to be long term.

Some of my friends had accepted even lawn-mowing work. One could earn 35 cents an hour. Some had taken up housekeeping for apartments and shops. This would fetch only $10 a month. I was not physically fit to take up laborious jobs and there were no sedentary jobs, or posts that could use my knowledge. I had applied to many places and also gone for several interviews, but without any success. The situation had gone from bad to worse.

One day, I saw a ray of hope. I had applied for a clerical post in *The New York Times* magazine. The weekly wages were $35, with a few other allowances. I passed their written test. But I also had to pass an interview. I was confident of success since I was fond of writing and had prior experience at *Campus*. With great hope and anxiety I reached the magazine office for the interview. I was asked very nominal questions. A person from the interview panel gave some details about the job.

'This is not a stationary job. We will ask you to visit locations and you will have to give a complete report of an incident. You also have to take photographs; sometimes, you may have to carry heavy cameras. Just writing skills are not sufficient. You also need physical stamina for such type of hard work. I am not sure if you are capable of all this.' He glanced at me meaningfully.

I had understood by then that I was not being selected. All my hopes were shattered. I sat still in my seat. A bleak future blinded my eyes.

The following week, I met Dad. We would meet once a year but we never talked about alimony. Even though he was my father, I did not want to ask him for money.

Most of the times, we would meet at Barney Greengrass on 86th Street. It was a small, ordinary restaurant, but a quiet place, away from the hustle-bustle of the main street. It was popular for its Jewish food. We discussed about the current recession and my unemployment.

'Albert, everyone faces ups and downs in life. You should not be depressed. Look at me. You will not be able to guess the losses I suffered when the markets crashed this October. But I managed to recover. Now I am into the real-estate business.' Dad was very calm. He seemed to like his piece of chicken.

I could neither remain calm nor relish my favourite dish which was lying in front of me. I was facing a very critical question: 'What next?'

'Albert, don't let the situation affect your eating. If you stay composed you can find a solution. I have an idea. Tell me if you like it.' By now the sturgeon smoked fish he ordered was on the table.

'I have a friend called Robin. He manufactures boards for the game of bridge. These boards are different from those available in the market at present. Today, one can play only by the famous

Culbertson method, but the special feature of Robin's board is that one can play all by oneself, with the four ace method.

'We can do business, selling these boards in partnership. We will buy them from Robin and sell them to dealers and bridge-clubs in the city. I am sure, Albert, that fans of this game will be very glad to buy this board. You will be surprised to see how they fall for it.' Dad was busy with the sturgeon as he talked.

I listened with great interest. Soon, I too began enjoying the fish in front of me.

'But Dad, who will give us money?' I voiced the main issue.

'You leave that to me. I have already talked to some dealers. They are anxiously waiting for our boards.' He had finished eating.

'When shall we start?' By now I was impatient.

'Immediately, from tomorrow. On Monday, be at the main gate of the Central Park at sharp 10 in the morning. Robin stays close by. We will buy a few boards and begin work immediately. In the meanwhile, I will have a word with Robin and find places where we can sell the boards.' Dad was visibly excited with my response.

We finished eating. I took a city bus from Barney Greengrass. My imagination was already running loose. I began dreaming. I saw myself as a famous businessman with my name and photographs everywhere. I saw myself surrounded by a crowd begging to interview me. I was telling them, 'This novel board has brought a revolution in the game of bridge. This board....'

'183rd Street.' My dreams were broken by the announcement

of my halt through the bus-speaker.

That night I was dreaming only about bridge.

I began my sales-work from the next day itself. I made a list of all the clubs in New York where bridge was played. Only a few of them were run independently. Most of them were affiliated to bigger clubs. A majority of these clubs were located in an area that spread from North Chamber Street to South Canal Street in Manhattan. This area was mainly known for its elite and affluent inhabitants. So the club members were also, obviously, from this class. Although my college was in Manhattan, this area was new to me. So I studied the subway route up to Chamber Street from the maps. We purchased 50 boards from Robin for $30. We fixed the price of each board at $1. Now we were all set to sell these novel boards.

Only Paul knew about my partnership with Dad. Paul and Manny had finished school and both of them were in City College, like me. Paul was busy studying for his last semester.

When we actually began our marketing, Dad did not appear enthusiastic. I was not able to meet him. I tried calling him a number of times but he remained unavailable. I was perplexed. The sight of the boards lying in the house began to irritate me. I had to take some action urgently. Instead of waiting for Dad to introduce me to the dealers, I decided to try selling the boards myself. I began visiting dealers every day. I also started making the rounds of clubs like The Manhattan Club, Cavendish Bridge Club, Honours Bridge Club, and others located in this area. I even lost count of the number of times I visited The New York Bridge Association!

When I would start my talk about the board, some would examine the board and say, 'Oh, what a novel board. We will definitely buy.'

This would boost my morale. I would keep pursuing such clients. But they would keep me waiting for hours. Then I would realise that they had shown fake interest.

Most of them would instantly start giving reasons for not buying it.

'The board is good but the price is a bit high. One can get the same board for 70 cents in the market,' they would say.

'Even if we approve your board, we are bound by rules. We have to float tenders for purchase of every item. We will get in touch with you once we receive the tenders.'

I would return home, dejected. World is very different, I would tell myself. No dealer was waiting for me! In reality, most of the dealers would be in a hurry to put me off! I told myself that, henceforth, I should not be carried away by sweet talk from any person; even from Dad, for that matter.

All my dreams of becoming a successful businessman withered away. Finally, after strenuous legwork for six months, I was successful in selling all 50 boards, but only for a total of $32.

Suddenly, one day, I got a message from Dad asking me to meet him urgently. Reluctantly, I reached the Barney Greengrass. I carried $30 to return his investment.

'Albert, you may keep the money. I called you urgently because I sincerely want to apologise. How much I wished to help you in the board-business! I am sure you will understand me. Perhaps you may be aware of the different schemes President Roosevelt has started to generate employment. This has shaken the market. There is a big boom in the construction business and a great demand for houses. The past six months have been very hectic you know. I did not have a single moment to breathe. I made a mistake, son. I should have told you this earlier. Albert, I am extremely sorry.' Dad choked up while talking. I felt very bad. I had been wrong in my opinion about Dad.

'Albert, I have now decided to make up for my mistake. I have to admit that I made a blunder in selecting the bridge-board. Few people play this game. How big a profit can one make by selling them? But now, after careful thought, I have hit upon a product that I am sure, will be a great success.' Dad seemed to have regained his enthusiasm.

'What is it?' I was anxious to know.

'A Beer-Cooler Cleaner. Just see, every household has beer bottles, every restaurant stocks beer. You may have noticed those keg coolers to cool beer, not only in restaurants but also in homes. But it is very troublesome to clean these coolers, especially to clean between the barrel and the outside frame. Many a time, coolers are thrown away just because they are clogged with dust. I have seen a beer-cooler cleaner that is so good, that within a short time the cooler shines like a new piece. People are not aware of this cleaner and I am confident that it will sell like hot cakes once it is known.'

I felt inspired by Dad's talk. We finalised the idea. Dad introduced me to a Mr. Sunny, who made these cleaners.

He agreed to deliver the cleaners to the customers. We pooled our money. I gave my savings of $30 as contribution. Together with $70 from Dad, we raised a total of $100 as our capital.

With my hopes rekindled, I resumed my entrepreneurship, and once again, the earlier situation repeated itself. Dad vanished from the scene; he was unavailable at the time of actual selling. It was extremely necessary to recover at least the money we had put in. With this sole aim I decided to try out on my own. It was a bitter, cold January. The temperature had plummeted to minus fifteen. I would wear six to seven layers of clothing and set out to make rounds of various hotels and shops.

One evening, the door-bell rang. I was at home reading a book. Paul was studying in his room. Mom had gone to the Central Synagogue. She was a life-member of its community centre. It was at the corner of the 55th Avenue .The synagogue had a hall for social activities. Cultural or social functions were held almost every day in this hall. This was Mom's favourite place to meet friends. Her evenings were exclusively reserved for this and as usual, she was not at home.

'Has Mom returned?' As I was about to get the door, the bell rang again as if the caller was in a great hurry.

I quickly opened the door. A middle-aged man was standing outside. He was looking uncomfortable in his heavy winter clothing.

'You are Henry's son, I suppose?' He asked.

I nodded.

'I am Stevenson. I have some work with you.'

I ushered him inside.

'Henry is my friend. I have loaned him money two times so far. The first time it was $30 and the second time $70. He had promised to pay me back within two months, the entire amount. Today, even after six months, I have not received a single penny from him. I tried to see him a number of times, but he is not to be found anywhere. I feel sorry to ask you, but I desperately need some money for my kidney operation. I remember Henry speaking about some business run by both of you together. That is why I was compelled to search for your address. I have great hopes from you, son.' He was talking very politely, without anger.

I was shocked. My self-respect was torn into pieces. It was shameful to receive creditors at the door. It became clear that our business had started with loaned money. I hated Dad at that moment.

He was watching me anxiously. I recollected myself.

'Mr. Stevenson, I am extremely sorry for this. But please give two months. I will return the $100. Let me have your address, I will deliver the money myself. You will not be required to call on us for money anymore,' I assured him.

Apparently convinced with my words he left, but I was extremely disturbed. The $100 haunted me day and night. Yet undaunted with this new development, I sold all the remaining cleaners. I sold some even at a lesser price. But even after adding my savings, I was not able to manage $100. Finally, I borrowed some money from my friends and repaid Stevenson.

While coming back from his place, I thought of the lesson I had learnt.

'Henceforth, I will not be influenced by Dad. It is not possible to work with him anymore. There is a vast difference in our basic philosophies. I will never see him, however urgent it may be. Henceforth in life, I will never depend on him or anybody. I will always work independently.'

From that moment I deleted the word 'dad' from my mind forever. But I had to start looking for work again.

***

It was eight in the morning. I pushed the revolving glass door of Distinctive Creations and went inside. It was a gift shop on 112th Street and Broadway. Its yellow and red illumination was bright enough to catch the attention of passers-by. Various items, cards, albums, gift articles, cutlery and so on, were displayed attractively on the glass shelves. There was a small office at the back for sales, purchase and accounts work. At one corner of the office was the cabin of Mr. George Roderick, the owner of the shop. On the right corner, in front of his cabin, was my table. I was appointed as an Assistant Accountant, and allotted the work of keeping records of the daily sales, maintaining the sale–purchase register, and preparing vouchers.

'Even if this is your main work, you are expected to do any job as the need may arise. In the beginning, it will be a part-time job. If you work satisfactorily, we will convert it into a full-time job. Your wages will be $15 a week at present.' This was what George Roderick had said to me during my interview.

I had to agree. I had to bag whatever job came my way and try not to lose it. That was my priority at that moment.

I had decided on two things when I joined Distinctive Creations. First, I needed to save a few dollars regularly to repay my friends—and I was successful at this. Second, I decided to talk only minimally with my colleagues. I had decided not to while away time chatting, gossiping or in small talk. I was not going let my work be affected by anything, by any incident or even the weather. I had learnt to concentrate on reading and writing amidst noisy surroundings or chaos. I was determined to see the fulfilment of my ambition of becoming a successful writer.

I continued my routine visits to The New York Library every evening. I would finish my work fast and use the spare time for writing. My mind was constantly restless. It would calm down only when I put my thoughts on paper. The economic and political system of the country agitated me. The shortcomings of a capitalist economy incited me to revolt against the system. The economic climate of the country petrified me with a fear that in such an environment my ambition of becoming a writer was perhaps going to remain a dream forever.

Writing became my passion. I wrote extensively on topics close to my heart. I had simplified and abridged all three volumes of *Das Kapital* by Karl Marx, into one single book. Of course I had not glorified him. My main purpose was to point out the shortcomings in his ideology. Instead of analysing the principles of communism, I openly professed a revolution. I was never inclined towards the Communist party because I could never approve of its staunch dogmatism. I disapproved both- capitalism and communism. Socialists too had disappointed me with their policies. I was getting drawn towards democracy, which I found to be more liberal and progressive. I agreed neither with the Left nor with the Right. I did not want to bind my ideology by aligning myself with any political party.

I wanted to publish this. I got a list of publishers in New York City from the library. With great aspiration, I started meeting publishers such as Lynn Book Publishing Company, Alpha Publication, Bowen & Co, and Simon & Singer.

I had written one more volume of around half a million words, named *A History of the Dark Ages: The Twentieth Century*. I had done an exhaustive study and had come to the conclusion that the Middle Ages were definitely a dark period characterised by a complete lack of knowledge. But, fortunately for mankind, this ignorance was lessening in the twentieth century. However, we were still blindly following a few outdated traditions in politics, health and religion, which I proved in my book with examples.

But the manuscript of this book was returned by each and every publisher. Finally, I had to give up hoping that my book would be published during my lifetime.

I had started writing at the age of twelve. So far I had penned nearly twenty big manuscripts. These consisted of fiction, drama, and poetry, too. But no publisher seemed to be impressed by them. I had also written a book, *The Art of Never Being Unhappy*, which was about self-development. My worst experience when Omega Publications, instead of publishing, misplaced my hand-written manuscript itself.

The attitude of the publishers baffled me. I had read several stories about writers having burnt their fingers with publishers. Their experience proved true in my case too. The leading publishers were absolutely not ready to entertain a newcomer like me. They would show me the door saying they already had a back-log of two to three years. Nobody showed interest in reading my manuscripts. It disturbed me to think that if every publisher decided to publish only established writers, when would a new writer like me get an opportunity? How and when could a new writer establish himself if he was denied a chance? How can one break this vicious circle?

The attitude of the leading publishers, and even those in the mid-level category, was similar. Why do they take so long just to decide on the acceptance or rejection of a manuscript? Of course, they had the right to any decision whatsoever. But none of them informed their decision in time. This attitude was unethical, according to me.

These publishers would keep the manuscripts with themselves for several months and I would keep on making the rounds to know about their decision. I could not approach other publishers until I got back my material from the first. This situation was agonising. Besides, there was always the fear of manuscripts getting misplaced, as with Omega Publications. I could only hope that my original work eventually made its way back to me. Publishing a book seemed like a mirage after these demoralising experiences.

I had also from the experiences of other writers that even if a publisher accepts your work, one cannot heave a sigh of relief.

You really cannot guess when your manuscript will see the light of day. Also, a writer never finds out the true number of copies sold.

I got fed up with the process. Although all of them had rejected my work, I was sure that no one had sincerely taken the effort to read it.

The Creative Publishing Company on 3rd Avenue was a reputed publishing house. One day, they called for me. I reached their office very anxiously. They made me wait for a long time. At last, the publisher sent for me.

'I will first explain our policy. We have a team of experts who will scrutinise your script. Wherever required, it will be re-written by them. You may give us the manuscript only if you agree to this clause; else you are free to take your manuscript and leave.' He spoke very bluntly without allowing me to respond.

I came home with the manuscript and several questions in my mind.

Without actually reading the script, how could he predict the possibility of rewriting? Publishers give re-writing a pretentious glorified name of 'editing'. But do these so-called editors have expertise in my subject? If they do, why don't they write on it themselves? Rewriting a work amounts to snatching away a writer's freedom of expression. The response of the publishers perturbed me extremely.

My thoughts were independent. They were a misfit in the present system. I was not interested in getting my work published at a place where I had no freedom of expression.

I was very dejected when I returned from The Creative Publishing Company, but not anguished. I was confident of my thinking and my writing. I did not wish to lose my focus because of such events. No amount of rejections was going to shake my confidence. My inner voice was more powerful. It superseded all these rejections and told me, 'Albert, this does not mean you are being rejected as an individual. Let the publishers reject your books or your views. I, Albert Ellis, will never reject my totality.

***

Since many days, I had been keen on writing a scientific and revolutionary book on sexology. I wanted to bring forth information which was researched and proved, and I was prepared to take whatever efforts this study called for.

On the seventh floor of the New York Public Library was a large reading hall—number 315. It had sweeping glass windows and huge chandeliers, which gave a regal look to the hall, especially when lit in the evenings. The book-racks were arranged such that it was very easy and convenient to locate a book in a very short time. Table number 21, which was near a window and in the centre on the hall, was my favourite. I would sit there for hours. For nearly two years, this was my second home. Without caring for wind, rain, sun or snow, I would voraciously read 30 to 50 books every month, several of which were on sexual behaviour. I also read a thousand papers on marriage, sexual relations, and love.

Along with the New York Library, I became a member of the Mid Manhattan Library too. It had a rare collection of literature necessary for research work. I took a Metro Referral Card from the New York Library. This helped me access books from other libraries, if they were not available in the central library. The New York Library had 39 branches all over the city, and as a Referral Card holder, I had free access to any library. I began taking full benefit of all the facilities offered by the Central Library.

I did some extensive reading after becoming a card-holder. I read *Marriage and Morals*, a work well researched by Bertrand Russell. His bold views made me lose sleep for a number of days. I found the views expressed by Havelock Ellis and Magnus Hirschfield very liberal. I learnt to think and write scientifically only after reading their views. Masters and Johnson, Alfred Kinsey, Alex Comfort, and Vatsyayan from India also influenced me with their theories. The result of all this reading and study was the creation of a huge volume I called *The Case for Sexual Promiscuity*.

Once again, I made an attempt to publish this book and faced the same response. I approached several publishers but this time it was even more difficult. The name of the book itself would deter them.

'This subject is very explosive. We do not publish anything like this.' They would almost drive me out with this statement.

'You have used words 'fuck' and 'shit' very often. These words are highly indecent and objectionable. Do not hope to get your book published until you remove these words or change them.' This was the suggestion from the famous Mark & Noble.

No publisher was courageous enough to accept the name and also the words in the book. I had to fight their mental barriers. I would listen with utmost restraint. With great tenacity, I would explain my views, but unsuccessfully.

Then, I would console myself: 'I have used these words because there is a strong and a definite purpose in using them. These words are not used by respectable people, because any thought, any act, anything written about sex is considered taboo in our society. We are paying a heavy price for suppressing our curiosity in order to follow social norms. We have also created many hurdles in our path to gaining more knowledge about sex.'

This belief that it is shameful and also a sin even to utter this word is very deep-rooted in our minds. I wanted to eradicate this and undertook a mammoth study on this subject. Finally, I arrived at one truth. You do more harm when you create an aura of secrecy around sexuality, than that by allowing an open expression of the so-called vulgar words or other expletives and actions. There is no reason to hide these words under the garb of secrecy. The more you deem a thing as 'prohibited' or 'non-permissible' or 'secret', the higher is the level of curiosity and attraction. It has been proved that, in spite of making strict laws, men and women, even from highly-cultured families, maintain an air of naivety, but do enjoy pornography or salacious talk, at some or the other stage of life. But they do not have the courage to admit it openly, because of social inhibitions.

As long as we do not get rid of these inhibitions, we will never think independently. Once we accept our sexuality without any inhibition, we will realise that there is nothing shameful. Words are neutral. Shame lies in our minds. When you cast away this shame, you will see your true self behind the veil of decency. You will experience the satisfaction of remaining honest to your natural instinct.

I remember when I would give public speeches for Young America and New America, my seniors would call me and warn, 'Albert, you are a good orator, but you tend to use indecent words very often. Please do not use such words. Our audience is a discerning audience. Its members come from a respectable class.'

I would nod in affirmation and deliver the speech without using those so-called objectionable words; but occasionally I would say, very casually:

'Friends, to describe this feeling, I actually have a different word in mind. But since all of you are very decent and respectable, I cannot spell that word out before you.'

Upon this statement, the word I implied would be instantly conveyed to everybody, even without my uttering it, and would arouse loud laughter from the audience. None of them had the courage to say that word openly, but I had succeeded in making each one of them utter it in his mind. And then I would have the last laugh. But there was also another reason behind my laugh. Who had created an aura of obscenity around these words? Sycophants who hide their true faces behind the mask of phoney decency? If you tear away this mask, you will find that no one is decent and nothing is vulgar. It's only one's true self exposed. So when these 'respectable' individuals followed their natural instinct and laughed heartily, throwing aside their masks, I would also join them in their laughter even if for a few moments.

Most of the time, the information about sex available to us is about its physiological aspect. It indirectly sends a message to the reader that sex is a kind of science and there is nothing pleasurable in it. The aim of my book was not to arouse the reader but to enable him to get maximum happiness from sex. If my writing does arouse somebody, I do not blame myself, because I do not have control over what can arouse a person.

In the earlier days, when women covered their bodies fully, even a glimpse of their ankle was capable of stimulating a man. Now, when the trend is to dress less, even an exposed knee fails to arouse men. So, if in the future, the fashion trend changes to going around undressed, even a nude woman will not arouse any man. Therefore, the rational derivation is that the interest people have in obscenity only minimally of a biological nature. It is generated purely from their attitude towards sex.

If this interest was a biological phenomenon, the change in fashion trends would not have influenced the issue of which part of a woman's body arouses a man. Vulgarity is also not found in all societies. It varies from person to person. What appears obscene to a person may not appear so to another. What arouses one person may not arouse another. This is because every person has a different view towards sexuality. The same rule applies to literature. It is difficult to decide accurately which words could provoke a person. Therefore, instead of thinking about this conflict of opinions, I stress only on the thoughts I want to convey. I plead that people should confront their own opinions. My writings, my words, are very direct. I do not approve of beating around the bush. If I have to suggest the act of 'intercourse', I do not simply say 'physical relations'. Since there are various kinds of physical relations, the reader is likely to remain in doubt about the exact nature of relation referred to. Therefore, although the word 'fuck' is objectionable to the so-called respectable, decent people, it is still the most apt word of expression. More importantly, it is easily understood by the common man.

The words I use in my writing, and while expressing my views, are in direct conflict with the views of learned people. When I was in college, I attended lectures by scholars in several seminars and conferences. They would use a language full of bombastic words, which are totally alien to laymen. Sometimes, the lectures were so full of such mystical and incomprehensible words that it became difficult to make any sense of them. When you read their articles, written in traditional style, interspersed with heavy words, you know that they lack soul and are devoid of humanity. You feel convinced that they are written with the sole purpose of adding more feathers in their caps. These intellectuals fulfil only personal motives while writing, with no genuine regard for the society per se.

Conventionally, the higher the level of complexity in writing, the higher the recognition it receives. In fact, it is more difficult to write in a simple and easy style that can be understood by everybody. The writing style should be reader-friendly. One should write so brilliantly that it grips the mind of the reader. It should stimulate him and provoke him to examine his or her beliefs. When such thoughts are put on paper, they become a self-created-force. They have an inbuilt strength to them.

It is this strength that empowers me to write. Even if others call my words provocative, I strongly believe in their power; because they are born out of sincerity. Therefore, I am not afraid to use these words time and again.

In my book, I have advocated sexual freedom. I have written: 'From childhood itself, children are subjected to strict behavioural rules by society, religion and moralists. Undue stress is laid on the difference between the genital organ and other organs of our body. They are taught not to touch the sexual organ or ask any questions. If a child does ask a question, he or she is often silenced and reprimanded. Most of the times, an answer is cleverly avoided. Many a time, the child is given an unscientific explanation about the process of birth, that he or she was brought from a hospital.

'The consequence of this attitude is that the curiosity about sexual relations in children goes on escalating. It also gets impressed upon their minds that sexual relations cannot be talked about openly and should be always kept secretive. If their curiosity does not get satisfied directly, they tend to try other ways. As a result they get information about sex in a distorted form. Moreover, they try to obtain this information by undesirable methods. Parents hide their sexual relations and are ashamed of it. This makes children believe that sex is an obscene act. This belief eventually gets rooted in their minds. Later, this belief becomes so strong and powerful that even in adult life, a feeling of guilt and surreptitiousness consistently pricks their minds while enjoying sex.

'Open up your minds and thoughts. If you search for the origin of your guilt, you will find that our so-called religious masters and moralists have systematically planted a certain attitude about sex , that sexual relations between a man and woman is unholy, a sin. But according to these authorities, this sin can be washed away by reciting some religious verses during marriage. This is done just to retain their hold on the society, to enslave the society, to strengthen their position.

'Let them subject us to any extent of the onslaught of their views; we have the freedom to accept or reject. Even if there is an attempt to force mental slavery upon us, we have the freedom to shun this attitude. Throw away this slavery; open your eyes, and you will see that this attitude is totally baseless. Do not embrace it and suffer all your life. Form your own opinions about sex. Do not accept because someone wrote about it, because someone spoke about it, because someone brainwashed you with it. Follow your own mind. Enjoy fully the freedom of sex. I call this "sexual freedom".'

But sexual freedom does not mean free sex. My concept of sexual freedom is somewhat similar to the views expressed by Bertrand Russell in *Marriage and Morals*. I honestly feel that there is not much difference between the regressive philosophy of self-denial of orthodox thinkers, and the modern-day advocacy of absolute freedom of sex. These orthodox men have excessively glorified morality. In the process, they have done as much harm by preaching control over sexual desires as done by those who endorse modernity and free sex. To support instant gratification of sex and to keep sexual desire out of the purview of morality is not right, because no judgement about social behaviour is fully immune to principles of morality.

Although I have recommended sexual freedom in the book, I have also discussed social norms which should be observed simultaneously. Both partners should be genuinely aware that they have to respect each other's bodies. No partner should touch the other without his or her consent. Obviously, this implies that one should be honest and not offend his or her partner knowingly. It is necessary to include these norms in our sex life.

According to me, if we follow these principles, then sexual relations cannot be termed immoral. One cannot be assured of a happy marital life, just because the man and the woman love each other. Both of them should ensure sexual compatibility as well. Such a precaution is considered immoral by most people. But if an individual follows such rules in his personal sex life, then any consensual pre-marital sex between two willing partners, is not immoral, by any rational criterion.

Even in consensual sex, certain norms need to be observed. First, it is necessary that the person and his partner are adult, mature, and mentally sound. Second, both partners should be truthful with each other. It is also important that sexual relations do not lead to unwilling conception, or transmit venereal diseases. The man should not force himself upon the woman or injure her in any way. In my opinion, partners who observe these restrictions do not behave immorally.

Does pre-marital sex fall into the same category as adultery? In adultery, at least one partner is lawfully wedded to another person. Conventionally, a married man is expected to have sex only with his wife. In a matrimonial contract, there is a commitment to faithfulness in sexual relations. An adulterous person not only betrays his or her legal partner but also breaches their trust. This does not apply in cases where a partner gives their consent to such relations. But such cases are rare. Most often, adultery is committed surreptitiously, without the knowledge of the legal partner. In such cases, adultery is definitely a violation of the loyalty-clause of a matrimonial contract, even when it is not explicitly included.

This is broadly my stance about public behaviour and sex which are presented quite frankly in my book. I have not written for the sake of making my views and opinions known to the world, but because they are an integral part of my personality. They are reflected in my behaviour, too.

I am an advocate of personal freedom. Every person should have the right to freedom. But freedom is bound by some duties and responsibilities. I am conscious of this, and nonetheless, determined to follow this path all my life, even if I am alone in the journey.

*****

6

Karyl! Just the name made my mind and body resonate. Her fond memories overwhelmed me whenever I thought of her. Even at work, remembering those romantic moments with her would make my surroundings pleasant. Passion and desire would drive me crazy with an uncontrollable urge to hold her that very moment. Till then I had read love poems as a piece of literature, but it was only now that I actually experienced the romance expressed in these poems.

I was entirely drenched in her love. I would yearn like Browning and call her 'Oh, my love'. I wanted to assure her of my faithfulness, by saying 'Never doubt my love,' like Shakespeare. Shelley's words hinted at union in love. I too longed to ask her 'Why not I with thine?'. I could now relate to Robert Burns. His words 'My love is like a melody' would keep reverberating in my mind. Day and night, I lived in a world of love and romance.

Her name creates a tempest in my heart.

My first encounter with Karyl was the most romantic experience of my life. It was towards the beginning of December in 1937. Winter had set in, and although it had not started snowing, chilly winds were blowing. After finishing my work at Distinctive Creations, I was standing, as usual, at the 110thStreet subway station, when someone pulled at my jacket. I turned around; it was Jason from the Panther Gang, whistling behind me. I was seeing Jason after a long time since college. He was in the area for some work.

Jason was a great fan of theatre and he was the one who had introduced me to dramatics. It was from him that I had learnt that commercial theatre is called Broadway and experimental theatre is called Off-Broadway. The tickets to a Broadway would be normally very expensive but Jason would manage free tickets through his contacts. Thanks to him, I had seen Broadway shows like *Jubilee, On your Toes,* and *Leave It to Me,* at Times Square.

'Albert, you must see Off-Broadway shows instead of Broadway shows. Broadways are for the commoners, Off-Broadway are for connoisseurs. When there are no Broadway shows at a theatre, they have Off-Broadway shows, mostly as a matinee show. But to know this we have to keep an eye on the schedule.' Jason would often tell me.

We were lost in memories of our college days as we walked back from the subway.

'Albert, what a coincidence. I remembered you just a few days ago. You have not yet seen Off-Broadway, have you? There is some good news for you then. *Dream Girl* is running at the Imperial Theatre. It is a Vincent Johnson production. Their shows are based on very good themes. And it's on a Sunday, so you need not take leave from work. Now please don't miss it. I have a free ticket. Do you want it?'

Jason had not changed a bit. I took the ticket from him. I had heard about the Imperial Theatre from Jason earlier. It was located on 45th Street in midtown Manhattan and was famous for Broadway shows. The *Dream Girl* was scheduled for one in the afternoon.

I reached the theatre much before showtime. I had a seat in the front row. The first few scenes were quite dull. I was disappointed but hoped that it would get more exciting later. Right then the lead actress appeared on the stage. It was Karyl as the 'Dream Girl'. Oh, she was just beauty personified! What a curvaceous body! How striking were her blue eyes! Her blonde tresses caressed her face. What an attractive body! She was an ethereal beauty. Her expressions kept me arrested to my seat. The entire stage brightened up with her presence. I hardly paid attention to her dialogues; I lost interest in the theme of the show or the other characters. I had eyes for only Karyl, and Karyl alone.

For the first time in my life, I understood the inexplicable joy in appreciating a woman's beauty. I sat mesmerised till the end of the show.

Afterwards, Jason and I were to leave together, but I excused myself and sat in the hall. I wanted to see Karyl again and anxiously waited outside her green room. Soon after, she emerged, looking extremely beautiful, even without make-up.

'I liked your performance very much. In fact, I liked you very much.' This was what I wanted to say to her.

But I, Albert Ellis, who was capable of talking to 130 girls so boldly, was unable to string even a couple of sentences in order, when Karyl actually stood before me. The reason behind this became clear later. Out of those 130 girls, I had not got involved emotionally even with a single one. But Karyl proved to be an exception. I do not remember what I spoke to her about, but her sweet 'Thanks' kept ringing in my ears for quite some time. The woman who had mesmerised me was just a few inches away from me, talking to me; it was all quite unbelievable! I nearly stopped breathing.

'Karyl!'

A harsh voice called out, rupturing the delicate silence between us. It was a friend of hers waiting in a car. Karyl ran towards him impatiently and disappeared in no time.

Even in my disoriented state, the contour of her friend's body and his voice reminded me of someone. I kept trying to recall his name all the way home. Suddenly, the blurred image of his face cleared and it struck me…Ryan Richardo!

Ryan used to be my senior in college and was notorious as a flirt. An expert at fooling girls, he would ply them with sweet nothings to get intimate with them. Jason at our recent meeting had said that Ryan was married six months ago. I was worried. Did he tell Karyl that he was married? Or had he trapped her deceitfully? How far had they gone in their relationship? Did anybody warn Karyl about his ways? All these questions pestered me and I could not sleep that night.

Next day, I went to Imperial Theatre again. The show was scheduled for two more days, which meant that I would have the opportunity to see Karyl at least two more times. By now I was a full-time assistant at Distinctive Creations with long, regular work hours. Nonetheless, I would finish fast and run to the theatre. Nothing mattered—neither chilly winds nor snow or ice.

Eventually, I started visiting whatever theatre the *Dream Girl* was running at. Capitol, Princess, Shubert, anywhere. I would stand outside for hours, waiting to talk to her.

'Karyl, I want you. I am crazy about you.' I had lost count of the number of times I must have rehearsed this in my mind.

At last, one day, I gathered the courage to confess how much I loved her. I even told her that Ryan did not deserve her, that he had gotten married six months ago. Although she listened to me calmly, her expressions betrayed her shock.

'Albert, until I verify what you said about Ryan, I cannot accept what you say.'

Thus began a game of hide-and-seek; of hope and delusion. My mind was constantly preoccupied over whether she would accept me or not. There were so many ways by which I tried to convince her of my love. I would wait for long hours just for a glimpse of her. I showered her with various gifts. I strived to fulfil her every wish. I would hover around her and, at every opportunity, I would plead for her love.

I was happy to do all this. It kept me spirited even at work. I was an avid lover of literature. Now I was getting more and more inspired to write down in words about the love blossoming in my mind.

Karyl reigned over my mind, she was the queen of my heart. I wrote long love letters. Words became flowers and my letters were like bouquets. I wrote innumerable letters. Some of them were twenty to thirty pages long. One was ninety nine pages!

Soon, the relationship between Karyl and Ryan ended, but I could see no sign of my efforts bearing fruit. Karyl's behaviour was incomprehensible.

'Albert, you write very well and I love to listen to you'. Whenever she said this, I would feel elated.

'Can you guess how much I love you Albert?' She asked unexpectedly one day, bowling me. This question simply bowled me over.

'Much more than Juliet loved Romeo.' Her reply nearly made me lose my mind.

Yet, whenever I broached the topic of marriage, she would keep mum. 'I have not yet decided,' she would say curtly.

The same typical answer each time! It was stifling to hear this answer every time. The ambiguity of our relationship was suffocating. I was intrigued by her behaviour. Sometimes she was amicable, sometimes cold, sometimes loving, and at times, full of hatred. Often she would talk animatedly but also very arrogantly. Such unpredictable behaviour both confused and hurt me. My nights became sleepless with the agony of this uncertainty. But I could not think of a way out. She was evading a firm answer while I lived in deep anguish, unable to stay away from her even for a moment. I was very much disturbed. Why Karyl, why are you doing this to me? Why are you staying at a distance from me?

At last one evening I got my answer. It was Easter Sunday and Mom had gone to attend an Easter Feast at her friend's place. Paul and Manny had left home in the afternoon to see the Easter Parade. This magnificent event was held on Fifth Avenue.

Karyl was much occupied for the entire week, deciding on the right dress and a matching hat to flaunt at the parade. But I was indifferent to all the excitement around me. Nothing interested me. I wanted to spend the day at home in peace.

The uncertainty in my life was a result of Karyl's enigmatic behaviour. But she was not the cause of my emotional disturbance; I had created it. How can another person be the cause of my disturbance without my compliance? My mind was inflamed by the turmoil within me.

I could no longer sit at home. I walked out of house, wandering aimlessly for a while before I found myself at our favourite Bronx Botanical Garden.

The garden was blooming with flowers. Cherries and magnolia had blossomed beautifully. The garden pathways were thickly carpeted with pink and yellow petals. A light shower had made the soil moist. The scent of the wet earth had blended with the fragrance of magnolia. I began strolling on the walkways deeply inhaling the fragrant air. Perhaps this refreshed my dejected mind.

Karyl was playing with my emotions. But why was I dancing to her tunes? Why was I begging for her love? She obliges me with a few moments of love, like an act of charity. Why do I cherish those moments and carry them like a gold crown? What had made me so desperate? Her beauty? Or was it my infatuation? Was it because of her attitude? No. The answer to this desperation was not Karyl. I have definitely been infatuated by her beauty. But the cause of my desperation lay behind some ideas I was holding on to tightly.

If I just say that 'I want Karyl' then shall I become so desperate for her? I do not feel so. Because a person does not get intensely disturbed just because he 'wants' something or someone; at the most, he may be disappointed. But I was not only disappointed, I had become desperate. This clearly indicated that unknowingly I had decided I *must* get Karyl; I could not live without her. My life would become meaningless if I do not get her and I would be totally worthless. It was this thinking that made me feel desperate and helpless.

I had converted my 'wish' into an 'absolutistic demand'. To wish means to 'want' something or to expect something. But to say I 'must' have is unrealistic. When I identified the difference between a wish and a demand, I calmed down a bit. I was now able to think peacefully. How reasonable was it to say 'I must have Karyl'? When I say this, I am presuming that there is an unwritten and unchangeable law that says I 'must' get what I want. I laughed at myself. How misleading were my thoughts.

Next, I began to confront some other ideas deeply set in my mind.

Oh … that I cannot live without her? Was Karyl a basic biological necessity like water, food or air? How did I survive until I met her?

Why should life be horrible without her? It will still continue as it did till today. Perhaps, I will miss her if I do not ever find another person to love. But this was far more preferable to the anguish caused by pursuing Karyl. I was torturing my mind and body for her. Perhaps I may yet meet someone in the future who will love me consistently, unlike this fickle-minded Karyl.

Then does this imply that I should forget her? That would be an extreme view. To deny that I want her is self-humiliation. It would mean betraying my own feelings, because I do love Karyl. To stop thinking of her will mean a total disregard of for my true feelings! Therefore I will definitely wish for her love. But if I treat my wish as an absolutistic demand, this desire takes the form of an essential need. In order to get her, I may have to go to any extent, perhaps even at the cost of my self-respect; and even that may not guarantee success.

Therefore, I must permanently erase my unrealistic thinking that I desperately need her love and that life will become unhappy without her. I will be glad if she willingly gives her consent in marriage. But if she refuses me, I will not become desperate, and I will not plead at her door.

After this marathon contemplation, I felt unburdened. The pain became easier to bear. The sky was clear; dark clouds had disappeared and soft twilight painted the horizon in gold and orange shades. I felt rejuvenated and started for home with new optimism.

I understood now the reason behind our sorrows. Knowingly or unknowingly, a person transforms his wish into a necessity. To wish or to want something can become the cause of disappointment but not the cause for intense grief. Treating a want as a necessity can become the cause of grief. Consequently, the suffering results because we presume that unfulfilment of the desire will ruin our lives. One suffers because of the thought, that if you cannot fulfill such a necessity, you will ruin your life.

Some thinkers and philosophers believe that the origin of human suffering lies in our wishes, desires, and aspirations. You can end your suffering by destroying them. But does it not mean that one has to sacrifice happiness to get rid of suffering? A man without any wish or desire is a cold mass without humanness. The cause of human suffering is not in the desires one may have. One only needs to ensure that they do not treat their desires as necessities. We have to learn to liberate ourselves from the clutches of the words 'must have'.

Only then will the royal path leading to happiness seem wide open.

***

The next day, I told Karyl honestly about my new philosophy, including the difference between 'want to have' and 'must have', and about the decision I had taken. I felt relieved, good. The pressure was off my mind. I could even sense that I was speaking precisely, logically, and explicitly.

'Albert, I like listening to you. You can really cast a spell on the listener and it is this quality of yours that I am really fond of. I have made my decision: I will marry you'.

I could not trust myself or believe what I just heard. Finally, I had a firm commitment from Karyl. I had suffered a long torturous wait for these few magical words. As if in a daze, I repeatedly asked her the same question—whether she was firm in her decision—and she, too, repeatedly answered, 'Yes'.

'Karyl, in our family we make our own decisions. I am financially independent as well, so there will be no problems about our marriage from my family. But you live with your father; what about his consent?' Karyl had lost her mother when she was a child.

'Albert, will you meet my Dad? I will speak to him about you,' she said.

I agreed immediately. I did not want to lose any more time, now that I knew her decision.

Soon, we decided to meet at Karyl's place. She lived in the TriBeCa area. TriBeCa was the abbreviation of Triangle below Canal Street and it housed the elite of Manhattan. I had limited information about this place.

I met Karyl at the Franklin Street subway and we began walking towards her place. It was my first time in the Lower Manhattan area. There were no street-side vendors or food joints, nor was there a crowd of closely clustered buildings. One could only see antique shops, designer boutiques, studios of famous artists, posh restaurants, and furniture outlets; it was very calm and quiet.

'These places were earlier bought by big business houses who built large warehouses here. These were later converted into luxury apartments. They are called "loft apartments". We also stay in one such apartment. My grandpa had purchased the entire floor but now Dad has rented half the floor out and we live in the other half. Grandpa looked after production in the film industry, and Dad also works in the film industry like him. Many others from the film industry live in the neighbourhood.' Karyl informed.

120, Hudson Street, Powell Building. We had already reached Karyl's apartment. She lived on the 14th storey, the topmost floor of the building.

We took the elevator. 'Daddy is out for some work. He will return soon, but there may be delays. So, he has asked us to start eating and not wait for him.' Karyl said as we reached her apartment.

I was spellbound. I had never seen such a beautiful house. The furniture, the walls, the velvet curtains, the art pieces, the terrace garden; the entire place was impeccably decorated. I could not stop staring.

I went to the terrace. From the 14th floor, I had a panoramic view, right from the south of Canal Street up to the east of Broadway. In the centre was the Hudson River, a shining, jewelled, stream. On one side of the river was a circular construction.

'What is that?' I asked, pointing towards it.

'That is the famous Holland Tunnel. It joins New York City to New Jersey. Thousands of vehicles pass this tunnel every day.' Karyl said animatedly.

'Karyl, you are fortunate. Your house is really beautiful. It is decorated very aesthetically too,' I said frankly.

'Thanks. But I should be thankful to grandpa and Rick. Grandpa, because he bought this property, and Rick for beautifully decorating it. Rick Harrison is one of the most famous interior decorators in this area. This furniture is called Warehouse Furniture. He is an expert in this style of design,' Karyl said.

I was astonished. I had been under the impression that interior decoration was limited only to large offices. But the concept of having our houses done up by an outsider was new to me.

We sat down for dinner. Brown bread, Waldorf salad, fried lobster and other delicacies were laid on the table. Due to my diet restrictions, I wasn't permitted several dishes but I could definitely partake the pleasure of looking at the beautiful array.

'This is Pumpernickel. This is Bolillo. That is Bagel. And oh, this is Rye.' Karyl picked up the breads one by one from their impressive display while I made fun of their different shapes.

Just then the doorbell rang. We both stopped laughing. The steward opened the door and Karyl's father entered. He was very tall with a sharp nose, wide jawline, and penetrating blue eyes. He had an aristocratic personality.

'Apart from the piercing look in his eyes, Karyl looks very much like her Dad.' I noted.

'Daddy, he is Albert, Albert Ellis. Didn't I tell you about him the other day? He has done his B.B.A. from City College and is working as Chief Accountant with Distinctive Creations'. Karyl hugged him affectionately as she introduced us.

He did not respond. Wiping his hands with a tissue, he drew out the chair in front of me. I greeted him but he did not reciprocate, only observing me with his stern blue eyes. His gaze penetrated my body. There was a complete still at the dining table.

'Where do you live?' He broke the silence.

'The Bronx.'

'What about your family?'

'Mom, two younger siblings, and me.'

'Father?'

'He does not stay with us. Mom and Dad are divorced.'

I noticed a frown appearing on his face.

Silence fell again and continued for a while. I was feeling awkward. I looked at Karyl. She understood my predicament and started chatting about *Dream Girl* and the reactions from the audience. But he appeared disinterested. His mind was elsewhere. He responded faintly, murmuring intermittently 'yes, yes,' to her questions.

Suddenly, he interrupted Karyl and asked me, 'Do you attend church regularly?'

I paused for a moment before answering. 'I am a Jew. But I do not visit the synagogue. I do not believe in god.' I looked straight into his eyes as I spoke.

Immediately, his expression changed. He grew even more serious. The frown lines on his forehead became further visible.

'Jew? Then how is Ellis your last name?'

'Our original name is Grutes. Daddy changed it to Ellis before coming to New York.'

There was silence once again. By now, we were done with our dinner and waiting for him to finish. As he rose from his chair, he asked, 'Where is your family from originally?'

'Mom was born in Philadelphia. Her family had migrated from Germany. Dad is from New Jersey. His family is from Russia.'

He headed straight for the living room. Had he heard me? Or did he just pretend to listen and then ignored me? I could not guess. He had picked up a magazine and started reading. We also followed him to the living room and sat on a sofa before him. How should I initiate the topic of marriage?

After sometime, I gestured to Karyl. She started speaking.

'Dad, we both want to discuss something with you,' she said, looking at me.

'Yes, speak.' He did not look up. He kept reading.

I waited for a while for him to put the magazine down. Then giving up on that idea, I kept my tone steady and said, 'We want to get married'.

Hardly had I finished saying this, than he threw the magazine away. There was fire in his eyes and a scornful expression on his face. His voice shattered the peace in the hall like lightning.

'Marriage? With Karyl? Are you in your senses? Do you understand what you are saying? Did you take a look at yourself before asking for Karyl's hand in marriage? You and Karyl? Ha! You don't deserve her at all. You neither have the looks nor a good family lineage. And what family history! Son of divorced Jew parents! Education? Only a degree. A small-time job and additionally the responsibility of a family! Even you cannot survive on your earnings. How can you afford a girl like Karyl?

She has been brought up in riches. Get out of my house! Never ever try to meet her! Don't ever think of marrying her in your life! Remember, I will never let it happen. You may go.'

Without giving me an opportunity to respond, he asked me to leave. Although I had been somewhat sceptical about securing his approval, I had not anticipated that he would insult me in this manner and show me the door..

This was a rude shock. My head spun with fury and frustration. I was boiling with anger. I decided never to meet Karyl at her place.

I was unaware of the direction in which I was walking. I took the subway. I was in a dazed state. I got down at 200th Street and started walking again. When I stopped, I realised that I was near the Bronx Botanical Garden. The bitter words spoken by Karyl's dad haunted me. He had referred to my looks, my family with utter disdain. His contempt was as painful as the piercing of a thousand needles. As I paced up and down the walkway of the garden, I was tormented by a single question: How could he speak so rudely? He could have conveyed his rejection in simple words without insulting me. But who gave him the right to humiliate me by talking so indecently, so contemptuously?

My thoughts ran wild in anguish. I tried to bring them under control, afraid to lose focus on the main issue, which was my marriage with Karyl. At this moment, it was more important to pay attention to that issue than think about her dad. This was the time to stop myself from self-destruction

But was it correct for me to think about him in this way? Now that he has already made those statements, it is futile to think of whether he had the right or not. Is it wise to say that an incident should not occur when it has already occurred? It is stupid to want to be 20 years of age when I am 24. You cannot change reality. It is useless discussing how a person should speak when he has already spoken.

The question about how he could talk in the manner that he did contains a hidden presumption that he should not have talked in that manner. But even this statement is not in concurrence with the reality. Because, thereby, I am presuming that Karyl's dad must behave according to my expectations. But who am I to decide how he should behave? It is also childish to say that I should have control over him or he should have my consent to his behaviour. Just as he has the freedom to speak as per his own wish, I too have the freedom to not be hurt by his words.

I wanted to use this freedom.

If you are hurt by somebody's words, it indicates that you believe he speaks the truth. You may think so, only if his words are supported by facts. But if they are not, then it is not necessary to believe that person.

What was the reality in my case? Do I become worthless because he calls me so? Not at all. I was earning while learning; I was working honestly; I was working hard and I also took on the responsibility of my family. I was definitely not worthless. Then why should I suffer?

I decided not to pay any importance to her dad's words and lose my emotional balance. A quote by Eleanor Roosevelt flashed in my mind: 'No one can insult you without your permission.'

I repeated this several times to myself. Be it Karyl's dad or anybody else, I would feel insulted only if I agreed with them. And only I would decide if I should agree or not.

***

There was a show of *Dream Girl* announced at the Capitol Theatre. I was doubtful if Karyl would perform in that show, and also afraid that her dad might accompany her that day. I reached the theatre and sent her a message through Jason.

'I want to meet you. Tell me the time and the place –Albert.'

She replied: 'On Sunday, at two in the afternoon, at the Franklin Street subway, near the ticket counter.'

We met as planned.

'Albert, dad did not calm down even after you left. He came just short of slapping me. He kept insisting that we were White Americans, Protestants, that our lifestyles were different. He did not stop at this and also gave me a strict warning that he would throw me out if I continue our relationship. He keeps a watch on me day and night. A man from his office follows me all the time. Today, dad left for some work and I somehow threw off that stalker to come see you.' Karyl was sobbing.

'What have you decided then?' I asked her.

She continued crying.

'Karyl, try to forget what he said, just for a while. Please tell me what you feel, honestly. Do you want to marry me?' I directly put forth the question that haunted me.

'Yes.'

'Are you sure?'

'Yes.'

'Then you must remember that your dad will never give his consent to our marriage and we will never be able to marry if we decide to wait for his consent. You may have to sever your relation with him if we get married. Are you ready for this?'

'....'

'Karyl, you have to make a decision on way or the other. But please say 'yes', Karyl. I want you. If you agree, we can start our lives anew. Look, we can have a civil marriage without your dad's knowledge. He cannot do anything once we are legally married. We are both adults in the eyes of the law. No one can object. Please think again. Please say 'Yes' Karyl.' I made one last frantic attempt to woo her.

'Of course, it's a 'yes', Albert.'

I heaved a sigh of relief. I could not believe my good fortune, but I dreaded her fickle mind. I asked her again and again if she was firm in her decision and each time she replied, 'Yes'.

I decided not to waste a single moment and immediately began planning our future course of action. My first priority was to acquire a marriage license. It was necessary for both of us to appear before the government officer, but it was also very obvious that her dad would make every effort to prohibit her from meeting me. We had to act very cautiously and without arousing any suspicion. There was only one way. We had to stop meeting each other so often.

'Karyl, you have to be extremely careful. At any cost your dad should not know about our plan. Henceforth, we cannot meet every day. Send a message through Jason whenever possible. We shall meet only then. Let me first enquire about the procedure for obtaining a marriage licence. Jason will inform you about the day,' I explained.

I felt very sad as I wished her good-bye. I was not going to see her as often as before. But I had to bear with this parting for happier days ahead.

I also began searching for a good rented apartment for us. I preferred one close to our house, but since it was a busy area, the rents were beyond my reach. In the end, I finalised an apartment on 138th Street off Wills Avenue. It was a small furnished apartment with just a living room, a bedroom, and a half kitchen. But it was comfortable for the two of us. I even signed the agreement for a monthly rent of $45. Now everything was in line with my plan. I began dreaming of my married life with Karyl in that apartment.

The Department of Marriage Registration for Bronx County was situated in the Supreme Court building. I made the necessary enquiries. The procedure for a civil marriage was simple. We could marry within a week of obtaining the license. I met the officer personally. Two people were necessary to be present on that day as witnesses. The date for the appointment was for two months later.

Those two months were a great torture. I could meet Karyl only a few times, but every meeting would leave me distressed. Fearful thoughts made me lose sleep. Karyl continued to confuse me with her behaviour. After we stopped meeting frequently, she had befriended a new guy called Ronald. Many a time she would talk about him very animatedly. But at the same time she would also shower her love upon me. Then again, quite casually, she would remark, 'Albert, you are not at all charming.' Sometimes she would keep singing praises of her dad. This would lead me to doubt whether Karyl was capable of being a strong and supportive life-partner. Such uncertainty would keep biting my mind day and night. But I was confident of winning her with my deep love and optimistic about a successful married life.

Time flew by in this precarious state of mind. The day of our appointment drew close. The officer from asked us a few simple questions and immediately gave his approval. My joy knew no bounds. I had half won the battle. Now only the formality of registering our marriage was left. We decided to get married within the next two days. No one except Mom, Paul, Jason and Manny knew about our plans. I was afraid that if the news reached Karyl's dad, he would sabotage our plan. I was desperately anxious to get over with the marriage ceremony. I spent the next two days and nights in anxiety and fear.

The night before our wedding, I was wide awake but contemplating happy thoughts about our future.

***

Mom, Paul, Manny and Ronald, Karyl's friend, were present at the marriage ceremony. Everyone congratulated us. It was a joyful event. Paul and Manny gave us a surprise gift. Both of them had recently started working as accountants. Paul was employed by the shipping corporation and Manny was working with a private company. They had saved money from their salaries and booked a suite at the Palm Court hotel for our first night as man and wife. We planned to move to the Wills Avenue apartment the morning after. Finally, my restless mind was able to find some peace. We arrived at the Palm Court. It was located on Madison Avenue. How magnificent it was! The furniture was made of oakwood, with merlot finish, which gave a beautiful shine to the exquisite carvings. It was very cool and quiet inside, although it was one of the hottest days in July.

It was past noon when we entered our suite. The room was decorated with blue, yellow, and purple asters which looked soothing in the hot weather. I was excited. Karyl and I had only enjoyed a limited intimacy with her so far. We had not reached the stage of intercourse yet. But even the memory of those intimate moments was very stimulating. I was eager to unite with her in every sense.

We were very tired and stretched out to rest on the king-sized bed. My mind was in a state of bliss. Karyl was actually lying next to me. Was it a dream? No, now Karyl was truly mine. She was my legally-wedded wife. I was the happiest man on the earth. I was lying in a surreal world unaware of the surroundings. My mind was floating in some ecstasy. I was roaming in a virtual world where I saw and felt only Karyl.

I wanted to touch her, to feel her. How would she respond to my touch? Was she also excited with the idea of our union? My anxiety again reached its peak.

I stretched my hand to pull her towards me but she was beyond my reach. I stretched my hand further. Karyl was not there. There was nobody near me. I sat up. Where was Karyl?

An empty bed stared at me. Was I still dreaming? As I came to my senses I looked around the suite. She was nowhere. Karyl had vanished! I took some time to recover from the shock.

Perhaps she had gone out to bring something. Or perhaps she had gone to take a short walk. Maybe she did not wish to wake me up. I tried to console myself.

My gut told me that she had not left for a casual purpose. Something unexpected had happened. Just a few moments ago I was at peace. Now my heart began pounding. Karyl! Karyl! I searched for her in every nook and corner of the suite. Finally, on the small coffee table, I found a piece of folded paper. As I read my heartbeats became faster. I started trembling and broke into a sweat.

The note was from Karyl. She had written, 'Dear Albert, I want to see Dad. I cannot hide the news of our marriage. I am leaving.'

For a while, I was unable to grasp the meaning of her words. Slowly I began to understand the gravity of her decision. The realisation that the repercussions of this action were going to be very serious tore my heart into pieces. I had taken every care to avoid such a situation, but Karyl herself had invited a crisis. What could I say of this unexpected development? My inner voice had always warned me of her unstable mind, but my intense love for her had forced me to ignore the truth.

I ran towards the lobby of the hotel. It was empty. I approached the receptionist. I described Karyl and enquired anxiously if they had noticed any woman like her. Yes, they said. Such a lady had just left the hotel. The answer left me devastated. Their reply sucked life out of me. My limbs weakened and I collapsed on a sofa in the lobby. I felt as if someone was hammering me in punishment! After some time, I collected myself.

No, the situation was not that scary, I convinced myself. We are married now. I am her lawfully-wedded husband. Even if she has gone back to her father, it is my duty to bring my wife back respectfully, I told myself.

I got up and started for her home. I had decided not to enter that house again when her dad had insulted me. But now this was the need of the hour. The situation was such. My love superseded my resolution.

The 23rd Street subway station was right opposite Palm Court. As I walked towards it, several thoughts were at war in my mind. I do not remember when and how I reached Franklin Street station and the Powell Apartment. I took the elevator and rang the bell.

Her Dad opened the door. The moment he saw me, he broke into a volley of anger.

He began blasting me.

'You! You rascal! You have ruined my Karyl's life. You fooled her into marriage with your sweet talk. You have maligned her forever. I had warned you to stay away from her. Still you followed her shamelessly. You have poisoned her life. But mind you, you have to deal with me. Sign these papers which say that you do not have a relationship with Karyl and you are willingly divorcing her. Mind you, if you do not sign these papers, I will lodge a complaint against you with the police for kidnapping and marrying her forcefully. Go and enjoy jail-time for the rest of your life.'

I was stupefied with this unexpected bombardment.

'You cannot force me. We are married now. We have married willingly. We are husband and wife by law,' I replied boldly, with great courage.

'Which law are you talking about? I can reverse Ronald's statement as a witness. I can prove that there was no witness at all from Karyl's side. Then which law will legalise the status of your marriage? And mind you, Karyl has written the note herself before coming back to me. Is it not clear then that she too was against this marriage? Remember carefully, all this evidence and Karyl's statements are against you in the court of law. Remember, if I lodge a complaint against you with the police, you will spend the rest of your career and life in jail. I can even get you dismissed from your measly job and ensure that you remain jobless all your life. I do not want you to beg on the streets but if you do not sign the papers I ask, unfortunately, I will have to resort to taking this step too.' He kept shouting furiously at the top of his voice.

I was stunned with this surprising turn of events. His words hit me like fireballs. With some determination I got up. Karyl was sitting on the sofa, next to him.

I went up to her and said 'Karyl, I am your lawful husband. We are both adults according to law. It is not necessary to pay heed to your daddy's threats if you wish to come with me. I will never remind you of this incident where you came here without informing me. But please be bold at this moment. Have courage.

Come with me. I will make you happy. I will never leave you. Come with me. Leave this place right now. Every moment is precious. I need your support, Karyl. It will give me strength. No one can harm us if we are together. But at this moment, Karyl, I need you very much.'

I desperately pleaded for her support, choking up as I spoke. I could barely control my tears. I looked at Karyl. There was absolutely no change in her expression.

'No, Albert. I do not wish to come with you. I feel like I have definitely made a mistake in marrying you. Please obey dad' she replied in a determined tone. She appeared very composed.

Her words pierced my heart. My entire body became a hotpot of sorrow. All my delicate feelings turned into ashes. The harsh truth that I had lost her forever burnt into my heart. I understood that I was alone and weak without any support. I surrendered to the situation.

I took the pen and those papers from her dad and signed wherever he asked. Pushing the papers into his hands I stood up and left without looking back. His words followed me: 'It will take at least three months to get the divorce document. I shall post all the necessary documents to your address. You need not see us anymore. You are not connected to us in any way from this moment.'

I walked out like a zombie. How pitiable my life had become. I had to sign divorce papers on my wedding day. Such a situation is ridiculous and rare. In the morning I had been so blissful, but the afternoon and the pain it brought forth were beyond my imagination. The events since the morning were more sensational than a movie! All my dreams were shattered. This unexpected chain of incidents pushed me into a whirl of depression.

I had almost filled my cup of happiness, but a cruel stroke of luck had snatched it away. I could not contain my anger towards Karyl anymore. I had a simple wish: I just wanted to get married and live a happy life. But Karyl's actions had ruined my life. It had set my heart on fire and 'Albert' was burning with it.

Should I return? I was still her lawful husband. How can she defy me? I had every right to take her backtoforce her out. I shall take her to the hotel; rape her till she screams in pain. I must punish her for betraying me, a punishment so severe that she will grieve in pain the rest of her life.

My trauma became so unbearable that, as I walked, I kept kicking the small shrubs by the side of the walkway. I vented my anger on small stones. After a while I looked around. I was in the Botanical Garden. Perhaps I had taken a cab to come here. I was not able to recollect anything.

Soon, I consciously stopped thinking violently about Karyl. For me, it was immoral to touch a woman against her will, even if the woman was my wife. Before marriage, I had many intimate moments with Karyl where I would be anxious to get physical the moment I saw her. Although I never considered pre-marital relations to be immoral, I never forced myself on her against her wish. These ill-feelings had risen out of grief. I could have never behaved this way in real life. Whatever I want, I want it to be given willingly.

But did Karyl respect my feelings? She had torn my delicate

love into pieces. She could have denied my marriage proposal in clear terms. Who had given her the right to play with my life?

While my mind was caught in these thoughts, it occurred to me that Karyl alone was not responsible for this mess. I had also allowed her to play with my feelings. I had allowed her to hurt me. I had the freedom to not be humiliated by her. But I had ignored this freedom. A feeling of defeat engulfed my mind. I had failed. I was a complete loser.

I collected my belongings from the Palm Court and returned home. As usual, Mom was not home. Paul was in his room. He was shocked to see me but I was not able to explain what had happened. He also did not pester me with questions. I had no energy. I was completely exhausted. I threw myself on the bed. With the soft familiar touch feel of my bed I could no longer hold back my tears. As I silently wept, Paul came into my room. He had guessed that something very serious had happened. He simply kept patting my shoulder.

I badly needed somebody to comfort me. With Paul's affectionate touch, I let myself go. I lost control over the restraint I had managed so far and blurted out the events of the day. I had to reveal how my self-esteem had been shred into bits. I was overwhelmed with sorrow.

'Albert, to be honest, you do not deserve such a fickle-minded girl. It was you, wasn't it, who always said that our lives are not so small as to be limited by a person or by an incident? It is much bigger. In your words, we have to make our life big ourselves. Albert, your life is much larger than Karyl's rejection.' Paul was still patting me warmly.

I was unable to express what I felt with his reassuring words. I wanted to thank him and say, 'Paul, you reminded me of my words at the right time, thanks,' But I was in absolutely no state to speak with anybody.

We sat in silence for quite some time. I was half asleep with mental fatigue. The night passed in agony and restlessness. I kept suppressing bouts of grief in the darkness of the night. Once again, my habit of contemplation came to my rescue. My mind said: 'Albert, you have to learn to bear such calamities in life. In some situations you have no alternative other than to suffer silently. But, yet, you have a choice before you – whether to keep suffering to the extent of self-destruction or whether to accept gracefully and move on in life.'

I tried to switch to optimistic thoughts for the rest of the night. By early morning, my mind calmed down, and soon I was fast asleep.

***

I received the divorce-documents by post. I had tried to bury all the bitter memories of the past six months, but that piece of paper painfully revived them again. The divorce of a marriage which was never consummated! I had recovered from that crisis but the wound was very deep. The days would pass in work but the nights were long and sleepless, with the pain growing unbearable every hour.

Late at night, as I would lie down sleepless, a storm would rage within me. Karyl. I would yearn for her. My unfulfilled desire for consummation would set me on fire. Every inch of my body ached for her. A feeling of incompleteness hounded me. Nights became restless with my burning desire. I was almost on the verge of a nervous breakdown. Night after night, alone in the darkness, I suffered silently.

Any work near 138th Street would remind me of the apartment on Wills Avenue that I had booked. For no fault of mine, I had lost the money I paid as advance. Karyl had destroyed my dreams of a happy life in that apartment, I fumed. To add to this, I had to appoint Mark Baker, a lawyer, to complete the legal formalities of the divorce and pay a huge fee to him. It was her dad who was responsible for this additional burden. I would go wild with frustration. Day by day I grew cynical about the whole world as such. Nothing good was happening in life.

While I was promoted in my job, often along with typing and clerical work, I was made to do lowly jobs like sweeping the shop floor, which I could not refuse. My inner voice would scream in denial, 'This is not your job, Albert. You are wasting your intellect.' My mind would protest against George Roderick's exploitation. He was already paying me poorly and extracting impossible hours. But I was not successful in getting a better job elsewhere. My intelligence and knowledge were worthless. I was disenchanted with the entire world.

I had written so many books. All those manuscripts were gathering dust. No publisher was interested in them. In spite of my merit I had to beg for work, I had to beg for books to be published.

I had started the two business ventures because of Dad. Even if the ventures went into losses, it was I who had made up for it, without any help from him. But Dad had never acknowledged this. I would boil in anger thinking about his ungrateful attitude. He had neglected his responsibility towards his family and never cared to send the alimony money. I kept simmering with anger.

All my dreams of a happy life, of becoming a writer had been shattered. I was totally disappointed with the world, which seemed full of indifferent, cruel people. My wife had disowned me on the day of the wedding. I thought to myself, 'Everybody despises me; everyone treats me with contempt; my talent, my intelligence, is ignored everywhere.' I was enraged with fury and hatred. I could not bear the harsh reality any longer and prayed for a single stroke of punishment to end this slow suffering.

Some days it would become impossible to contain the ordeal. I would get violent. I would scream in frustration, hit the wall hard till I injured myself. Kick anything that came in my way. Strike the bed in exasperation. This would wake up Paul. He would watch me in horror, wide-eyed and scared.

I would go mad with anger. Paul never intercepted. He was scared lest I hit him in the heat of that moment. But he knew that I got such bouts intermittently and would cool down after sometime. He would then pat me affectionately. Drained out, I would then collapse in his arms and cry out unabashedly. Men do not cry, I knew. But in that situation it would become impossible for me to control my tears. Sometimes, on hearing the noise, Mom would come to pacify me. She would sit near me for a while, cover me with a blanket and then leave silently. This would bring some comfort to my agonised mind and I would manage to sleep after some time.

I would often break into such fits of anger, and every time it would leave me completely exhausted. With great effort I would gather back my energy, only to lose it again in the next attack.

I would need enormous energy to gather this strength! After every outburst I would calm down but only for a short period.I was able to suppress my anger but it would always be simmering inside me subconsciously. Any incident, however minor, would trigger its eruption like a volcano and reduce me to ashes.

I wanted to put an end to this cycle. I believed that if we are able to control our feelings of worry or hatred, we should also be able to control our anger.

Although I worked in office as usual, this thought would occupy my mind. We are creators of our emotions. Then to what extent do external factors contribute to our anger? I was anxious to find out. As per my habit I turned to the library one evening. But I could not concentrate on reading. It was necessary to first clear the mess in my mind.

I closed my eyes and pondered over the recent events. As I relaxed in the chair, the scenario began getting clearer. Of course the circumstances around me had contributed to my anger but that was not the main cause. If it were so, all the people in the world who faced such situations in life would have been prone to hysterical attacks of anger. I had read biographies of many great persons who had suffered like me in their lives. Did they too have such outbursts like me? Most probably, not. So the main reason for my anger was not the external circumstances but it was 'I' myself. My thoughts seemed to be getting aligned.

Why does my anger keep on escalating? This is perhaps because I keep on telling myself something. This self-talk was probably the reason for my simmering anger. I began examining my attitude. 'I want this world to be the way I wish. If it is not, I am not able to bear with it.' This was the attitude I had nurtured. I had to check if this attitude was rational. I began asking myself some questions.

Was it wrong in saying that this world is not the way I want it?

'No. It is not wrong. That is the reality.'

Is it wrong to say that the world should behave according to my wish?

'Yes, it is wrong to say so. One has to accept the reality around us. There is a difference between these two statements: "It would have been better if the world was as per my wish" and "The world must be as per my wish". The first statement expresses my wish and the second my obstinacy. Because of my obstinate approach I had ruled out the possibility that the world may not be how I want it to be. Such a rigid attitude is, of course, wrong.'

Was it wrong to expect that people around me should behave according to my wishes?

'People around me do not plan their behaviour after consulting me. I have no control over their decisions. Even if I wished very strongly, nobody can assure me of their behaviour.'

I had some more questions: Does my statement—that the world should be according to my wish—have any support? Am I the ruler of this earth and of the living beings? Have I bestowed this designation upon myself? Why should the world agree to my unilateral rule? Do I possess any extraordinary power required for such a rule? Who am I that I can expect Karyl, her Dad, the publishers or the owners of other companies to lay a red carpet and wait for me?

There was only one answer to all these questions. What I thought about myself was an exaggeration. I am an ordinary person. I do not have any divine power. I do not have any special authority. So it was definitely wrong to expect them to behave as I wished.

The question that automatically followed was: Why is it wrong to say that it is unbearable to live in a world that is not as I want it to be?

This statement is not consistent with reality. In reality I had learnt to bear with the situation. I could definitely say the situation was unbearable, had it led me to death. But that had not happened. So it was obvious that it was within my capacity to bear with the situation. How could I then say that it was beyond my capacity?

And the final question. Was the situation really so dreadful?

Now the answer was very clear. The situation was definitely very difficult but not dreadful. No calamity had befallen upon me. Many people have to face far more severe situations in life. In earthquakes or accidents, many lose their entire family or wealth. One can call such a situation dreadful. But the one before me is definitely not that.

I was convinced from this disputation that the circumstances around me were bad but not as horrible as I considered them to be. I had no logical reason to insist that others should behave as I wish. I would be wasting my energy in grumbling, complaining and fretting, in fits of anger, as long as I kept demanding that everyone should behave according to my wishes. My anger was not going to change them. Instead, it was ruining my health. I should have focused my attention on solving the crisis objectively rather than wasting my energy in this manner.

I remembered the words of the famous psychotherapist Virginia Satir: 'We have to live in the world as it is, and not as it should be.'

We have to live in a world which is not ideal in all respects. So I chose to accept the people around me and the world, unconditionally.

This was not an easy task. I would constantly get angry, feel anguished. But then I would review this disputation; this also helped me make a thorough study of anger.

When we express our ire about others and show our annoyance, unconsciously we keep thinking about them. We keep talking to ourselves about them. We cultivate hatred and anger in our minds and expressing these feelings again and again. As a result, we become what we hate in others. We imbibe in our personality those same qualities which we dislike, about which we are displeased. The person who makes us angry is not affected at all by our outburst. In fact, most of the time he is unaware of our anger. This makes us angrier. In the end, it is we who lose our mental balance.

I made a conscious decision—to remain happy. I told myself that my happiness did not depend on other people or circumstances but only on myself. I started training my mind to think that it was good if all the people in this world behaved as I wanted, but I will not insist adamantly that they should.

This attitude lessened minor problems but I would still occasionally find myself sometimes drifting towards irrational thoughts.

To overcome this, I found a novel method. I prepared three cards with a message on each, which would bring my wayward thoughts back on the right path. Whenever I read the message on the card, it would break the chain of irrational thoughts. I trained myself to use this method to keep a proper mental balance. I kept these cards in places where they would be easily visible. I placed one of them in my room, another in my wallet, and one in my shirt pocket. Whenever I had a self-talk session, the messages on these cards would guide me. This method would help me control my wayward thoughts, which created anger.

The message on the first card was: 'No gain without pain.' It would remind me that success needs hard work, that there was no shortcut. Hard work is important for a better future. On reading this message, I would feel more inspired to work harder.

On the second card, I wrote: 'Adversity is a blessing in disguise.' A situation may appear very difficult outwardly, but it makes you tough as you grow. You make progress only when you face the situation bravely. This card would give me courage and increase my willpower.

The third card read: 'This too shall pass.' This card would tell me that nothing is permanent in life. Situations keep changing and this is nature's law. Remain hopeful of a better future. You do not have to work hard all through your life. You will definitely be free of it sometime. I would feel inspired on reading this card. It would give me new energy to work.

Gradually, I increased my endurance level. This was the only way of learning to accept the world unconditionally. I learnt to be patient and control my mind.

Confucius, the great Chinese philosopher who lived two thousand years ago, had written: 'Do not be desirous of having things done quickly. Do not look at small advantages. Desires to have things done quickly prevent their being done thoroughly. Looking at small advantages prevents great affairs from being accomplished.'

I had noted this in my diary. I would read it every morning before leaving for work.

***

'432, Block No. 5, Seventh Avenue, Greenwich Village.'

I was holding the chit on which this address was written. There was an unexpected shower of rain. There had been no forecast on the radio and I had left home without an umbrella. I was completely wet. I tried to find some shelter but I couldn't find any among the old houses on that street. The road had become very muddy. Water dripped from the bottom of my pants. I folded these up and walked through the mucky path.

I was very irritated. It had taken quite a few months for me to recover from the Karyl episode. But hardly had I recovered than she sent a message through Jason asking to see her urgently.

I ignored the message, treating it as one of her usual tantrums. But she sent the same message two more times.

'Albert, please see her at least once. Karyl is really in a bad shape,' Jason pleaded as well.

His words touched me. I took her address, but only after resolving not to be a victim to her histrionics. This place was to the west of Broadway, far away from Manhattan. The arches and the traffic islands looked like historical ruins. There were billboards of a few Off-Broadway shows in some lanes. The small cafeterias, shops, bars and clubs gave the streets the air of a metro, but the discipline and town-planning one found in Manhattan was missing. There was no area-map anywhere. Dirty and drenched, I searched for Block no 5. Finally, I saw an old single-storey construction, with all apartments placed along a single common corridor. There was knee-deep water at the entrance. Wading cautiously through the puddle, I managed to reach Apartment 432. All the while I kept wondering: What had made Karyl leave her Daddy's posh house in the TriBeCa? Why had she moved to such a place?

The door was opened by Karyl herself. I was astonished to see her condition. There were dark circles around her sunken blue melancholic eyes. She looked very weak, like a withered flower.

'Albert!' She ran forward to hug me.

Karyl was unable to speak coherently. She sobbed uncontrollably. Her frail body was trembling like a creeper in a storm. She was in a very sorrowful state. Her trembled and her eyes flooded with tears as she spoke.

From her outburst I could gather that she began a new affair with Ronald after ending our marriage. But her dad did not approve of this relationship either, and asked her to leave his house. So she had to move to this rental place. To add to the misery, she was dismissed from the lead role of *Dream Girl* because of her frequent absence. She was compelled to accept work as a mere backstage artist for survival. The final, most cruel blow was when her new lover Ronald deceived her and left for China with his new girlfriend.

She looked very exhausted. Perhaps she had not slept since many days. She said she had lost her appetite. Whenever she remembered how Ronald cheated on her, she would cry in fits. She confessed that she was seriously contemplating suicide. I understood. She was unable to think logically because of the trauma of betrayal. Karyl was heading towards a nervous breakdown.

'Nervous breakdown' is actually not a medical term. It is a phrase used by lay-people but it implies many types of mental disorders. Many a time, mental upheavals cause changes in the nervous system. Very often a person shows symptoms of mental imbalance much before he actually gets afflicted by a nervous breakdown. But since these symptoms are mild, they are often ignored. The main symptom is mental instability. Inconsistent thinking, frequent change in decisions, mood swings, experiencing intense and contrasting emotions are some such symptoms.

Now I understand the reason behind Karyl's unpredictable behaviour with me. She had displayed these symptoms even during our courtship. Her mood would always keep changing.

She would praise my gifts sometimes, and ignore them completely at other times. She would admire me and for no reason also deplore me. She was always indecisive about marrying me. I was now able to understand the contradiction in her behaviour. The process of nervous breakdown had already begun during those days. Ronald's deception had given her a shock, which caused those symptoms to be aggravated, and result in a breakdown.

'Albert, please forgive me. Please help me. I need you very much. I feel so comforted when I talk to you. Dad has closed his doors to me. I have no one in this world except you, Albert. If you also choose to reject me, I will end my life.' Karyl pleaded with desperation.

I was moved by her words. After knowing about her nervous condition, sympathy had replaced the anger I had for her. With great effort I tried to forget that only a few months ago, I had also pleaded before her similarly and she had rejected my plea with utter disregard.

In our relationship, it was I who had always surrendered to her whims. This raised her self-esteem in her eyes, since it was she who had rejected me. But in this case, the situation had reversed. So, when Ronald deserted her for some other girl, she felt devastated. All her self-esteem was torn apart. That formed the onset of a nervous breakdown.

Our relationship was not bound by law anymore. I decided to help her without getting entangled into a relationship. I did not make this decision out of sympathy; there was definite thinking behind it.

First, I still loved her. Although she was the cause of my angst and even though I did not wish to renew ties with her, I loved her very much. I sincerely wished a happy life for her. So out of humanity, I decided to help her in every possible way. By refusing help I did not wish to carry the guilt of pushing her to self-destruction all my life.

Second, I felt that in helping her I had an opportunity to test my skills as a counsellor, and also my knowledge of psychology. If I succeed in resurrecting Karyl, I could say that the counsellor in me had won. I did not want to miss this opportunity. I instantly assured her of my help. Even an assurance seemed to comfort her considerably.

I first located the attitude that had harmed her self-esteem: Ronald leaving her and finding a new lover. This had created a feeling of self-depreciation. She was filled a kind of inferiority-complex. Karyl felt that she had failed in sustaining a man's infatuation. Her complex was not limited only to this. She also felt that this lack made her worthless not only as a woman but as a person. This self-damning thought which she nursed had brought her to a stage of nervous breakdown.

When I had suffered from inferiority complex earlier, I had written down my thoughts about the possible beliefs that had caused it. I had also examined them thoroughly. When I found that I was denigrating myself because of wrong beliefs, I created new beliefs and replaced the old, misguiding ones. I had consciously revised my self-talk accordingly.

I used the same method in dealing with Karyl's depression. I helped her to write down her thoughts, to analyse every statement she made. To get rejected by somebody was definitely not a small incident in one's life. But in a larger perspective, it is not a fatal incident.

She had unnecessarily enlarged the purview of this event and was giving undue importance to it. In the process she was paying a heavy price in terms of the quality of her life. Gradually I convinced her that she had perhaps failed in holding Ronald's attraction for long, but this did not make her inferior in any respect.

I made serious efforts to draw Karyl out of her complex. I eventually succeeded in convincing her that her thoughts were unrealistic and a creation of her mind. She too realizsed that unless she herself made special efforts, she would not be able to control her turmoil.Karyl cooperated with me with great sincerity. The result was soon visible. She began glowing as before, and was the vivacious, lively Karyl once again.

I would frequently go to Greenwich to counsel her. We had uninterrupted privacy in her apartment. In the course of our meetings, we became physically intimate. We had absolute freedom. We could shed all inhibitions. Our passions needed no control. The fire of desire was difficult to douse. The awakening of our suppressed desires in that exclusive privacy was very powerful. One day, the inevitable happened. The union of two excited bodies. That was my first experience of sexual intercourse, my first experience of womanhood! I was in a trance. Such an ecstatic experience! Every inch of my body was stimulated! Every part of my body oscillated in excitement! I now understood why this pleasure is called sublime.

Undoubtedly, the pleasure one derives from sexual intercourse is several times more than that from masturbation. Of course, a climax can be reached in both; but the quality of satisfaction in an intercourse was definitely superior. The subtle responses of the female partner, the exciting foreplay, the variety of sensuous moves, which grow with the intensity of desire, sometimes very bold, add significantly to the pleasure. You definitely feel the absence of a partner in masturbation. Satisfying sexual desire by the mere imagery of a partner adds a limitation to the pleasure you can derive from it.

To keep physical relations with your ex-wife is not permitted in religion. It is considered a sin. But it did not violate the rules of my principles of morality. It did not make me feel guilty. Let the religious leaders or other authorities treat this as immoral. It was my conviction that it is not immoral when a mature adult has consenting relations with another.

I was strictly following the rules about morality I had set for myself. I never touched Karyl against her wish, not ever enquired about the nature of her relationship with Ronald. Even though we were no more husband and wife by law, I would have never made this enquiry even if she were my legally wedded wife. I personally believed that every person had the right to choose another person and the type of relationship he wished to maintain. I began enjoying Karyl's companionship without any reservations.

***

As a result of Karyl's re-entry into my life, I began seriously studying the institution of marriage and marital relationships. I arrived at the conclusion that both husband and wife should have the right to freedom in sex. This opinion was based on extensive reading and contemplation on this subject.

The concept of freedom of sex within the limits of a marriage is not confined only to the act of sex, but also includes the right to choose a partner in sex. Once you get married, you are expected to be loyal with your spouse even if you do not wish to. I did not approve of this binding and the suffocation that it entails all through your life.

I was convinced with my views about marriage even though they were unconventional and shocking. Loyalty in sexual relationships should not be mandatory for sustaining a marriage. A man and a woman should marry to make each other happy, but according to me, it was not right to force one to seek happiness only from the married partner.

When there is willingness in a relationship, there is spontaneity. The relationship stays free and natural. But when you put a constraint, it loses these qualities, and turns into a cold, indifferent affair. This development becomes inevitable when you are forced into a relationship. It is inconsiderate to expect your partner to fulfil all your requirements all the time. Even if Karyl were my wife, I would not have forced my expectations upon her.

Man is not monogamous by nature. He can desire for more than one partner. The institution of marriage will become stronger if we accept this reality. Since this is not acceptable to the society, however people tend to have extra-marital affairs which have to be kept surreptitious.

In spite of religious restrictions or strict laws, people are brazenly engaged in extra-marital sexual relations behind the garb of decency. And this number increases day by day. The reason behind this is just the unrealistic expectation that once you marry, you are not permitted to like anybody else.

When both the partners in a marriage have the freedom of sex, besides other freedoms, they will be able to accept their respective needs with an open mind. They will also respect each other's individual freedom. One can enjoy this freedom and also keep their marriage intact. I did not consider this as adultery or sexual infidelity. On the contrary, I thought it was improper to curb the freedom of one's partner under the authority implied by the legal status of marriage. When one enforces such restrictions in marriage, he or she is unknowingly encouraging the partner to opt for surreptitious relations outside marriage.

When you are afraid of acknowledging your own desires, you are tempted to fulfil them secretly. I was against such secretive or furtive relationships. I had accepted my natural instinct. I never felt the need of behaving cowardly or secretively.

Whenever our action is supported by thinking, we are able to confront our real self. We remain honest with our feelings. Even if our views are clashing with those of society, we are not afraid to fight against convention.

I had this courage. Therefore I was never cowed down by the societal pressures. I did believe in social rules and regulations which are necessary to maintain discipline and to keep society homogeneous. But I was never afraid of defying those social norms which were unjustified and extremist.

I put into practice all that I was convinced of. I found my happiness by my own chosen ways. Since we were already divorced lawfully, there was no legal risk. I had relations with many women to fulfil my desires. All these experiences enriched my knowledge about sex. But of course, I always followed the rules set by me. I never deceived anybody. I always took precaution so that it did not lead to unwanted pregnancy or venereal diseases. I never forced myself upon them or hurt them in any way. I was always cautious that I did not violate any law.

No sex is perverted when both the partners enjoy a sexual relationship without exploiting or hurting each other. I experienced great benefit when I defied all those norms which were a hurdle in my search of happiness. I was able to enjoy different ways of deriving pleasure. I realised that it was very important to open up a woman sensually. Once her passion is aroused, she participates wholeheartedly, from foreplay to coitus.

I discovered various techniques of arousing a woman mentally. Many a time one hears complaints of a woman being cold or frigid in bed or reluctant for sex. I realised that the reason for this is more often psychological rather than physical. It is a result of sexual inhibitions which are deep seated in their mind.

I devised different methods to uproot them. I understood that women have a great power to arouse themselves as well as their partner. But these inhibitions are so strong that they turn cold and dispirited. They lose their will to explore their sexuality.

When I started to remove the layers of misconceptions gathered on their mind one by one, their response was enthusiastic. The outcome of my adventures was that instead of following women, I began getting followed by them.

While I enjoyed the company of different women, I reviewed my feeling of love for Karyl once again.

Love is immortal. Love is sublime. This is what literature writes about love. But in reality, love is a worldly feeling. A person may love another person just as he loves mathematics, science, philosophy or some other subject or even some abstract concept, for that matter.

Love is a feeling similar to other feelings, like happiness, grief, anger, fear. It is not necessary to treat it specially. Just as other emotions arise and disappear, the emotion of love can also fade away. Like other feelings, even love may go through the cycle of creation, development, sustenance, and destruction. To love means to get involved totally in another person and to evaluate him or her positively. There will be changes in that feeling if there is a change in this evaluation. But you have to take the decision entirely yourself whether to entertain the feeling of love constantly in your mind or to get rid of it.

We also tend to classify love as physical and platonic. We treat platonic love as supreme and superior to physical love. If you think rationally, it is not appropriate to make such a distinction. There is nothing to support this thinking and no reason to accept it. In fact love that is fulfilled both ways lends a unique quality to this experience in one's life.

The subject of love is the most discussed subject in literature. Writers have regarded love as the most supreme feeling and given love the most prominent place in their work. Great poets like Guttay, Shelley, Byron or Shakespeare have glorified love, depicting it as a dreamy emotion and have immortalized it in their work. But rarely has anybody noticed the difference between a healthy love and an unhealthy one.

To be very specific, love can be healthy or unhealthy depending upon the approach one adopts towards it. Romeo ended his life on hearing that Juliet was no more. Antony committed suicide because he did want to live without Cleopatra. He was a victim of the thought that life was meaningless without her and that his existence depended upon hers. These two examples demonstrate the intensity and depth of their love but only apparently.

These stories impress upon common people that one has to trivialize oneself in true or ideal love and go to extremes in order to prove it. This influence is so deep that it has not occurred to anyone so far that it is not healthy.

When a person sacrifices his life for his lover, he is presuming that he does not possess any identity of his own. He believes that the value of his life is determined only by his lover's acceptance or rejection. Such a person has very little love for his own life. Because of this belief he feels that life is worthless without his lover. This way of demonstrating one's total involvement or dedication in love is not healthy, in my opinion.

Total dedication and involvement does not imply that one should surrender one's entire life to the other person. When we make our existence dependent on someone else blindly, it means that we are devaluing our self and also encouraging the other person to exploit us. On the other hand, in healthy love, a person loves his lover more than anybody else, but to love or to be loved does not become one of his basic necessities in life. Even if one is madly in love, he does not denigrate himself.

He wants love, he wants it very much, but that does not become his dire need.

The belief that in true love or in an ideal love, one has to treat oneself as inferior, gives rise to emotional imbalance. This was evident in the symptoms Karyl showed during her nervous breakdown. We adopt many myths about love very blindly. I examined every myth thoroughly and rationally and noted down my observations.

The first myth about love I examined was: 'Love is some mystical power and therefore it cannot be expressed in simple words.'

My comment: 'Love is just a feeling like other feelings. It is an evaluation of a person which can be expressed in simple words.'

Another commonly believed myth was: 'One can love only one person at a time.'

I observed that a person can love more than one individual.

'Love develops automatically with your married partner.' This was another myth I checked.

My observation was: 'Love need not always bound by marriage. Many people continue their married life without loving the partner. As against this, many fall in love with a person outside marriage.'

We have associated feelings of love with sex so rigidly, that we expect that the person we love should be compatible in sex too. This gives rise to another myth that if we are in love with a person, we cannot have sexual relationship with someone else

This myth failed the test of rationality. What I had noticed was that although we love a person we can find happiness in having sex with someone else.

A common perception was that one can enjoy sex with a person only if their love is true.

The conclusion I drew from my observation was that some people can enjoy sex even if they are not in love with that person.

The last myth I examined was important: 'If you love somebody, you have to love that person incessantly.'

My observation was: 'However intensely he or she may love you, a person does not love every moment all the time. Even heavenly love gets discontinued intermittently.'

After writing down these thoughts, I wanted to analyze one more concept: 'Love at first sight.'

I had fallen in love with Karyl at first sight. When I tracked the psychological process behind this, I realised that before our 'first sight', our mind was already searching for love. It had been always eager to love someone. The qualities we wished for in a person were being already framed by our mind. So when we find a person close to our expectations we are convinced that we have found the right person.

In conclusion, neither is there any divine power behind falling in love nor is the feeling of falling in love spontaneous and unexpected. A longing of wanting a lover grows in the mind unknowingly and it is this feeling that makes one fall in love at first sight.

It is commonly believed that falling in love is beyond our control. But if we look objectively, we will notice that it is actually within our control and we cannot deny our contribution when it happens. We *decide* to fall in love. In the same way, we can also decide not to fall in love.

I found these conclusions very useful. Now I clearly understood that my thoughts had largely contributed to the love I felt for Karyl. I had gone crazy in her love as if it felt like an urgent necessity in my life. Now I could change my attitude and restore my peace. It also helped me in culminating our relationship without a heavy mind. Meanwhile Karyl too had found a new mate and decided to marry him. Thereafter I took a conscious decision of staying away from her life. I did not wish to sabotage her married life by maintaining our relationship. It was of course difficult to forget her and I never attempted to do so. I felt that after having a very intimate relationship it was against nature to make such an attempt. But I took care that I thought about her detachedly. This turned out to be easy because I was convinced of my rationally derived conclusions.

But in spite of these conclusions, I could not deny the importance of love in life. In fact it had the highest place in my life. My love for Karyl had not materialized into marriage but nonetheless it was only because of her that I had this wonderful experience of love.

In the beginning I did follow her crazily like a slave, because of some unrealistic ideas about love. But I do not repent this. It was only because of this experience that I realised subtle sensitivities within me. I had not loved with some intention or for some benefit.

Religion, social status or wealth were not factors which decided my love. It was intense love that originated spontaneously. In fact, to possess the capacity to love somebody wholeheartedly, to sacrifice one's life for sake of love, is a very extraordinary capacity and I am proud to possess it.

I experienced the power of emotions only because of my love for Karyl. I also discovered my capacity of experiencing intense love, an emotion in its entirety. I could unveil its different shades only because of my love for Karyl. But no amount of this positive attitude was able to lessen the agony of parting. It was as deep and intense as my love.

To experience such intense emotions is a proof of human sensitivity. To be emotional and sensitive should not be interpreted as a shortcoming or weakness. On the contrary, it is because of this quality that one can empathise with the other person, understand his or her feelings and experience the same intensity of emotions. This quality in fact is very useful to a psychologist. I realised this quality in me, in my potential as a psychologist, only because of Karyl. Perhaps it was this quality that was useful in curing her from her nervous breakdown. I am grateful to her for enabling me to experience love and to explore the psychological process behind this experience.

My love for Karyl, and later, the parting with her, reminded me of lines by the famous British poet Lord Tennyson: 'It is better to have loved and lost, than never to have loved at all.'

I had experienced this truth. I had recovered from my failure in love and started a new chapter in my life with renewed energy.

***

7

'Love and Marriage Problems Institute.' This was the name of the organization founded by me and its abbreviation was 'LAMP Institute.'

I had never planned to start something like this. But over the years, I had read so much about Sexology, that many of my married friends began consulting me regarding their sexual problems. They had begun to consider me an expert on this subject. Some did actually benefit from my consultation. Many began calling me a 'Living Encyclopaedia on Sex'.

I had a sizeable collection of personal experiences while writing *The Case for Sexual Promiscuity*, a book on Sexology. It was in doubt about the book ever getting published. But I was happy that it gave me an opportunity to study the subject in depth, and gather vast knowledge about sexual practices.

Eventually, I felt that I should use my knowledge professionally to guide people. LAMP was the result.

I was successful in establishing LAMP and simultaneously retaining my job. I would report at Distinctive Creations at eight in the morning like other staff members. I worked as sincerely as before; in fact I became George's right hand. He had begun relying upon me for every task.

When it was time to declare our annual raise in wages, I put forth a proposal. Instead of a monetary raise, I asked him to allow me to leave office after completing the day's work. He agreed without any hesitation. So I began reporting at work at half past ten in the morning. Without wasting a single moment I would begin my work. My stamina and speed was extraordinarily good. I would finish my entire work within 3 to 4 hours.

I wanted to utilise whatever spare time I got, very meticulously. I opened the LAMP clinic at our house at Andrews Apartments. A separate entrance for the clinic was arranged. I could furnish the clinic very sparsely, just with a table and a few chairs.

From the first week itself, I began receiving clients. I was happy. But on the following Sunday itself my happiness was eclipsed. It was the first Sunday of December. Noon. I was engrossed in listening to the live commentary of a football match on the Red Network radio station. It was being played between The New York Giants and The Brooklyn Dodgers. All of a sudden, the commentary stopped and a surprise bulletin was broadcast at around 2.26.

'Japan has attacked Pearl Harbour. Around 1,200 Americans have been injured and 2,400 have been killed in this attack. The seventh of December, 1941, will be the most unfortunate day in the history of our country.' Reporter Robert Eisenach was broadcasting this shocking news.

The news caused an upheaval in the entire country. Some new development would take place every day. War was the only subject of discussion everywhere, in every home, in every office, at every public place. Everybody remained hooked to the radio.

There was also a rumour of a likely bomb attack on New York, which was the financial capital of the country. People were scared to leave their homes. But one had to attend work. Everybody lived in terror of another attack. As a result, for some days, not a single client visited LAMP. It was, perhaps, the most difficult period in the life of the institute.

Soon, President Roosevelt declared that America was joining the Allies in reply to Japan's aggression.

These events created a wave of patriotism in the entire country. But, as the days passed, fear subsided and a trickling flow of clients began. Gradually normalcy restored. The flow of visitors to LAMP steadily increased later to such an extent, that I would begin counselling as soon as I returned home, without any rest.

People came from different places, from different age-groups, and from all strata of society. I would first try to gauge their views about sex. I was strongly convinced that their unhealthy attitude to sex was the cause of their sexual problems. There was another reason, and that was the socially-induced inhibition to speak openly about sex. I had discarded this inhibition long time ago. While speaking with clients, I would very openly and forthrightly talk about my views, and point out their faulty attitudes towards sex. I inspired them to think independently. I would try to revive their spirit of experimentation and make them aware of the power of imagination and invention. During my counselling sessions, I helped them to put all these qualities into use by removing the hurdles from their mind.

After studying several cases, I came to the conclusion that the psychological aspect of sexual desire is often ignored. This is the main reason for unhappiness and dissatisfaction in sex. Whenever I unfolded this perspective before the clients, it made them realise the significance of my views. I would help them explore their desires, which had been submerged in their preconscious minds by social restrictions, but were still in a semi-alive state. I would make them realise that exploration of one's sexuality is a way of developing one's personality. In order to motivate them, I would say, 'Sexual desires are common in humans and animals. But there is one difference between the two. In animals it is more dependent on external factors such as weather, season, or other such factors. But human beings are gifted with a brain which has an extraordinary power to arouse a person, simply by thinking and imagery. Therefore, even in the absence of a sexually stimulating object, one can be aroused by vivid imagery. We humans are very fortunate to have been gifted with a brain, but we do not use it during sex. Our brain, which thinks freely on all other subjects, stops thinking when it comes to sex.

'Restrictions on sex are so strong that they make our brain inactive. We avoid talking openly about sex. Traditional thinking has such a heavy bearing upon our minds, that we take pride in pretending as if we do not have any sexual desires. We have equated repulsion and disinterest in sex with simplicity and sanctity. This is so deep-seated in our minds, that we never realise that we are ignoring our natural instincts.'

Many a time, married couples came for guidance and help. I would find most of them incapable of discussing their sexual problems with anybody, even with their own life-partners, so hard would be the mental barriers in their minds. The supposedly informal and intimate relationship between a husband and wife remained formal, even after spending years of married life together. In matters of sex they would react as strangers, but act as partners in maintaining silence on the subject of sex.

Such couples limited their capacity for enjoying life. They had turned coitus into one of the formalities of life. These couples treated sex like a routine chore. They did not devote any time for tender foreplay, which is very necessary to excite a partner fully. And even when they had time, they would display a lack of will to use any imagination. They had closed all doors to think differently about sex.

What remained in their minds was a simmering dissatisfaction. Such cases would remind me of Leo Tolstoy's famous quote: 'The greatest wars in the world are fought in bed, not on the battlefield.' This quote definitely provokes us to think to what levels dissatisfaction in sex can reach.

To remove this dissatisfaction, I would tell them, 'Fulfilment of sexual desire is not an act to be finished in hurry. Sex does not mean only copulation. This is a very limited meaning of sex. Sexual satisfaction has a much wider significance. If a man and woman share a bed only for intercourse, then their sex-life ought to get dull. If you follow the same method of coitus year after year, you not only make your sex-life monotonous but you also miss some romantic moments in life. Remove your mental barriers. Allow your mind to roam freely. But this requires a will to experiment and innovate.

'You can innovate in two ways. One way is to change your partner. But if you want to remain faithful to your partner, there is a second way: To use different ways of sex-play. This needs a change in your mindset. You can explore new techniques to bring variety, but only when you do not condemn your sexual desire.

'When you search for this change, you will discover the different pleasure-points or the 'erogenous zones' of your body. According to physiology, these pleasure points are the mouth, ears and the area around the neck, lips, hair, back, armpits, breasts, shoulders, genitals, thighs, groin and anus. An act, which can stimulate the maximum number of pleasure points leads one to the highest level of satisfaction.

'If you have blinded yourself with orthodox and traditional dogmas, you will not be able to attain this level. If you relate sexual behaviour only to genitals, this traditional belief will make you seek satisfaction only from the conventional penile-vaginal penetration. The real reason behind this belief can be understood when you think deeply. There is persistent brainwashing in the belief that the conventional position should be the only way of copulation. This is a very conservative view towards sex.

'We are taught that sexual desire is a divine plan; it is nature's plan for procreation and inheritance. Procreation is, of course, the purpose—but not the only purpose—of intercourse. Happiness is also an important aim of sex. The joy you derive from sex is supreme. If you want to experience it, eradicate the belief that sex is only for procreation.

'Abandon the burden of these orthodox views impressed upon you so long. Get rid of the spell they have cast on your minds. Only then will you pay attention to your body. Only then will you stop feeling ashamed of your body. Only then will you realise that besides the genitals, there are other pleasure points, and only then will you begin to explore your body.

'You will be able to find out which pleasure point of your body is the most effective. You can then concentrate on that point and get maximum pleasure out of sex. You need not depend only on your genital organ for satisfaction. It will inspire you to imagine different methods of fulfilment. It will help you in identifying the method that can enhance your level of maximum satisfaction.'

I had observed that the couples whom I counselled carried an air of modernity and appeared to have a progressive approach, but, with regards to sex, they were very orthodox and rigid.

These observations were in total concurrence with the scientific conclusions I had read about sexual behaviour. The main observation amongst these was that 90 percent of couples follow the conventional 'missionary position' in which, during intercourse, the man is on top of the woman.

It is often pleasurable and exciting to engage in a variety of sex positions. But the conventional posture is most preferred because chances of conception are greater. People have been so influenced by the traditional view that the purpose of sex is only procreation and not enjoyment that they never think about the possibility of other postures.

I would tear away the mask of modernity of such couples. Why should we always follow the conventional position? Whenever I asked this question, the only answer I received was that because it was the most commonly used position.

Even if they did think of other positions, they did not have the courage to try them out. It worried them that their partner might consider this a perverted sex act. Consequently, apart from the common missionary position, these couples neither tried any other posture of copulation, nor attempted any different method of erotic play. I would tell such couples,

'In order to show this courage, free yourself of the thought that every sex act should culminate in the climax of intercourse. Then you will realise that even without intercourse, you can find pleasure in other kinds of erotic play like oral sex or anal sex.

'If you think that some sex acts are perverted, then you are depriving yourself real pleasure. In fact, we have seldom thought independently about which sex acts should be termed perverse. The traditional view is that any type of sex that is not related to procreation is perverted. We never doubt this view, mostly because we do not think independently. Even if we do think independently, we do not have the capacity or courage to apply it in matters of sex.

'Throw away your veil of hypocrisy about sex. Eradicate your unhealthy feelings about sex. Feel the freshness and purity of your mind. You will realise that you have obtained a clear vision of your sexuality. When you get this vision, you will have a healthy outlook towards sex.'

I would repeatedly tell them about the truth I had understood from my research: 'Besides the level of intensity, happiness in sex also depends on an important aspect, and that is to bear a healthy attitude towards sex. If you feel guilty and sinful, you will deprive yourself of the happiness you deserve, in spite of having a strong sexual desire. On the other hand, if you have a healthy attitude, even in the absence of an intense desire, you will derive much more and varied happiness.'

I would teach them how to adopt a healthy attitude towards sex. I would motivate them to concentrate on the psychological aspects of sex. In humans, it is natural to have sexual desire, but like animals, the sex act is not entirely a natural instinct. I would motivate them to learn about sex and guide them in developing a mindset for this learning.

While stressing the importance of psychological factors, I would tell them, 'If you want complete gratification of your desires, you have to first arouse your partner mentally. The absence of mental arousal will mean only physical mating. Before seeking sexual gratification, it is necessary that both the partners are aroused mentally.' I would teach them some useful techniques to arouse a partner by way of dialogue, imagery or exchange of thoughts, and make them practise these techniques.

Most of the couples often asked me this question: 'How many times can we have intercourse in a day, week or a month?'

To train their minds to fight such incorrect presumptions, I would tell them, 'First, it is wrong to assume that all individuals are basically equal and that certain techniques give the same level of satisfaction. Each person behaves differently in sex. Therefore, there is difference in the methods he or she chooses. There is so much variety in the sexual behavioural patterns of couples that we cannot designate a particular method as 'right', and recommend it.

'The second erroneous premise is that satisfaction from sex entirely depends on the frequency of sexual encounters.

Satisfaction from sex also depends on other factors; for example, the 'quality of sex'. During sex, you should not carry the burden of comparing yourself with some standard set by your mind. This thought will deprive you of real enjoyment. Do not try to fit yourself in any standard of performance. This would mean that satisfaction is of secondary importance to you. So forget comparison and enjoy sex to the fullest.'

Another frequently asked question was: 'Does satisfaction depend on size of the genital organ?' I would explain,

'Certainly there are advantages and also disadvantages of the size of the genital organ. But happiness in sex does not depend only upon the size of the organ. See how deep-set is the influence of the thinking that sexual happiness is related only to the sex organ. Besides the genital organ, even by using other pleasure points you can make yourself and your partner happy. Not only this, just by using stimulating words to arouse yourself and your partner, you can get satisfaction. But you have to learn some skills. The joy of sexual satisfaction does not depend on the body, but on the art of love-making. Physical attributes are given by birth and, generally, cannot be altered, but love-making skills are not inborn and have to be acquired. Once you learn them, you will never worry about physical inadequacies. But if you adhere to your strong belief that because of your physicality you cannot fully enjoy sex or make your partner happy, then, irrespective of the size of the organ, you will definitely fall short in giving or taking joy.'

Many persons who had homosexual relationships would come to meet me. In order to clear their misunderstandings, it would become necessary to go deeper into the nature of their relationship. I would tell them, 'Do not feel guilty about your relationship. Whether your sex life is homosexual or heterosexual is entirely your personal preference and this choice cannot be labelled as perverted or abnormal. So the question about its suitability does not arise at all.

'If I say I like the colour yellow more than green, then that is my preference. I have the freedom to choose a colour and, obviously, I need not feel guilty about it. But in case of the choice of a homosexual relationship, the approach is not so straightforward. The thought that such behaviour is immoral, and I should never behave immorally, is uppermost in people's minds and it creates guilt. Therefore, homosexuality is viewed with this feeling of guilt. Behind the statement that 'morally it is wrong to behave in a certain way' hides the thought that we are behaving differently; that such behaviour is not acceptable to society, that it is perverted and, therefore, we must avoid such a relationship.'

I would ask them to search the core of their thoughts.

'If a person does a sex-act persistently and obsessively in the same manner, his act can be called 'perverted'. But such behaviour is found not only in same-sex but also in opposite-sex relationships. Therefore, we need not designate it differently as perverted. If two mature individuals have sexual relations with each other willingly, with mutual consent and without harming each other, then even if the relations are between the same sexes, these relationships cannot be labelled as perverse, by any rational criterion.'

A person opts for same-sex relations because of two main reasons. The first reason is that some are biologically inclined towards such relationships. The second is that some learn after some practice. Whether it is biological or learnt, a person's attitude towards his relationship influences his behaviour to a great extent. If he is obstinate, he creates problems in his sex life. The obstinate attitude is that one can get satisfaction only from same-sex relations. Such individuals are afraid to try any other type of sex and, in the process, narrow down their experience of a sex life.

I would help such people to change their attitude. Apart from same-sex relations I would teach them to enhance their joy by showing them other types of love-making. If they showed willingness, I would talk to them about different methods of heterosexual sex. Heterosexual relations are likely to be more satisfying than homosexual relations. The quality of happiness is also likely to be superior. I would tell them my opinion that male and female bodies are more suitable for hetero-sex. But at the same time, I would also tell them that there is no valid proof by which we can state that it was superior to homosexual sex.

I would help also those homosexual persons who wanted to change themselves and try heterosexual sex, or heterosexuals who wanted to experience homosexual sex. I would give guidance to persons who practised both types of sex, but wanted to change. My main aim would be to make a person accept his sexuality, homosexual or heterosexual, without feeling guilty.

Problems of homosexual men and women set my thoughts rolling.

Many sexologists agree that homosexual relations cannot be considered abnormal. It is just a matter of individual preference.

When I examined this view, a truth emerged. Modern research says that very rarely is this choice an outcome of biological factors. It is mostly based on the views impressed by the society upon us, directly or indirectly.

In the case of some people, an inclination towards a particular type of sex is inborn. But it is not unchangeable. Physiologically, a majority of us have a natural instinct for both types of sex. But because of social conservatism, we do not think out of the box. We think that such relations are perverted because they cannot lead us to procreation. Because of this view, we consider heterosexual relations superior to homosexual relations. Since we consistently practise heterosexual sex, we consider it to be natural. Consequently, we refuse to experience homosexuality, treating it as unnatural.

After arriving at the inference that homosexuality was a matter of individual preference, I went further and concluded that it is necessary for every person to experience homosexuality at least once in his life. The very fact that we have very negative feelings like hatred and repulsion about homosexuality and despise it proves that we have not cleared the cobwebs from our minds. It shows that we still do not have an unbiased perspective. The only way to remove these cobwebs is to experience homosexuality ourselves.

In fact, I was of the opinion that a will to experiment is also an important aspect of self-realisation. According to me, it is more appropriate to pass a judgement about something only after experiencing it. I felt that it was not reasonable to refuse an experience because of some prejudiced thinking.

I experienced homosexual relations without any guilt or prejudice, and discovered that one can reach sexual climax this ways as well. But it lacked the romance and excitement of a heterosexual relation. It is capable of satisfying a person only when penetration is the sole objective. But according to me, penetration alone is a very limited objective of sex. Apart from this aspect, I was more interested in foreplay and in the pleasure I got from a female partner. A male partner obviously fell short in giving the pleasures of a female body. So same-sex relationship did not appeal to me much. But I was aware that other homosexual persons were entitled to have a different liking than I.

After all the experimentation, I took an important decision about my sex life: My first preference would always be a heterosexual relationship.

*****

LAMP gave me an opportunity for introspection. I felt happy counselling others. I felt I was serving society. Although I still had an urge to write, I preferred counselling, which was more direct. Reaching people through books meant dependence on publishers. Counselling did not require any middlemen.

Writing is a one-sided process. Only the writer communicates. But counselling is two-way communication. We learn more and we are able to broaden our vision. I found that while I went deep into the minds of other people, I could study my mind also. The process of counselling was just in line with my nature.

It was my aim to train people in sex through counselling. I was ready to take whatever efforts it called for. I was confident that LAMP had a bright future.

As LAMP began prospering, I thought of getting it registered. I approached Mark Baker, the lawyer who had helped me during the divorce proceedings and, unexpectedly, a new calamity befell upon me.

'It is illegal to run an institute like LAMP without any professional qualification in psychology. Even though you have a B.B.A. degree, you are not eligible for a license to run such an institute. You will have to first undertake a postgraduate course in psychology. It is a legal offence to start an institute without a license, and you could be jailed for this,' Mark explained.

He was right. I was against any illegal activity. I had only one option before me: To shut down LAMP.

With a shattered mind I removed the nameplate. I thought my heart had turned totally insensitive after facing so many hardships. Nevertheless, there was some softness still left in its core. It was assuring me,

'I made you tough to face life,

But do not forget that inside you,

There is a small tender shoot,

Green with life, nourishing you,

Because it knows when you fight, it's every atom tries its might,

It knows it's every atom has power,

And the strength to break your stony cover!'

I gathered my strength and told myself: 'Albert, now your only aim in life is to get a postgraduate degree in Psychology.'

***

8

/ **M**orningside Heights.'

This county extended from Morningside Park up to Riverside Park and housed many institutions like Bernard College, Manhattan School of Music, Bank College of Education and other places of higher education. No doubt it was considered an educational centre. Each of these institutions had created their own identity in the field of education. After walking through this county, I understood why University of Columbia relocated itself from Madison Avenue to Morningside Heights. I was outside the Department of Psychology of this university, waiting to be interviewed.

After deciding to acquire a Masters degree in Psychology, I began making enquiries about this course. There was no postgraduate course in psychology at City College. In the list of colleges offering it, the University of Columbia was highly ranked. The Columbia School of Psychology was among the world's top seven institutions. Famous psychologists like James Cattle, Edward Thorndike, and Robert Woodworth had been among its reputed heads of department.

The current head of the university's department of psychology was Dr. Henry Garrett. He was such a reputed authority that students of psychology would memorize his books. There were very few seats for the Master's course; therefore, Dr. Garrett was personally interviewing students. Like many others, I was also waiting for my turn with him. Stress, worry, willpower, ambition, confidence—my mind was full of mixed emotions.

'Albert Ellis!' The clerk outside the cabin announced.

I picked up my file and entered the cabin. It was very spacious. Dr. Garrett was sitting behind a large semi-circular table. Knowledge and wisdom radiated from his face. He asked me to take a seat and began going through my file.

'Albert, first let me congratulate you for your success in the Bachelor's course. But it is important to bring to your attention the fact that you do not have a degree in psychology but in business administration. It is necessary to have a degree in either psychology or in some allied subject such as sociology. Your B.B.A. degree alone is not useful to study psychology.' His forthright talk at the outset itself was like a bomb that shattered my morale.

'Sir, although I do not have a degree in psychology, I have a great desire to study psychology. I will work hard and makeup for my lack of knowledge.' I collected myself and replied courageously.

'Even if you study hard, you do not have any background in science. How will you make up for this? Psychology is a science. It is a branch of the social sciences, which studies the psychological processes from a scientific angle. A student of psychology should have a strong fundamental knowledge of science. It is difficult to admit you for this course.' He made his point more clear.

'I have studied physics in my B.B.A. course.' I said pointing towards my degree certificate.

'Yes, but besides physics, you did not study any other science subject. Also, you studied physics only for two terms. This is far less than required. To develop a scientific viewpoint and to strengthen it, it is necessary to have a thorough knowledge of science. I do not feel that studying a subject like science for such a short term in a superficial manner will enable you to think scientifically. You have absolutely no background for a Master's course in psychology. In spite of your success in the Bachelor's degree course, it is very difficult to grant you admission.' His tone was decisive.

I was taken aback. But without getting demoralised, I began speaking. I spoke briefly, but in precise words, about the various books on psychology that I had read, about LAMP, about my ambition to become a psychologist, about rational thinking. He listened patiently. After a few moments he said, 'You seem to be passionate about subjects like love, marriage and sex. But mind you, these subjects are good only in literature. If you want to make a career in the field of education you will have to select subjects that can be studied scientifically. You have read extensively but to be frank, this will not be of any use here because you choose books randomly. Such reading, which has no definite direction, is not done scientifically and systematically. Without a strong fundamental knowledge of science, it will be difficult to study modern psychology. Chances of your admission appear very bleak.'

With these words from Dr. Garrett, I lost all hope. I was extremely disheartened. But I stopped myself from feeling depressed. I sat quietly before him recollecting my thoughts. Suddenly, an idea occurred. As I was getting up to leave I decided to make one last attempt.

'Sir.'

He looked up from the papers.

'Sir, I have a request.'

He looked questioning.

'Sir, it is very clear that at present it is difficult to admit me. But will you grant me one last opportunity? The new term starts only in August and the summer term has just begun. I have two months at my disposal. If you allow me to attend the summer course, I will choose two credits in psychology and appear for the examination. The result of this examination will be known before August. If I get good grades, will you reconsider your decision about my admission?' I asked him politely. He looked at me for some time and said, 'Alright. I will allow you to attend the summer lessons but the decision about your admission will depend upon how you score in this exam.'

I could not hide my happiness.

'Thank you, sir, thank you very much.' This was all I could utter at that moment.

'You are welcome. All the best.' He wished me as I took his leave.

I came out of his cabin and realised that I had undertaken a great responsibility. From his straightforward demeanour, I had not expected him to accept my proposal. But now it was necessary to think about the next action, instead of wasting time thinking over his surprising behaviour. Dr. Garrett had challenged my intelligence. Although this challenge was really tough, I decided to make it a success.

Deliberately I selected two subjects that Dr. Garrett taught. I studied very hard. I secured an A+ grade in both the subjects. I also broke the earlier record by getting 100 percentile marks in one of the subjects. I had proved myself. I showed the result to Dr. Garrett. He was happy. He congratulated me but he also said that he still maintained his earlier opinion about my inexperience in the subject of science. He compelled me to take some science subjects along with psychology and at last gave consent to my admission.

When I went through the curriculum I realised that it was designed to create professors for clinical psychology, whereas my ambition was to practise as a professional psychologist and not as a professor. My purpose of taking a postgraduate course was to be qualified to work independently as a professional psychologist through an institute like LAMP. But with this post-graduate degree, I would be eligible to work only in the field of education. This qualification was of no use to me. The situation was disturbing, but without losing courage I decided not to retreat.

I took a calm appraisal of the situation. I was aware of the effects of mental upheaval on decision-making. When we are disturbed we tend to overlook options that are available to us. Once we clear the fog around a problem, we are able to look at it more clearly and objectively. With this clarity and objectivity, I started evaluating other options. In the meanwhile, as an alternative, I also took admission in the Department of Psychology of New York University.

During my search for credits, I came across a new avenue towards my goal. The Teachers College in Morningside Heights had just started a fresh professional course in Clinical Psychology. This college was affiliated to the University of Columbia. I went there to enquire more.

Its faculty consisted of some great professors like Irving Lorge, Goodwin Watson, Bruno Klopfer, Percival Symonds, Esther Lloyd-Jones and Rollo May. Each one of them was an eminent authority in psychology. It was a great opportunity to study under these professors. The admission process was also simpler than that of Dr. Garrett. They had no objection whatsoever as regard to my B.B.A. degree. The college authorities believed that when a student is genuinely thirsty for knowledge, he excels himself with hard work, even in the absence of any prior training.

I was admitted in the first year. This degree course consisted of thirty-two varied study-credits. I decided to make the most of this opportunity. I would attend morning lectures and report to Distinctive Creations by 10.30. Since I had shut down LAMP, I had ample spare time. I stopped hanging out with friends and spent every moment in studies. My sole ambition was an M.A. degree in psychology. I was successful in finishing all the thirty-two credits within one year. I passed with flying colours. I secured honours.

Our house in Andrews Apartments now displayed a new name plate: 'Albert Ellis. M.A., Psychologist.'

I had already earned some fame as a marriage counsellor. The new name plate as ◉Psychologist◉ began attracting more people. I started getting 3 to 4 cases in a week for psychotherapy. Even in LAMP I was counselling people for their problems. In those days I had only my knowledge, experience and analysis to assist me. I did not have the foundation of any theory. I realised that without such a foundation, psychotherapy tends to become directionless and unmethodical. Sound theoretical knowledge was the main pillar of psychotherapy. If this pillar is weak, psychotherapy is reduced to commonsense advice. The difference between psychotherapy and such advice now became clearer.

You neither require knowledge of psychology nor any professional training to give general advice. Any person with experience can offer advice on the basis of his experience and intelligence. Many times such advice proves useful, but yet it cannot be treated as 'psychotherapy'. Also, there is always a likelihood of this advice turning into mal-advice.

Psychotherapy is much more rigorous than plain advice. For example, if a person is facing difficulties in getting married and is disturbed because of this reason, then searching a suitable bride is not the purpose of psychotherapy. This is a practical problem and solving practical problems is not the aim of psychotherapy.

The true aim of psychotherapy is to clear away the emotional disturbance created by a practical problem. Such disturbance is an obstruction in approaching the problem neutrally. Psychotherapy helps in removing these hurdles. It teaches a person to handle a situation objectively, with a calm mind. It strengthens his efforts to solve his original problem.

Now I had an opportunity to keep this in mind while treating my clients. With the foundation of strong knowledge of psychology, I could think of applying the various psychotherapies I had studied during my M.A. course.

There are many psychotherapies, but mainly two are often used. One of these, developed by Carl Rogers, is 'person-centred'. In this therapy, it is presumed that a person is capable of solving his or her own problem. It involves only directing a person with suggestions and hints, without giving him/her a direct guidance. According to this therapy, to guide a person directly implies enforcing the views of the counsellor upon the person.

It was Rogers who began the practice of addressing persons who came for treatment as 'clients' instead of 'patients'. The word 'patient' implies a diseased or an unhealthy person. A person who comes for psychotherapy is not diseased, but he is a person whose capacity for overcoming a problem is temporarily frozen. He is in need of some help to revive this capacity, and, according to Rogers, the role of the psychotherapist is only to extend this help.

I fully agreed with this humanitarian view of addressing a person as 'client'. I was also entirely in agreement with the need for empathising with and understanding a person. But when such a person approaches a therapist, he is in such an emotionally disturbed state of mind that it is not possible for him to think about the problem with a stable mindset. In such a situation, according to me, it was important and very much necessary to guide and direct him; I was in disagreement with Rogers on this point. In his opinion, at times it is not inappropriate to give direct guidance during therapy. On the contrary, in my experience, this turns out to be helpful many a time.

It is necessary to train the person directly in the beginning of the therapy itself and in such a way that he is able to improve his mental health. In my opinion, the earlier one starts such training, the earlier will he become capable of restoring his mental balance. Because of this viewpoint, I was not interested in following Rogers' therapy.

The other method used by psychologists was the method of psychoanalysis developed by Sigmund Freud. Most of the psychologists I knew were tremendously influenced by his psychoanalysis.

According to Freud, a human mind can be divided into three levels. At the first level, we clearly experience our mental process. This is the 'conscious' level of mind where we are aware of all that happens in our minds. The second level is called the 'sub-conscious'. At this level we are not fully aware of all that is going on in our minds, but with some effort, we can become fully conscious. But the major part of our mind, nearly two-third parts, according to Freud, lies in the third level, which is called the 'unconscious' level. We are totally unaware of the activities of mind at this level.

It is deemed uncivilised to express many of our wishes, desires or other instincts before others in their natural form. So we suppress them. Since the pressure to suppress is highest in the case of aggressive or sexual drives, our suppressed feelings are predominantly related to these two. However hard you may try to suppress them, these desires do not cease to exist in our minds.

They keep rising to the level of the 'conscious' mind. But the conscious mind keeps rejecting them because of social pressures. Finally, they find place in our 'unconscious' minds. Since we are not aware of our feelings in our unconscious minds, we assume that they do not exist at all.

Every person suppresses some of his desires to a certain extent. But if this happens to a great extent, then these suppressed desires cannot remain dormant even in the unconscious mind. Subsequently, this suppression gets manifested sharply in the form of a mental disorder.

Psychoanalysis tells us that the origin of mental disorder is in these aggressive emotions and the sexual desires suppressed in the unconscious mind. To identify these emotions, a person is persuaded to remember the forgotten incidents that took place in his childhood. His dreams are analysed. He is encouraged to speak freely, without any inhibitions. The main aim of a psychoanalyst is to make a person aware of the thoughts in his subconscious mind and to teach him to accept them, that is, to make him aware of his inner vision or his 'insight'.

From my experience at LAMP, I was aware that sexual desires were deeply buried and this always caused a serious obstruction in satisfying these desires. I had already drawn the inference that this was the chief cause of sexual problems. The theory presented by Freud was very much in concurrence with my inferences, so I felt it relevant to follow his method of psychoanalysis. But even if I followed his therapy I was not his staunch follower.

Whenever we take an extremist view of a principle or value, or of an ideology or individual, our thought process becomes one sided. As a result, we accept everything without studying it independently. The theory put forth by Freud was definitely revolutionary, but it had to face severe criticism as it failed in its scientific evaluation.

Unlike the prevalent methods of psychotherapy, the method of psychoanalysis was very exhaustive. Of course, there were certain aspects with which I did not agree. I felt that I would be able to clear my doubts if I studied psychoanalysis more in depth. The prevalent methods had many weak areas but I was unable to find a better method, and my mind remained in search of such a method. Until then, I decided to follow the method of psychoanalysis.

***

I felt my M.A. education was falling short in making me knowledgeable about the mental processes involved in psychotherapy. I wanted to take higher education in psychology to update myself with the latest developments.

I secured admission at The Teachers College for a Ph.D. course. Dr. Percival Symonds, a reputed professor of the college, was my advisor. I selected 'Emotion of Love in College Girls' as the topic of my research and it was sanctioned by the department. I started my research in full swing.

According to the university rules, a mere sanction for the topic was not adequate. It was also necessary to appear for a pre-qualification test. I prepared well and appeared for this test.

But when I received the questionnaire, I felt sympathetic towards the professors who had prepared it. The questions in the first part required comprehensive answers but the second part consisted of 200 questions of an objective nature. These questions were very trivial, such as questions about the date of birth of a psychologist, about his native place or about the names of books. I felt it was very childish to ask such questions to students who have completed studies up to the postgraduate level. Students who intended to do doctoral research were mature in age and knowledge, and they should be examined for the depth of their knowledge in their subject.

It is more important to test students for their knowledge about a psychologist's thinking rather than his date of birth. One can answer such insignificant questions after learning answers by rote. But it is unfair to ask students aspiring to do advanced research, to waste their valuable time in memorising answers to such questions. This process of assessment was simply childish.

I could not stay indifferent to this scenario. After answering all the questions, I wrote a note at the end.

'Was it really necessary to ask such trivial questions to post-graduate students? One of the principles of psychology is that knowledge gained by understanding is superior to that gained by memorising. Then why have questions requiring rote learning being asked?'

I was confident that I was not unfair in commenting on the nature of the examination but I did not expect that it would become the subject of discussion among the professors. On learning about my note from Dr. Percival Symonds, a senior professor Dr. Arthur Gates called for a special meeting of all the professors to discuss the issue.

'The student who has made this comment has exceeded his limit. He is definitely a communist. As a punishment for his action, he should not be granted admission,' Dr. Gates took this aggressive stand.

The Senate had recently passed the 'Smith Act', tabled by Senator Joseph McCarthy, and there was a wave of anti-communist sentiment throughout the country. Even though the Second World War had ended, Cold War between the Soviet Union and the United States had begun. Any protest against the establishment invited arrest or inquiry, on grounds of suspicion of being a communist; this law facilitated this action.

Dr. Gates was sure that since I had shown extraordinary courage in making such a comment, I was definitely a communist. He was repeatedly insisting against admission. But he was facing difficulty in pushing forth his recommendation because I had obtained the highest score, not only in the subjective questions, but also in the section of objective questions. I had not only broken earlier records but had also surpassed the earlier highest score.

Other professors were not inclined to decline admission to a student who had scored so highly. Finally, Dr. Gates reluctantly withdrew his objection and I was admitted into the doctorate course.

But this sequence of events surprised me. My comment was about the format of the questionnaire. It was not aimed at any individual professor. Why, then, was only Dr. Gates irritated? I got the answer to this from Dr. Symonds. That questionnaire was prepared under the guidance of Dr. Gates. I had unknowingly hurt his ego and invited his fury.

I learnt a lesson even as I put away this episode from my mind. The words we use while speaking or writing are neutral by themselves. Our reaction depends on the meaning we attach to words. So if we want to know what is going on in a person's mind, then, instead of trying to understand the situation, it is important to understand how he evaluates that situation.

I began my doctoral research under the guidance of my advisor. Although my topic was 'The Emotion of Love in College Girls', it also included the topic of sexual desire. My emphasis was actually on the different dimensions of the emotion of love and sex. One can experience sexual desire without feeling love, but when love is blended with sexual desire, the experience reaches a different level of intensity.

I wanted to research the inter-meshing of these two emotions among college girls. I prepared a list of questions to test these emotions. I compiled the data. Along with this work I also read several books and journals. I was also successful in holding workshops to discuss the subject, as required. Ready with all this preparation, I began writing my thesis.

In my life I had faced several hardships and I had also experienced that there was a great difference between planning and execution. My Ph.D. thesis work was no exception to this. My path was not easy and I would have been surprised had it been so. I was prepared to face any adverse situation.

Some orthodox moralists of the college took objection to the topic of my study. They were of the opinion that such a research would defame the university for supporting 'vulgar' topics. According to them, some newspapers might possibly publish explosive news about this research and harm the reputation of the college.

A meeting of twelve professors was called to review the approval given on my research topic by the previous committee. I was also called to this meeting along with my advisor. Dr. Percival Symonds had been my advisor but since he was sent to Washington as a consultant to the Armed Forces, Dr. Goodwin Watson was appointed as my advisor instead. I presented my research and the entire work I had done, before the committee. I was confident about my work. I also presented information about the research methodology I had used. I put up a strong defence. After my presentation I was asked to leave.

I was definitely concerned about the decision of the committee but I was able to keep myself from getting disturbed. This was possible only because I had studied in depth the mental process of a person in adverse situations.

When we have to face an adversity unexpectedly, we get so disturbed by the situation that we lose whatever courage that is left within us to tackle the situation. Then we come to the irrational conclusion that we are totally incapable of facing the adversity, and push ourselves into a den of worries. Sometimes we also hope that some miracle will improve the situation. When this does not happen and when reality boomerangs upon us, we collapse due to frustration. This indicates that not the situation but the thoughts about a situation are more frightful. But if we train our minds to think differently about a situation, we can save ourselves from self-destruction.

That night I convinced myself about this thought. I decided

to wait patiently for the outcome of the meeting without getting disturbed unnecessarily. The next day, Dr. Goodwin Watson informed me about the decision. Eleven members had voted 'For' and two had voted 'Against' me.

I was accused of spoiling girls and tempting them into love and sex on the pretext of questioning them on these topics openly. The two senior professors who voted against felt that if I was not controlled, more girls would go wayward. This trend would ultimately harm the reputation of the University, according to them.

I was relieved that although two members opposed me, the majority opinion was on my side. But this relief was short-lived. Dr. Goodwin Watson warned me of an imminent danger.

'Even if there are only two professors opposing you, these two professors are so powerful and obstinate, that it is almost impossible to get your thesis approved. Even if you are successful in presenting it, they are examiners of the viva that follows the presentation, and they can easily fail you in this viva. I will advise you to forego this subject.'

Dr. Watson did not disclose the names of those two professors but I could easily guess who they were. One of them was Dr. Arthur Gates. I had already displeased him by commenting on the nature of questions in the qualifying examination. So I was not in his good books. During my admission he had to retreat from his rigid position because of the support I got from other professors. But I was sure that being provoked once, he would retaliate at the first opportunity. Especially in the present situation when my future was in his hands, I knew that he would use his authority to corner me.

Even a good psychologist is ultimately human. Sometimes the human qualities in them are so powerful that they cannot free themselves easily from some common human emotions like anger, love, jealousy or hatred. So even if I wished them to behave differently, I was not so naive as to expect any different behaviour.

The other professor who opposed me was Prof. Ruth Strang. She was 55 years of age and a spinster. She believed that love and sexual desire were detrimental to mental health. She held the firm opinion that these feelings have to be completely removed. So, it was but natural that she opposed my subject.

A person can have a difference of opinion. However, I felt it was unjust for a person to use his authority to enforce his individual opinion on others.

The main purpose of education is to teach a student to think independently in every situation. Are not the teachers themselves placing hurdles in the path of education by carrying prejudiced views about a subject?

No subject should be taboo for a true teacher and a true teacher is never hesitant to discuss any subject with his students. But when a teacher is unable even to think about the feelings of love and sex because of some fear, then such a teacher is not honest to his profession.

Even though my expectations were very reasonable, I had to accept the reality—and I did so accept the reality very rationally, without getting disturbed.

But this was not easy. All the efforts I had taken for my doctorate project were being rendered futile. It was very agonising. I had not worked only for the sake of the thesis. I was totally involved in my work. I was emotionally connected and it was difficult to remain untouched by the developments. I was overwhelmed with disappointment and depression. But I realised that unless I overcome these emotions, it would not be possible to think about the next course of action.

I started warning myself: You may fight with all your might but if the circumstances are beyond your control, it is wise to make a compromise.

I added one more card to the earlier three cards. 'Accept and cope, rather than condemn and mope,' was the message on this card. I consciously began to put this message into practice.

Gradually, things became clearer. I realised that these two professors had objected to the subject of my thesis, not to my doctorate degree. Obtaining the doctorate degree was my ambition. So I still had one more option—of changing the topic and choosing some other neutral and harmless subject for my research.

If I changed the topic, it would become difficult for these senior professors to interfere in granting me the degree in the absence of any valid point of objection. If at all they tried to obstruct, that would prove their prejudicial attitude and this would malign their reputation. Also, if I changed the subject, they may become happy with my gesture and calm down.

I also analysed my worry that my entire work on the earlier topic was being wasted. By thinking in this manner, I was limiting the utility value of my research only up to my doctorate degree. But I could definitely use this knowledge elsewhere.

After taking a broad overview of the situation, I took two important decisions. The first of these was to change the subject to a new topic. I selected 'A Comparative Study of Different Personality Tests.' The second decision was to complete my research paper on the emotion of love among college girls.

I put my decisions into action immediately. I completed my research on 'Love' and wrote papers on the basis of this work. These were published by some journals devoted to psychology and sociology and were widely acknowledged.

While I was working on these topics, I also finished research on the sexuality of transgender persons. This research paper attracted lot of attention from the psychologists. Some of them appreciated my work, saying that it was a valuable piece of research. Many discussions were held on this paper. This helped in establishing cordial relations with many of the distinguished professors.

Meanwhile, I got approval for my new topic and I started working again with full enthusiasm. I updated myself with the earlier research on personality tests. After an exhaustive study, I wrote a long analytical paper on this topic. It was published in 'Psychosomatic Bulletin', which was a highly acclaimed journal. This paper became so famous that I was invited by other professional journals to write two more papers, which got published later. In due course, my research paper on the Ph.D. topic was also published. These developments made me famous and gave me the status of 'an eminent psychologist.'

After obtaining my doctorate degree, it was now necessary to decide about my career. Someone has said, 'If you cannot decide what to do in the future, then first decide what you do not want to do. Then it will be automatically clear what is to be done.'

To decide what I did not want to do, I began studying the field of 'Psychometric Testing'. There were many advantages to working in this field. I already had my doctoral research in support. Also, by now, I had become known to the research scholars. There was definitely more scope in this field than in other topics in psychology.

But this could not be my profession for a lifetime. I did not believe in assessing the characteristics of a personality by various tests. In my opinion, these tests were of a superficial nature.

One can evaluate a characteristic only when it is stable in nature. It is difficult to make an assessment if it changes or fluctuates. It is presumed that the personality of a person is stable during such an evaluation. I disagreed with this presumption.

Personality is an ongoing process of change. It is incorrect to designate a changing personality with a specific character. This amounts to denying the possibility that certain characteristics can be changed wilfully. This approach is harmful to the development of that personality.

The personality of a person is very complex, multifaceted and inter-meshed. In my opinion, to fit a personality into one or more types of labels determined by these tests was not correct. It was incorrect to assess or judge a personality in totality by this method, and I was sceptical about how deep one could reach a person's mind by such tests.

To assess or evaluate a person's total personality by these methods can be compared to guessing the depth of an ocean or the level of its tides from a single drop of its water.

So I decided not to work in the field of 'Psychometric Testing' and began exploring other avenues.

I realised that to study a personality thoroughly, we must study a person's philosophy of life, instead of assessing his characteristics. Every person, knowingly or unknowingly, follows some specific philosophy and his behaviour is consistent with this philosophy.

From childhood, we cultivate certain attitudes towards our own self, towards others, and towards the entire world in general. These get expressed in the life-philosophy we adopt. Some of these attitudes are healthy for our mental health and help us to face problems. But some are harmful and they aggravate the problem.

When a person has an emotional problem, the unhealthy attitudes become more powerful than the healthy ones, and the person acts in a self-destructive manner. So if we want to study the psychological problems of a person, we must first trace the destructive life-philosophy, which is at the root of these unhealthy attitudes. Thus, it became necessary to work in the field of psychotherapy. I decided to focus on psychotherapy for my future research.

I remembered the musical album, 'Rhyme with the mind', by my favourite musician, Friml, as I took this decision. Its lyrics reflected my thoughts. Composed in a unique unusual tune, the lyrics went:

'If you forget your wish and do what others want

'You can pass life, but will not be calm

'Feel your heart, ask your mind

'Sing your tune, then you will find

'The song on your lips

'Is the song of your life.'

As I sang this song, I asked myself, 'When will I find the song of my life?'

***

'Hurricane Erina is arriving at a speed of 60 miles per hour and has reached east of Long Island. It may hit New York at any moment. Erina is rated 1 on the hurricane scale, which means severe. Its wind is blowing at 33 miles per hour and around nine inches of rainfall is expected. Citizens are alerted of heavy floods by the meteorological laboratory. Mayor William Odewire has requested citizens not to leave their homes. Hospitals, police and the subway have been asked to prepare for the emergency.'

For the past two days, the news about the hurricane was being broadcast day and night on the radio. The Mayor had declared a holiday for two days. June to November was the usual season for hurricanes originating in tropical countries. But the 'Great Atlantic' hurricane of five years ago, had caused severe loss of human life as well as of property. So the mayor had taken extra precautionary measures to face Erina.

It was late afternoon, around four. I was extremely bored at home. Sitting by the window, I looked outside. It was still sunny and bright. The sky was clear. There were no signs of Erina. I wanted to go for a stroll, but the botanical garden as well as the library, and all public places, were closed.

'Albert...' Paul called out.

'I have an idea. Let's go to Manny's place. He has called us. We three have not met for a long time. His mother has gone to Boston and she will be away for a week. He is alone at home. We may not get this opportunity again.' Paul was excited.

The way to Manny's place was now very easy. It was no longer necessary to squeeze ourselves through the hole we had made. Now we could just jump over the fence. Within a few minutes we were inside his house. Time flew as we talked, reviving our childhood memories.

A lot had changed in the past few years. We did not meet as frequently as before. Paul and Manny were settled in their jobs. They were about to end their bachelorhood. Paul was dating Esther and Manny was engaged to Anna. I teased them about their impending married lives.

I was the fall guy among the three. I was single but they knew I was not a true 'bachelor'.'Albert, you have many lovers and we appreciate your faithfulness with each one of them.' Paul and Manny were in a jovial mood.

They knew that my definition of faithfulness did not fit the traditional concept. I did not approve of binding myself with one person for my entire life. My interpretation of faithfulness was very simple and that was to be faithful to one person at a time. Whenever I loved a woman, I loved her intensely and faithfully without engaging my mind with another woman or loving her. I had enjoyed the company of several women and whenever they asked me about my commitment, my views would shock them. I was against deceiving anybody or behaving hypocritically. But in spite of this, many women would be eager to offer their hearts to me happily; this was definitely satisfying my male ego.

'Albert, do you know magic? Please tell us. Why do so many women follow you? What is the secret?' Manny asked jestingly.

There was no such secret but I was aware of the magic in me. In the company of my favourite women, my talent of engaging them in talk would bloom. I would unravel the subtle nuances of love and sex. The awareness of opening up to their innermost desires would stimulate them. Then the romance would turn into a blissful experience. Physical intimacy is an inevitable stage in the process of understanding each other. I would shower my love on the woman's body and mind without any inhibition and the woman would offer herself to me with the same intensity.

'But do you have any particular type?' Paul joined Manny in ragging me.

Of course I did have preferences. I preferred intelligent women. I mostly liked those who were younger to me by five or more years. I found them more attractive and amicable.

I was about to share these thoughts overtly with them, when the doorbell rang. Manny opened the door and I was stunned to see the guest. It was Gertrude, the same Gertrude I had seen a year ago. She had not changed at all.

'Gertrude? Here, at this time?' I wondered.

'I have come to see you Albert. I had told Manny to inform me when you come but not to tell you about my visit. I wanted to surprise you. Haven't I?' She spoke with the same old exuberance.

'You have not surprised me, you have shocked me. This is great, Gertrude! There has been non-stop warning on the radio broadcast asking us to stay indoors. Why did you come all the way from Morningside to the Bronx?' I was really surprised.

'What? Haven't you heard the 5'o'clock bulletin? They announced that Erina has changed its direction. It has moved to the north, so now New York is safe. How is it that you guys don't know?'

This was a surprise to us. We had been so engrossed in chatting, that we had completely forgotten to hear the radio or the news about Erina.

'I heard the bulletin and left immediately. Can you guess why?'

I looked at her. Her eyes sparkled with happiness and excitement.

'Shall I? You are engaged, isn't it?' I looked into her eyes.

'Albert, only you can read my mind. I have talked so much about you to Warren. You are truly a magician of mind. Warren is eager to meet you. You must attend my wedding. I have brought the invitation with me today specially for you. I am getting married next month.' She gave me the card.

'Sure. Congratulations!' I shook hands with her.

'Gertrude, this is very unfair. Albert is given a special invitation but how can you ignore cousin Manny and Albert's brother Paul?' Manny poked at her laughingly.

'Of course not. I want to invite you two also. But you are very impatient.' She retorted with a smile.

She began talking animatedly about Warren, his nature, about his job and his future plans. She came and left like a hurricane, but not without reminding us several times to attend her wedding.

After she left, we had dinner at Manny's and returned home. I lay on my bed but it was difficult to sleep. Gertrude's visit had stirred up many memories. Five years had passed. I had many girl-friends before Gertrude. I never expected any relationship to last long, however pleasant they may have been. After suffering so much in life, I was aware that there was a vast difference between dreams and reality. I enjoyed the present without carrying any burden of the past and without worrying about the future. Some of my relationships were very short-lived. I would bid goodbye to those that were agonising. Amongst all my relationships, the one with Gertrude turned out different. The emotional impressions it left in my heart lingered for a long time. Her memories were vivid in my mind even after five years.

It had been the second week of March but the mornings were still chilly. The last term of my M.A. course at The Teacher's College was almost about to get done. To my surprise, Manny came to see me in college.

'Oh, it's nothing serious. One of my distant cousins, Gertrude, stays close by. She lived in Texas but she has moved here recently after marriage. She is a teacher in some school. Mom had been to Texas for some work. She met Gertrude's sister there, who gave a parcel to Mom for Gertrude. I just came to deliver that to her. Actually, we will be meeting after a number of years. I doubt if she will recognise me. Since your college falls on the way, I thought I could see you too.'

I was happy to see Manny. We hadn't met too often in recent times.

'Shall I accompany you? We are also meeting after a while.' I asked.

Manny was glad. I decided to skip the next lecture. The address said: La Celle Street and Amsterdam Avenue.

'It is close to 123rdStreet and Broadway.'

We located the house without much effort. It was an old four-storied building, with shops on the ground floor. We climbed the wooden stairs up to the third floor and rang the doorbell. Gertrude opened the door. I was a bit surprised to see how attractive she was. Manny introduced himself.

Her face brightened.

'Manny. It's been ages since we met.' She welcomed us inside.

'Gertrude, this is Albert, my friend. He is finishing his M.A. in Psychology from The Teacher's College. He is planning a Ph.D. too.'

'Psychology? Oh, it is a very interesting subject. I would love to know more about it.' She said to me.

'Albert, you are always busy getting questionnaires filled. Gertrude can help you in this. She can get them filled from the other teachers at her school,' Manny suggested.

They both began chatting about their childhood. Manny told her about his job, while she spoke about her school and her husband Kevin. Kevin was in the army and posted in Europe, so he could not visit home often. I observed Gertrude as she talked.

She was wearing light-blue trousers and a sweater with a floral design. The body-hugging sweater made her shapely figure quite noticeable. She had left her blonde shoulder-length hair loose. Although she was in a hurry to leave for school, she prepared coffee for us.

Later, for some reason or the other, I kept bumping into her. Once I met her at the gate of our college. She had come to enquire about some course. We went to have coffee at the West End restaurant near the college. In the following week, I went to her place to give her my questionnaire. After that meeting she invited me to dinner.

Gertrude was three years younger to me. She was quite intelligent and also well-read. She thought independently and had her own opinions. I liked discussing various topics with her. We would spend long hours in discussion. We began meeting more frequently and soon became very good friends.

'Kevin and me, we are not compatible, physically and mentally. I am seriously thinking of separation instead of carrying on in this fashion,' she confessed one day.

'Have you met anybody else?' I asked.

'Not yet, but I am waiting to meet someone.' She said.

Is that 'someone' me? My mind began racing.

Gradually, we were drawn towards each other. One day we crossed the boundary of plain friendship and grew physically intimate. We began meeting almost daily, sometimes in the morning before my college or in the evening after office hours. We would meet at her place most of the times. Her house was small but well maintained. We enjoyed complete privacy. Our love was so fiery that even with the slightest memory, I would get excited while working or attending lectures. Her erotic love-making drove me crazy. The romantic moments spent with her would keep me charged throughout the day. They would make me forget all the hardships of life. Apart from Gertrude, none of the women I had met, had taken a lead during sex. She was distinctly different. She was so uninhibited, that most of the times she was the one who took the initiative without any hesitation. She always found innovative ways of wooing and foreplay, and it was almost a challenge for me to satisfy her.

I had come across some of the latest research while reading about sex for my doctorate. I would tell Gertrude about those research papers. Through this relationship I had the opportunity to check the veracity of several inferences. One research paper had reviewed four major types of sex.

The first was 'Intimate Sex'. This comprised soft, tender love-making. In this type, emotional satiety is regarded as most important.

The second was 'Exploratory Sex'. In this type, more emphasis is laid on finding new and different ways of sex-play, and romance is very important.

The third was called 'Impersonal Sex'. There is no change or variety in the sex-act and sex is performed by the same method, for a long period, like a daily chore. There was neither emotional involvement nor any romance.

The fourth type was named 'Sadomasochistic Sex'. One of the partners is subjected to sex forcefully and may even be injured in this process. Such type of sex results in giving pain and agony to the partner, who is forced into sex.

Research explained the psychology behind choosing a specific type of sex. Two persons are more compatible in sex when they are in agreement with the type of sex they could have. I found out why Gertrude and I were compatible in sex: We both were game for Exploratory Sex.

The main characteristic of persons inclined towards 'Exploratory Sex' is an enormous power of imagination. We both were gifted with this and used it wholly while experimenting. We used our energy in a variety of sex-acts without suppressing it.

Normally, when a woman experiences an orgasm, she stays calm for some time. This state is called the 'Refractory Period'. In this period, the sensitivity of her organs reach such a high point, that there is a possibility that she may be reluctant to a second orgasm. But women like Gertrude, who had a very high level of sexual energy, can experience multiple orgasms, one after another within a short period. Such women are called 'Multi-orgasmic Women'. They pose a challenge to the male partner's sexual prowess. But even this can be an enjoyable experience.

I could take on this challenge successfully because I was free of any mental barrier. Hence for me it was an easy task.

Thanks to Gertrude, I got an opportunity to study the female orgasm very closely. This is the topic of an ongoing worldwide research, but most of the psychologists were influenced by Sigmund Freud's theory, called 'The Dual-Orgasm'.

He had inferred that there are two types of female orgasms. The first one is 'Vaginal Orgasm' in which the vagina is stimulated. This is commonly called the 'G Spot'. The second type is called as 'Clitoral Orgasm' in which the clitoris is stimulated.

According to Freud, women in their adolescence or at a very young age experience the clitoral orgasm. This type of orgasm is an indication of immature sex. When they become adults, they reach orgasm by vaginal stimulation. Between the two, the satisfaction gained by the latter method is superior. In short, according to Freud's theory, women find highest satisfaction in sex by way of the vaginal orgasm.

I strongly felt like examining this theory before accepting it blindly. I began reading books, research work, and papers on this subject. I arrived at the conclusion that the satisfaction derived through both types of orgasms was of the same quality.

After thoroughly studying the female anatomy and sensitivity, I realised that the interior of the vagina is comparatively less sensitive than the clitoris. So there was no scientific proof for Freud's theory. I began writing a paper based on my finding, titled *Is the Vaginal Orgasm a Myth?* I decided to publish this paper after supporting my views with the latest research.

I would discuss the female orgasm with Gertrude many times. She was totally opposed to Freud's theory of 'Dual Orgasm'. She was a fan of feminist writers like Ellen Ross and Rayna Rapp. In her opinion, the theory which states that satisfaction obtained by vaginal intercourse is supreme was an orthodox view. Moreover, she also felt that it was strictly against the freedom of women. To accept such a theory amounted to admitting that intercourse with a male was superior. She said that by accepting and emphasising this view, women are being brainwashed into equating sex only with intercourse and not going beyond the stage of vaginal stimulation. In fact, she felt that there was a male chauvinistic view behind this theory. It would make women incapable of going beyond intercourse. This would restrict them from finding satisfaction by other ways. I always respected Gertrude's views. It was her ability to think independently and her intelligence that brought both of us together.

Our relationship was active for almost five years, from the days of my M.A. course till the completion of my Ph.D. During this period, she divorced Kevin, and we decided to get married. There was apparently no hurdle. We started looking for a new apartment to stay in after our marriage.

But when the time came to tackle practical problems, sparks began to fly between us. The issues were very minor. She was against allotting one entire room as a reading-room, whereas that was my top priority. She insisted on having dinner-parties at least thrice a week and also wanted my active participation at those parties. I was never fond of partying and opposed her suggestion. She was also keen on buying a car. To me, this was an unnecessary expenditure, when New York had a very good public transport system. I was forced to look at our relationship objectively. I found it difficult to say 'Yes' to the question as to whether Gertrude was the perfect life partner for me. When I removed the layer of romance from our relationship, I realised that although we were compatible sexually, our basic personalities were vastly different. I was an introvert by nature. I loved solitude. I was fond of serious literature. I would get involved deeply in various things, from books to individuals. I had very few close friends. Gertrude was the exact reverse of all this. She was extremely extrovert, extremely talkative. She was always surrounded with friends and was very much interested in having a social life.

In brief, I was a thinker and Gertrude was a doer. Although she had her own opinions, she did not have the perseverance to follow them through for a long period. So she would keep changing her opinions and also keep professing new opinions with the same fervour.

As against this, it was my practice to think, rethink, and contemplate, before presenting a view. I insisted on forming an opinion on the basis of strong fundamentals, whereas Gertrude had a tendency to get carried away and change with the current.

I found it difficult to continue our relationship. I started identifying the basic differences in our personalities.

If there are extreme differences between two personalities, it leads to differences in understanding each other and also in making other choices. Since their thought processes are distinctly different from each other, they are incapable of agreeing on several issues. This obstructs the emotional union between the two individuals and causes a rift in their minds. There was such a striking difference between mine and Gertrude's personalities that it would have overpowered our sexual compatibility and caused pain to both of us all our lives.

I agreed that one had to make some compromises in a long-lasting relationship like marriage. If this compromise is in alignment with one's basic personality-traits, it brings happiness. When it demands suppression of your natural instincts every moment, the same becomes painful. Instead of severing the relationship after it becomes stifling, it was advisable to end it on a happy note with pleasant memories. I was successful in convincing Gertrude about this. We decided to cancel our wedding and bid goodbye to each other cordially.

'My heart is broken.' Gertrude cried uncontrollably.

But I was sure that she would mend her broken heart within a few days. From my experience, extroverts take very little time to recover.

My observation was very correct. Which was true—her happy demeanour while handing over her wedding invitation, or her outburst of grief when we parted? I realised both were. For an extrovert person like Gertrude, joy and grief, both are equally intense and genuine.

But what were my feelings when I saw the invitation? Although it was I who took the decision of saying 'au revoir' to our relationship, I was shattered. Gertrude could easily wipe away the intimate moments we shared from her mind, but for me it was an ordeal. I sincerely wished to see her happy but my heart was not able to accept the decision easily. The fact that she could live happily without me was definitely hurtful.

Gertrude left but memories of her kept recurring. One question repeatedly circled my mind. Why did it take five long years for me to realise that our personalities were poles apart? There was a wide disparity in our personalities. How did I lose my objectivity when this was evident from the beginning? Why did I wait till the wedding to realise this truth?

I got answers to these questions in the inferences I drew from my research. After closely observing the behaviour of mentally balanced and unbalanced persons, I had arrived at one conclusion. The root cause of one's irrational behaviour is, to some extent, biological. Persons who are normally balanced and rational, sometimes behave eccentrically, and this tendency is partly a natural instinct.

I had gathered some evidence to support my conclusion. These were, broadly, thus: 'All human beings commit mistakes'; 'All human beings commit mistakes repeatedly'; 'All intelligent people commit mistakes'; 'All intelligent people commit simple mistakes'; 'All intelligent people commit simple mistakes repeatedly'.

And the inference about myself from this evidence gave me the answer: 'Although I behave rationally most of the time, I do tend to behave irrationally sometimes, because to behave irrationally is a biological characteristic of human beings. Therefore, my irrational behaviour is as natural as my rational behaviour. Or perhaps, to insist that I should behave rationally all the time is in itself irrational.'

***

9

The office of Distinctive Creations seemed to have had a complete makeover. The chairs and the work-tables had been shifted to create an open space in the centre. On one side was an attractive, big bouquet of fresh red and yellow roses. Its fragrance had spread through the entire office. On the other side was an array of various food items.

The occasion for this function was my send-off. It was my last day at Distinctive Creations. I had submitted my resignation and was soon to join Greystone Hospital at New Jersey. After getting my doctorate, I had applied to various places and Greystone Hospital had selected me for the post of clinical psychologist.

My job at Distinctive Creations was not interesting but my association with the firm had been for ten long years. My heart was heavy while bidding farewell to my colleagues. In these ten years, I had risen from the post of a part-time accountant to that of personnel manager.

Many of my colleagues spoke about me at the farewell. Everybody lauded me for my sincerity and for my habit of focusing only on work. The last person to speak was George Roderick. He rarely spoke and this was one such rare occasion. He praised me lavishly. He felicitated my work and integrity in my association with the company by giving me a gift. Everybody wished me a bright future. I also gave a small thanksgiving speech. Dinner followed and I returned home.

As I returned, George Roderick's words followed me. I could not understand why, but I was disturbed. The past ten years flashed before my eyes. I was definitely more intelligent than the other employees and more efficient too. Even George would ask me to handle many responsible jobs with great trust. He had always been supportive, by granting me flexible working hours and later relieving me of the menial housekeeping job of my earlier days. My salary was also raised during this period. While I recollected all this, I had to admit to myself that I had not been totally honest to him.

Many a time, I would finish work very fast and use the spare time for my personal work. Much of the thesis work was done in the office in George's absence and by using the office typewriter. I had observed that the other staff members would pocket extra money by purchasing stuff for office use at a higher price. Some would charge extra benefits for working overtime without actually working overtime. Gradually, I also joined these members in their fraudulent activities like changing the purchase bills or preparing fake expenditure vouchers. I had also colluded with some customers so that I got the commission instead of the company. When I applied for admission at The Teachers College, I had hidden the fact that I was working, because the course was only for full-time students and my application for a full-time course consisting of thirty-two credits would have been rejected. I had certainly exploited my job to suit my convenience.

Now I understood why I was disturbed. I had not been loyal to George. Therefore, I was troubled when he praised me for my integrity.

In those days, since so many persons commonly committed fraud and made money dishonestly, I would consider this behaviour was common and I too became a participant in such nefarious activities, I believed that the behaviour of the majority was always right and appropriate. I never checked the truth of this thought.

But the behaviour of the majority cannot become a criterion for its appropriateness. It was prevalent among men to treat women as subordinates until the 19th century in most parts of the world. Can we say that this attitude of the majority was right? Of course not. At the most, we can say that this behaviour suited men-folk. But even this cannot render appropriateness to such an attitude. An action may suit me, but this cannot be the proof of its appropriateness. An action that is in self-interest is not necessarily the right action. An action is right when, along with your own self, it is beneficial to others also. All the religions in the world preach the same ideal: 'Do unto others what you want them to do unto you.' One has to first place oneself in the shoes of the other person or persons, and then think about the rightness of their action. Your action is right if it is suitable for everyone.

Before colluding with my erring colleagues in office, I should have asked myself whether I would have tolerated such behaviour had I been in George Roderick's place. Definitely, the answer to this would have been a firm 'No'. I began to regret my behaviour, but it was too late.

I observed that everywhere around me people were misusing their authority and power. In fact, it was considered to be naïve if one did not take undue advantage of a situation. Such people conveniently ignored the fact they were exploiting others in the process.

Even the field of education, which is regarded as noble, was not an exception to malpractices. I had come across very learned professors exploiting students. They would ask students to do research on the pretext of project work, give some nominal guidance and publish the work in their own respective names as the main researcher, after making some changes in the presentation and deductions. This practice was so rampant that the students presumed that this was the regular procedure.

These so-called 'eminent' professors would create such an aura about their intellect and their position, that no student would have the courage to protest against them. In spite of knowing that the professor was snatching credit from them, the students had to stay silent. They had to be happy that their work was getting published, even without any credit for it. To inflate the number of research papers to their credit was the only ambition of many such professors. Most of them would be ignorant about the reference work and even incapable of answering any questions about the content.

Every university would get certain funds for educational projects. To avail of these funds, these professors would arrange lectures, seminars, symposiums and workshops. At these seminars and symposiums, they would present their research papers, which were often based on some nominal information. The sole aim of these programmes would be to publish as many papers as possible in their names. The longer the list of such papers, the higher was the status of that professor and the greater was the likelihood for his promotions.

'Publish or Perish' was the slogan of many professors. The only aim of this so-called research was enhancement of their careers. But in the process of achieving this self-development, they were quite oblivious to the fact that they were holding students at ransom and exploiting them. Besides, I had doubts about the quality of their work and whether the research was of any genuine use to society. Whether such work was useful for further research or why it lay unutilised in the library would, in fact, be a matter for research. Fortunately there were many professors, like my advisor, who strived for the good of the students. But their numbers were small. Very rarely did one come across true research work done zealously.

Like professors, even students followed foul methods. Once a research work was completed, its conclusions were validated statistically. The hitch in this validity was that the results obtained by one statistical method totally differed from that obtained by another method, if some of the data was changed. So if one did not get expected results by one method, instead of finding the shortcomings, these students created suitable results by using some other statistical procedures. They had become experts at this. They called this manipulation 'statistical adjustment'.

To make some valuable addition to the existing work should be the main aim of any research. But it was common practice amongst the students and professors to misuse statistical methods in the name of research.

This state of affairs among the professors and students was so disgusting that I lost interest in academics. I was interested in going to the root of a subject and doing fundamental research. I wanted my research to reach people and not to make the list of papers in my résumé longer. So I never tried any statistical compromise nor did any valueless research.

However, I was required to make a different type of compromise. As a part of my course, I had to treat a neurotic person under the supervision of my advisor Dr. Godwin Watson. He was a follower of 'client-centred psychotherapy' developed by Rogers, so he insisted that I should also follow Rogerian therapy.

I was not fully convinced but since Dr. Watson was keen upon it, I tried this therapy with my client. When the client did not show any signs of improvement, I became impatient. I stopped following Rogers' therapy and began treating the client in my own way. Of course, I took this course of action without Dr Watson's knowledge. I was sure he would never approve of it and would have refused to certify the treatment. He remained under the impression that because I followed the Rogerian therapy, there was progress in the client's health. He even patted me for my success and also gave a certificate of appreciation.

I was guilty of misleading Dr. Watson. But at that time, my immediate aim was to secure my doctorate degree at the earliest. Hiding this truth from him was to my advantage and, hence, I kept him in the dark. But now I was repented having taken undue advantage of his trust.

Whether it was George Roderick or Dr. Watson, the feeling that I had behaved wrongly constantly pricked at my mind.

To say that because I was in need of money or in need of the doctorate degree or to say that I did what everyone did, was a lame defensce. I decided not to absolve myself and to accept the mistakes. As a human being, I could also err at times. Therefore, I decided to learn from those two mistakes without carrying a feeling of guilt.

I made two decisions.

The first decision was to admit my mistake with the concerned persons. I sincerely repented my behaviour. I was utterly regretful. I was prepared to face the consequences of such an admission. This decision was a test of this preparedness.

The second decision was to never repeat such mistakes. But the prerequisite to start acting on this decision was to pass the test of the first decision.

Before starting my new job, I met George and Dr. Watson and frankly confessed my mistakes. George said, 'It's alright. Anyway, you are not working with us anymore. But do not commit the same mistakes at your new job. I appreciate that you spoke so honestly with me. Such honesty is rare these days.'

However, Dr. Watson was shocked to learn about my deeds.

'I did not expect this. I had a very high opinion about you. I feel very sorry to know this,' he said, and wished me goodbye. Before I took his leave, however, he added that it was now necessary to study the shortcomings of the Rogerian therapy more carefully.

This chapter was finally closed after my implementation of the first decision.

With the same perseverance, I decided to act by my second decision and not carry a baggage of self-damning thoughts. This job was going to give me an opportunity to establish myself as a professional psychologist. The year 1948 had opened a new horizon for me but it also invited new challenges.

***

The huge dome of the famous hospital at Greystone Park Estate was noticeable even from as far as Morristown. People there called it a mental hospital. The township of Morristown was in Morris County in the state of New Jersey, which lies between Pennsylvania and New York. My route to the hospital was long. From the Bronx, I would take the subway to Penn Station in mid-Manhattan. Penn Station was the metro's central station and connected to other transit rail services. It was the connecting station for six different subway lines. One could take the subway to go anywhere in New York City, but to reach New Jersey, one had to take the New Jersey Transit Rail. I would take this line and get down at Newark Station, which was at a distance of five miles to the west of Manhattan. From Newark, I would take a metro to reach Morristown Station. From the station, the hospital was at a walking distance.

The hospital building was a longish three-storey stone building. The population in the northern side of the county was developing fast in towns like Morristown, Parsippany and Newark but there was no hospital for psychiatric patients. Trenton, the capital of New Jersey state had the only one. Therefore, the government had built a new hospital in Morristown at a cost of ten million and forty six thousand dollars. There was also an underground tunnel connected to the Morristown station to facilitate speedy shifting of patients in cases of emergency.

A majority of the patients were soldiers, and most of them had returned from the war in Europe which President Roosevelt was now calling the 'Second World War'. They were victims of acute stress disorder, related to the trauma of war. Since the hospital was equipped with modern facilities like Insulin Shock Therapy and Electroconvulsive Therapy, it had a huge rush of patients. People flocked in not only from Morris County but also from the neighbouring counties like Sussex, Passaic, Union and Warren. Being a government hospital, only a nominal fee of two dollars a week was charged, which was fairly affordable to common people. Besides, it provided free treatment to soldiers and senior citizens.

After the war, the government had made significant changes in its mental health policy. Earlier, only serious cases were attended to, but following its new policy, borderline neurotic cases were also included for treatment. The government had taken urgent steps to change the approach to mental health. According to this policy, the states were required to take preventive measures, besides providing treatment. This policy gave top priority to community care centres under the Mental Health Act. It had also sanctioned funds to every state to open such centres. The Northern New Jersey Mental Hygiene Clinic at Greystone Hospital was started with this purpose and I was appointed as a Senior Clinical Psychologist at this clinic.

There were three different wards on the upper floors of the main building; and a reception counter near the entrance on the ground floor. On either side of it were two different departments, the Department of Physical and Medical Testing to the right, and to the left a department with several sections for various types of investigations. The Mental Hygiene Clinic was between these two, behind the reception counter.

In my clinic, there were two other psychologists. They had Master's degrees and their main work was to administer necessary investigations and questionnaires and diagnose the mental disorder. A patient was first examined by a team of physicians and psychiatrists. After various medical tests, the patient had to undergo psychological testing if he was found to have a psychological problem. After all these stages, the patient would be sent to me for psychotherapy.

There were also other patients who suffered from depression or schizophrenia, or those who faced problems in their everyday life. Although I had my own private practice as a psychologist, this job gave me the experience of treating a wide range of cases which widened my knowledge.

A separate case-file was maintained for each patient, in which a detailed record of symptoms and treatment was entered. There were several such files that had gathered dust in the cupboards of the hospital. I started unearthing them and studying those cases. I maintained notes of the records and other information in my diary. I did this not just to keep a record, but to study if I could use existing details to treat other patients.

I began writing my views on every treatment systematically.

I kept a record of the method of each treatment, its details, and my own experience. Within a period of two years, around twelve research papers written by me were published in different professional journals. Besides these papers, close to thirty-four essays about psychotherapy, and book reviews were also published.

This hospital was under the jurisdiction of The New Jersey State Department of Institutes and Agencies and there would be an annual inspection of the hospital by this department. Mr. Nelson Stuart, the commissioner of this department, came to inspect the hospital. He called for reports from all the departments and conducted meetings with the officers of each department. A review of the work done by every department was undertaken at this meeting. He also gave his own suggestions for improvement. In the end he made a special mention of my name.

'I congratulate Dr. Albert Ellis for his remarkable performance in the past two years. So far I have inspected several government institutions, but in my opinion he is the only psychologist whose research is worth publishing. There has been no psychologist in the past, nor is there any at present, who has published as many research papers in a journal as him. In this respect, the work done by Dr. Ellis is really commendable.' Mr. Stuart praised me before everyone.

Before leaving, he called and briefed me about his department. He was in charge of the Department of Human Service, which covered mental hospitals, orphanages and paediatric hospitals.

'The Rahway State Prison is located in Avenel town. Prisoners who have committed sex crimes are sent to this prison. Recently, our department has opened a State Diagnostic Centre in the prison. We need a good psychologist to treat these prisoners. Would you be interested? If yes, I will appoint you immediately. The salary and allowances are better but you should be prepared to work with criminals,' he said.

I said 'Yes' without hesitating even for a moment. This offer was more challenging than the present one. It would give me an opportunity to expand my work experience further.

Within fifteen days, I received my appointment letter from the Department of Institute and Agencies as Chief Psychologist of the State Diagnostic Centre at the Rahway State Prison. I immediately took charge of my post at the centre, located in Woodbridge town in Middlesex County. My commute though, had not become any easier. The only change was that now, instead of Morristown, I got down at Rahway station. There were around 1,000 inmates in this prison housed in three large buildings. There was a grading system for the prisoners and as per this system, they would receive treatment according to the severity of their crime.

Soon I developed cordial relations with the chief of this centre, Dr. Ralph Brancale. He furnished me with all the information regarding old records and treatment given to the prisoners.

In my spare time, I started making rounds in the different wards of the prison. I observed the behaviour of the prisoners closely and studied their mental processes. Over a period of one year, I had collected substantial information. Since these prisoners had committed sexual offences, the prison authorities had a very negative attitude towards them. These prisoners were already boycotted by society. There was hardly any possibility of absorbing them back. They had serious emotional problems. Most of them were victims of depression and an inferiority complex, and the number of suicide cases was large.

While treating them, my perception towards these criminals began to change. It is perfectly right to punish a person for his offence after evaluating his offence. But to label him as a 'criminal' in totality was irrational and unscientific. It amounted to predicting that in future, too, he would commit the same crime. By this attitude, we were denying him an opportunity to improve. I felt it was necessary to change our approach towards such criminals.

In order to express my views, I began writing a book, which was eventually called *The Psychology of Sex Offenders*. Since Dr.Brancale had provided me with all the necessary information about the criminals, I agreed to add his name as co-author. I had almost finished writing the book when once again Mr. Nelson Stuart called me.

The post of Chief Psychologist in the State Department of Institutes and Agencies, of which he was the Commissioner, was vacant. This institute was located at Trenton. Of course, I could not reject such an opportunity. The ascending graph of my career was definitely satisfying, but the main purpose of my study was not just to enhance my career. I sincerely longed to do extensive research. Simultaneously, my career was benefiting while pursuing this aim. It did not require additional efforts.

As the Chief Psychologist of the department, my main responsibility in the institute was not to treat patients but to implement different schemes and projects for the mental health of society and form new government policies for mental hygiene.

My stance was that psychologists should keep updating themselves with the changing mindset of society while undertaking different projects. This was necessary in order to improve the mental health of society. I earnestly wanted research to be of a fundamental nature, and helpful to society. Due to this, I undertook a new project independently. The purpose of this project was to check how healthy the attitude of the American people was towards sex. For this, I collected all possible information of events which happened on the first of January, 1950, from magazines, newspapers, journals, movies, music albums, radio and TV broadcasts, available in the country. Using statistical techniques like 'Factor Analysis' I made a comprehensive analysis of this data.

The inferences I could draw from this was that in reality, actual sexual practices were quite different from those that were brainwashed into the minds of common people through religion, politics, and education. There was a great demand for sex in all print and visual media. Amongst all credits, it was sex which generated the highest revenue.

This survey indicated that people would even skip reading news headlines at times to read news or columns about sex first. In general, there was a great curiosity about sex in the society, and to satisfy this curiosity, various illegal ways were adopted on a very large scale. In fact, this situation encouraged hypocrisy and escapism on personal and social levels.

When I evaluated these results, I found that the stipulations about sex I had earlier made in my book, *The Case for Sexual*

Promiscuity, had been vindicated. I had written, 'As long as society refuses to accept sexuality, attraction towards sex is bound to keep lurking in people's minds. However strict the restrictions that religious fanatics may try to impose, nothing can curb this attraction. On the contrary, the intensity of this attraction will rise. Eventually, this can lead to perverted ways of expression. There is no alternative other than to advocate sexual freedom. Sexual freedom is necessary for healthy attitude towards sex. Only then we can ensure a mentally healthy society.'

The results of the survey, together with my conclusions, were sufficient enough to publish a book. I named this book *The Folklore of Sex*. Obviously, I expected it to be difficult to find a publisher for this book and I readied myself for this Herculean task once again.

A doctorate degree, the post of Chief Psychologist, and other extensively published material had definitely boosted my status in the eyes of the publishers. But to make them digest my bold views about sexual freedom was a monumental task. After some perseverance, Doubleday and Company finally accepted my manuscript and published the book.

My efforts to find a publisher had borne fruit after twelve long years. The tenacity I showed over such a long period made me tough enough to tide over any hardship. The biggest advantage of my perseverance was that I developed an exceptional capacity to overcome frustration. Without this capacity, I would have been disturbed by every incident; small or big, my mind would be entangled to such an extent, that it would have closed all doors to my growth.

***

'Mr. Sanford Bates- Commissioner
State Dept. of Institutes and Agencies
Trenton, New Jersey.'

The nameplate on the cabin door was quite prominent. I knocked gently. The previous commissioner, Mr. Nelson Stuart had retired, and Mr. Sanford Bates had joined just a month back. In this one month, I had spoken to him on very few occasions. So now, when I was asked to see him urgently, I was somewhat perplexed.

'Yes. Come in.' He answered loudly.

I opened the door and entered.

I could see that Mr. Bates was extremely angry. His face was red. The vein on his forehead had become taut. His eyes were emitting fire. He was holding my book, *The Folklore of Sex*. He threw it down on the table and screamed, 'Dr. Ellis, what's all this? What have you stated in this book? Your views are highly objectionable.'

'Sir, the conclusions in this book were derived during a project undertaken by me independently,' I answered politely in a controlled tone.

'That's exactly why I have called you. Have you decided to malign our institute by publishing them?' He asked furiously.

'Sir, how can it malign our institution? This research was done by me, independently, and these conclusions are the outcome of this work. This is not at all related to the institute in any way.' I remained calm while answering.

'What nonsense. What research are you talking of? Damn that research of yours! How can you say that it is not related to our institute? With such opinions you will make the institute notorious for encouraging vulgarity. Your writing can arouse public ire. We may be questioned by higher authorities; don't you understand this? You are a senior psychologist. I thought you would be aware of your position while writing. But we are totally disappointed by your careless attitude.'

'Sir, I have not written anything objectionable. My results have been derived after applying statistical methods. I can prove this. I think it is my duty to present the truth before the people the way I have seen it in society. I have written the book with full awareness. Therefore, I do not at all repent having written this.' I was blunt but modest.

'Of course, that is very obvious. You seem to be shameless. You are least worried about the damaging effects your book will have on society.'

'But, sir....'

Mr. Bates cut me short and continued his tirade.

'To hell with your sexual liberalism. You are maligning religion by advocating sexual freedom. Do you want to destroy the institution of marriage by recommending such unjustifiable freedom? This will create chaos in society, don't you realise? You are misguiding society by publishing such research.'

'Sir, misguiding society...how? In what way...?'

'Yes, misguiding society. Society needs the strong foundation of the institution of marriage. Why don't you do some research about what would strengthen this foundation? Instead, you are out to demolish the basic structure of our society. Your research paints a false picture of society. It should be banned.'

'Sir , I….'

'And what is your conclusion? That people should accept sexuality and practise sexual liberalism? Instead of controlling the waywardness in society, you have gone to the other extreme with your opinions. Do you understand how dangerous this freedom will be for society? It would be wise if you apologise for writing such a misguiding book. Or else, be prepared to face the consequences.' He was absolutely not ready to hear me.

When all my efforts to explain my stand were unsuccessful, I had no alternative but to leave. I returned to my desk but my head began spinning with his words.

How had I misguided society? In fact I had made an honest effort to put forth the real picture as I saw in my survey. It was not my personal opinion. It was deduced after scientific study. He accused me of wrongly portraying society because the results were not in agreement with his personal views. It showed his narrow-mindedness. In fact, he was ignoring reality, which was as good as misguiding society. Yes, I am against limiting one's sexuality within the framework of marriage. But nowhere did I express any opinion against marriage. On the contrary, I had suggested that restrictions deemed in a marriage should be relaxed and should include sexual freedom also.

The reality, irrespective of Mr. Bates' views, was that the institution of marriage was already in shambles. However romantic a picture one may paint about married life, most marriages are rotten from inside. The partners continue in the marriage because of social pressures but they are afraid to admit this openly. These marriages are devoid of romance, and the partners live a dry, loveless life under the guise of practical compromise.

The research done by social psychologists tells us that the original reason behind the idea of marriage lies in the social system. The psychological and sexual characteristics of a majority of people are not suitable for marriage, but the heavy social pressure on them creates the psychological need for marriage.

If a married person is asked to give an honest answer to the question of why he chose to get married, it will be evident that most people marry because it is a social custom. There is no specific reason or purpose. They do it to follow the trend and flow with the current. Sex is one of the requirements of marriage. Very rarely do we think about the purpose of marriage; whether it is our psychological need or whether our partner is mentally and sexually compatible!

Very few think beyond the aspects of physical attraction or romance and check if the partner is mentally compatible or not. This is an important factor which is often ignored.

Generally, physical looks, education, and social status are the major issues in deciding a match in most communities of the world. Social pressures compel people to sustain their marriage in spite of mental incompatibility. But such people do not have exciting sexual relations.

The truth discovered by social psychologists is that, irrespective of whether society is developed or underdeveloped, most marriages are influenced by social and financial factors. The institution of marriage itself is built by downsizing the limits of personal freedom. Hence, it is not surprising that society has been ridden with extra-marital relationships, sex-related crimes, perverted sex, and prostitution. This is inevitable. To stop the growth of these undesired practices, to make society healthier, we have to lay more emphasis on psychological factors. It was this opinion that I had stated in my book.

By psychological factors, I mean the awareness of the fact that the psychological and sexual needs of one's partner could be different from one's own. If both partners are aware of this fact, they will accept the right to individual freedom of their partner openheartedly, even while respecting their individual needs. Thereby, they will nurture a healthy relationship. Such a relationship is an indicator of good mental health.

I could now see the situation more clearly. Mr. Sanford Bates was chief of the institute. It was not advisable to incur his wrath. If I wished to get ahead in my career, it was necessary to apologise and compromise with him. Apologise for the sake of my career, or face the consequences of his anger? I was caught between the devil and the deep blue sea. Pleasing Bates would mean paying a heavy price for going against my basic instinct. But it was equally tormenting to face his wrath. It would definitely harm my career. The dilemma was very difficult.

As I began analysing the situation, I realised that rarely can one make a perfect decision. Every decision has its advantages and disadvantages. But we are always in search of the perfect solution, one that will have only advantages! The necessity of taking a decision would not arise if ever such a decision existed.

The fact that I was in a dilemma meant that it involved some advantages and disadvantages. Therefore, instead of finding a 'perfect' decision, I had to find out which compromise suited me best, in order to arrive at a decision. I had made many compromises in life but this situation was different. The compromise Mr. Bates had proposed was entirely against my principles. If I apologised for my work, which was based on scientific analysis and done wholeheartedly, it would turn out far more torturous than any other compromise. I decided not to apologise. I prepared myself for whatever repercussions this decision might have.

I was very sure that Mr. Bates would retaliate directly or indirectly. I was proven right. He contacted Dr. Ralph Brancale, Chief of the State Diagnostic Centre. Dr. Brancale had insisted on publishing his name as the first and main author of the book *The Psychology of Sex Offenders*. I could not fulfil this wish as he had helped me only in furnishing a list of criminals. This task could not justify his demand. The major work of the book was done by me. Mr. Bates and Dr. Brancale both were aware of it. Dr.Brancale had even hinted that he would send a negative work appraisal to Mr. Bates in connection with my work at the centre. I had ignored it.

At the time of declaring the annual raise in salary, I was informed that I was not eligible for one. Mr. Bates pointed out some technical errors in my work and levelled two flimsy charges upon me. The first was that since I stayed in New York, which is outside New Jersey and worked in New Jersey, it was a violation of service conditions.

The second charge was that I was running an independent practice as a psychologist even though I was employed in a full-time job, which was illegal. Additionally, he also attached a letter from Dr. Brancale, which said that he was dissatisfied with my work.

These two charges were so trivial, that I could have easily nullified them by complaining to the Civil Service Commission. I knew of several colleagues who came from faraway places like Philadelphia in Pennsylvania, and some also travelled daily from New York, like me. Besides, I had mentioned my place of residence as New York in my application itself and still selected by the institute. This clearly indicated that my place of residence did not matter.

As for the second charge, there was certainly a law which barred private practice for employed professionals. But this law was applicable only to physicians and psychiatrists. Service conditions were silent about psychologists having a private practice .The letter written by Dr. Brancale also did not hold any water. I had many certificates of appreciation by the earlier senior staff. Even Mr. Nelson Stuart, the previous commissioner, had given a letter of appreciation for my work. I had around sixty papers and essays published by then. All this was adequate for acknowledging my status.

But now I was thinking on different lines, wondering why I was stuck at this job. I was at such a stage in life where I had almost lost interest in money, fame, stability, and such materialistic benefits. I needed something more than this, which would provide inner satisfaction. It was clear that my job was incapable of giving this. Outwardly I had everything, but there was a big void inside.

While working at the institute, there had been many occasions when I felt that this was not what I had aimed for in life. But I

10

It was one of those chilly Saturdays in February. I was busy preparing lunch- tuna salad with egg and mayonnaise, chicken soup, and bread. Mom had brought banana pastry yesterday.

'There has been snowfall of two to four inches. More snowfall up to six inches is predicted. Citizens are requested to....'

I turned off the radio and drew aside the curtain of the kitchen window as I scooped the salad in my bowl. The snowfall had not ceased. The street had turned into a white carpet. There was so much snow on the cars parked outside, that it was difficult to recognise them. I did not expect any client in such weather. We both had no option but to stay indoors.

It was only the two of us in the house now. Paul had married Esther and had moved near Grammarcy Park on 18th Street. Janet had married Patrick and settled in San Diego in California. There was some sort of emptiness at home. I had settled in my profession. I was doing well in my practice as a psychologist in the clinic I had opened in our house.

Mom and I never communicated too well between ourselves. Neither was she interested in my activities, nor I in hers.

Now, even though it was only the two of us, we ate our meals separately, according to our convenience. We had not shared the table together for many months. But today the heavy snowfall made things different.

'Mom...,' I called her after I had set the table.

'Albert, you have cooked really well, especially the tuna salad.' Mom said genuinely.

'Thanks Mom.'

The food had really turned out tasty. Sipping hot, steaming chicken soup in that cold snowy weather was very comforting.

'Albert, since many days I've been thinking of a plan,' she said as she served herself more salad and bread.

I set down my spoon and looked at her. She looked serious.

'How about selling this place? Only two of us stay in such a large house. You hardly leave your room. There is nobody to share housekeeping. I am not of much help to you in this work. Earlier, you had Paul and Janet to help. Most of your holidays are spent in cleaning the house. What if we sell this house and purchase a smaller one? We can save some money too. This house is in a very good location. It will fetch us a handsome price. What is your opinion?'

What she said made sense. I was tired of looking after the maintenance of our house. We really did not need such a large house for the two of us. Since Mom was the legal owner, her decision was final.

wanted to sell because of a job transfer. I fell in love with the place instantly. It had tall windows and a high mansard roof. There was a small balcony from where one could see the garden below and the statue of Columbus on 59th Street.

The most attractive feature was that the subway station on 59th Street was at a walking distance. There was also a central bus station near Columbus Circle. I pooled my savings and Mom's contribution and bought the apartment for eight thousand dollars.

I booked Mom's air ticket to San Diego with Pacific Southwest Airlines. Her flight was at six in the morning and the airport was at a distance of fifteen miles. We took a cab. On reaching the airport, I checked in her luggage, took the boarding pass, and we sat talking in the lounge. Janet and Patrick were going to receive her. Mom had planned to stay with them initially for a few days. I asked her to call me as soon as she reached San Diego.

'Passengers going by flight number PSA 757 of the Pacific Southwest Airlines are requested to go to window number five for security check.' It was time for Mom to leave.

'Mom, take care.' I took her hands into mine.

'Oh, don't worry. I have Janet to look after me. Fanny is also close. But Albert, I am worried about you. Here, I could at least see you every day. Now I am really going to miss you.'

I did not know how to react. I was very sad. I did not want to let go of her hands.

'Albert, get married. Don't stay alone. Day and night you live amongst books. You don't even sleep properly, I know. Even if you go out, you go to the library. You have lost touch with the outside world. Paul, Manny, Janet, all are younger to you but they have kids. You have already crossed forty and you are still single. Why are you wasting your life because of one failed marriage? You have so many girlfriends. Don't you find even one of them suitable? Friends are only friends. The happiness of married life is very different, Albert. Loneliness is very bad. I have experienced it in the prime of my life. I do not want you to suffer the same. I am really worried about you.'

It was not an emotional outburst. She was calm and composed.

I was lost for a while. I felt as if I was little Albert once again with Mom around me, singing in her sweet voice. I wanted to scream, 'Mom, please don't go. Please don't leave me. Don't ever leave me, even for a moment.'

'This is the last call for passengers leaving by PSA 757 for ….'.

Mom left in a hurry. She waved till the last moment as she stood in line for Security Check. My eyes had welled up. From a distance, I could see only her blurred silhouette slowly disappearing into the crowd.

***

My practice began growing rapidly after moving to Park Vendome. The number of clients too increased. I would receive around sixteen clients in a day for at least three days in a week. I worked round the clock…nearly all twenty-four hours.

I was obsessed with my work. When I was employed, the number of clients did not affect me financially. I had a regular salary to support me. But now I was literally penniless. My income entirely depended on the number of clients. I tried to minimise my expenditure as much as possible.

I had set a routine. I would wake up at six and be ready by eight after cooking breakfast and lunch. Appointments would begin from eight sharp. Each session would be of forty-five minutes. Apart from a lunch break of half an hour, I would work almost twelve hours at a stretch.

At night, after the last session, at around eight, I would walk up to Columbus Circle. There was small shopping mall near the circle, from where I would purchase my daily groceries. At the end of the mall was Molly's Kitchen, a sandwich and pastry shop. One could get homemade food here, and cheaper too. Very often, I would buy sandwiches or pastry for dinner from this outlet. While returning, I would relax for some time on one of the benches in the centre of the circle.

The marble statue of Columbus was erected on a seventy-foot high granite pillar. On the platform of the pillar was Virgo with a globe in her hands. The park was illuminated with colourful lights which reflected elegantly on the statue. Its reflected brightness would bring alive the statue of Virgo. On the bronze pillar were carved Nina, Piñata and Santa Maria, the ships in which Columbus had sailed. These exquisite carvings were so beautiful that they took the viewer right back to that historical period.

In the evenings, the circle would be overcrowded with people, either rushing to catch a bus or a train. I would sit and soak myself in that madness, trying to draw its liveliness into me. The hustle-bustle of people would infuse fresh energy. After a while I would return, recharged with new enthusiasm.

Back home, I would eat dinner and resume working. I would maintain a record of every client and his or her problem, the details of the therapy given, and the techniques used. Then I would read up on other therapies and treatments given elsewhere for similar problems. I constantly thought about improving my practise. Past midnight by two, after reading, writing, and thinking, I would go to bed.

I had not discontinued my earlier routine of visiting the New York Public Library. On days when I had fewer clients, I would head for the library and stay there up to nine, the closing hour. I also brought books to read at home. Other than clinic-hours, I spent every minute reading, writing and studying. I was neck-deep into practice and research. I would refuse invitations to parties or entertainment programmes. Every moment was devoted to my life-goal. I was successful in steering my life according to my plans. But yet something was nagging my mind: a large void of loneliness.

I had virtually locked myself in my apartment. Loneliness engulfed me. I desperately longed for some company, a partner to share my life with, someone close to my heart. Every day, I met several people, but the talk I had with them was professional, a part of my therapy. This could not satisfy my need for sharing my feelings.

Occasionally, Mom would phone me. Although Paul and Manny lived in New York, we seldom met.

'Albert, nowadays we can meet you only with prior appointment.' Manny would say laughingly whenever he called.

Paul called me regularly every fortnight. 'Albert, you are so busy. Every time I call you I feel like I am wasting your valuable time.' Paul would complain.

Although there was truth to what Paul and Manny said, I had noticed a change. Either on phone or in person, whenever we talked, it would be very formal. This did not happen deliberately. We all were busy with our own lives. Each one had a small world of his own. The paradigm of our lives had changed.

The thread that should have bonded all of us as a family, was perhaps not as strong as it should have been. It was already weak. To expect it to grow stronger with the years was unrealistic. Perhaps this is the tragedy of human life. After a period, all close relationships gradually transform and turn formal. For me, this tragedy had become nightmarish. I feared that this loneliness, one day, was going to finish me. As the days passed, I began feeling suffocated.

I continued with my romantic escapades as usual. But I would often pay a heavy price for this. The concept of sexual freedom was quite attractive, but in real life it would often create complications. Some of the women did not have a firm attitude like me. Very soon, they would start feeling guilty over their 'immoral' behaviour. Some would get emotionally involved with me. A few would change their view and retreat at the peak stage of our relationship. I would explain my stand regarding a relationship between a man and a woman, very clearly. In spite of this, some would cry foul and accuse me of deception. These women would unnecessarily create misunderstandings over my behaviour and cause trouble. Solving the mess created in such situations was definitely painful. Of course, I was firm about my views. So, with some effort, I could prevent myself from suffering guilt that could have led me to self-destruction. But then, such short-lived relationships would put me in distress. Whatever happiness I derived from these relationships would fade away, leaving me yearning for a long-lasting, stable relationship.

At night, my body would burn with desire. All the romantic moments spent with different women would stir me up violently. I would then drown myself in the memories of those exciting moments. Fantasies of sex with those women would keep me company throughout the night. I would satisfy my desire by masturbating. Sometimes, when the urge became uncontrollable, I would let my imagination run amok. I would remember the bodies of the women I saw on the streets or in shops, and add my colours to the imagery. That would make me delirious. Like a maniac, I would create a great variety of imagery. I never suppressed my urge nor did I make any attempt to control it, or refuse its creation. On the contrary, I trained my mind to make maximum use of imagery to satisfy my desires.

I found that by focussing on the buxom parts of a woman's body, and on one's sexual desires in the imagery, one can experience climax with a greater intensity. I taught myself to use this technique to make climax more exciting. Once you ejaculate, the climax ends. I found out new methods to prolong the climax without allowing ejaculation to take place. Soon I became an expert in practising this technique.

I began writing a book based on these experiments. I wanted to disprove the myth that a single person does not have any sex life. Whether a person lives alone or with another, he has a personal sex life. His sex life with his partner, if he has one, is only a part of his personal sex life. Staying alone or without a partner should not mean depriving oneself of sex. I had the experience of deriving happiness from my own body, even while living alone, without any partner. Had this book seen the light of the day, I would have named it as *Sex and the Single Man*.

To add to my loneliness, I developed a sudden rash on my back. It turned into small boils, followed by severe itching. The more I scratched, the more would the rash spread over my back. This would result in abscesses along with unbearable pain. The day would somehow pass by in pain, but at night it would be impossible to sleep. New boils would appear in place of the old, if I tried to break them. This situation continued for quite a few days. I consulted doctors and was told that my diabetes had become severe. More investigation followed and I learnt that I had Type 1 Diabetes. I was asked to stop eating sweet and fried food totally. I did follow the diet recommended for me daily, but occasionally, for a change, I would have potato wedges, fries, and potato toast, or corn soup. Cakes and pastries were among my favourite food items, and I would have them sometimes when I was not able to control my craving. This was what had led to this condition. Now I had no option but to strictly follow dietary restrictions.

To cure the rash, I was supposed to eat protein-rich food and eat small portions eight to ten times in a day. My diet consisted of some hot dish, sandwiches with peanut butter or with low-salt cheese, and some fruits. Gradually, the rash subsided.

After getting rid of this problem, a new one appeared — premature ejaculation. The blood supply from the brain to the genitals causes a hydraulic effect, due to which the penis becomes erect. If there is some problem in this blood supply, one cannot hold the penis erect for a long-time and there is instant ejaculation. I knew this could happen because of diabetes.

When I studied this problem in depth, I realised, that the cause of this dysfunction is not only physical. The contribution of psychological factors is more than the physical one but also psychological. But till that point, there was no unanimity among the experts in deciding the proportion of these two factors.

I decided to review the psychological factors. Our thought processes are so powerful that when disturbing thoughts occur, even slightly, they adversely affect blood supply from the brain. This reduces the stiffness of the organ. These thoughts were powerful because they concerned deeply-embedded concepts about manhood. I also accessed inferences from previous research done on this subject. One in ten persons faced the problem of premature ejaculation sometime in his life. We have attached manhood to erectile capacity so strongly, that we are not able to look at this problem objectively. Therefore, we do not stop only at the thought or the explanation that this is simply an ejaculation that happened before the woman was satisfied; we go further and associate it with impotency. Further, instead of discussing the problem, many prefer to stay silent about it. As a result, the main cause of the problem is ignored. When the situation persists for a considerable period of time, it creates reluctance for sex in that person's mind.

To find the origin of this problem I decided to study my mental process objectively. This problem of early ejaculation had occurred only once with me. This was just the initial stage of the problem, but its effect lasted till the next sex act, where, a new thought was already occupying my mind—that 'my erection must hold for a longer time'. When the word 'must' entered this thought, it caused a change in my mental process. I bore the pressure of the demand that the erection 'must' last for a certain time, coupled with the worry of 'how long' it could last. Instead of enjoying sex, my mind remained engaged in keeping a watch on myself. Consequently, it gave rise to the worry of early ejaculation. As a result, I would ejaculate just with moments of worrying.

Subsequently, the guilt that I failed to control even after trying hard, and the worry of its recurrence, haunted me every day. My habit of premature ejaculation also continued. This situation prevailed for quite some time.

I realised that in any situation, when we think that we 'must' do something, the word forces upon us the absolute necessity to do a certain task. When we keep reminding ourselves of this necessity, it gets converted into worry. We become utterly disturbed and believe ourselves to be worthless if we are unable to do that particular task.

To overcome my problem of ejaculation, I first freed myself from this 'must'. I told myself that if I succeed, well and good; but I will not force the thought that I must not ejaculate prematurely. I decided to defy the fulfilment of conditions required to 'prove' my manliness. Thereafter, my mind stopped its vigilance and, once again, I began enjoying sex as before.

Apart from this problem, I realised that I would face other effects on my health because of diabetes. I was already taking one injection with seven units of insulin, daily. After some months, it became necessary to increase the dose to two injections. This heavy dose turned me into a skeleton. I improved in health but I was aware of a bitter truth—diabetes, had taken hold of my body. When I came to know that it was getting worse, the first action I took was to control my self-talk.

I had to stop the 'awfulisation' of my feelings in my statements. 'Awfulisation' means labelling an experience as the very worst. I was constantly telling myself that a serious ailment like diabetes is horrible, beyond imagination; it is the worst disease amongst all diseases. Naturally, it is beyond the limits of my tolerance levels. The word 'horrible' was making me emotionally disturbed. No doubt, managing diabetes was definitely not easy and I hated it; but it was not as horrible as I made it out to be. I was portraying diabetes as a serious disease by awfulising it. To stop this I told myself, 'The disease I am suffering is definitely a serious disease. But although it has eroded my happiness in life, it has not destroyed my happiness completely. Without feeling miserable, I can definitely find some joy and happiness in life.'

I had already started my campaign against 'awfulisation'. Even while speaking with others, I resolved not to talk in a tone of despair about my complaints and problems. Without being scared of what might happen in the future, I began practising my monologues. This brought a change in my fear of loneliness as well. If loneliness was inevitable, I had to learn to overcome it. I told myself not to 'awfulise' my loneliness. Gradually, I was able to prevent harmful thoughts.

I told myself to accept that diabetes and loneliness would be my lifetime friends. But dealing with them was within my control.

I immediately began to work in this direction. I decided to publish my experience in the form of a book, *How to Stubbornly Refuse to Make Yourself Miserable About Anything—Yes, Anything.*

***

I decided to train in psychoanalysis after my doctorate and contacted The American Institute for Psychoanalysts. This institute was located to the east of Manhattan. A well-known psychologist, Karen Horney, had modified Freud's theory and founded this institute. Here, although more emphasis was laid on psychoanalysis, the approach was not the orthodox Freudian. New developments in psychotherapy were incorporated from time to time. For my training, this institute recommended the name of Dr. Charles Hulbeck, who was an expert psychoanalyst. It was mandatory to get one's own psychoanalysis done before starting private practice as a psychoanalyst.

Dr. Hulbeck's clinic was near Battery Park to the south of Manhattan. I was working in New Jersey and would go twice a week to his clinic for my psychoanalysis. This analysis had taken nearly two years to finish and was now over.

I would still continue to meet Dr. Hulbeck regularly. I consulted him for my cases and he too was happy to guide me. It was mandatory to have a degree in medicine to be eligible for training as a psychoanalyst. But he treated me as an exception to this rule. 'I pay more importance to sincerity and studiousness as a researcher rather than the degree you hold,' he once said to me. I made special efforts to live up to his trust. Our relations soon became so close professionally, that we started referring our clients to each other.

I called myself a psychoanalyst and was using psychoanalytical methods for my treatment, but yet there were still some questions in my mind. The first was: what was the usefulness of my psychoanalysis done by Dr. Hulbeck?

This psychoanalysis had helped me in reducing my worries and irritability. But it was difficult to give the entire credit to psychoanalysis; there was also significant contribution of my own efforts.

Second, why were clients not showing any improvement with this therapy? To answer this query, I tried some other Freudian techniques. I also studied methods developed by neo-psychoanalysts, who had deviated from classical psychoanalysis and created their own camp, remaining within the framework of psychoanalysis. But even these methods failed.

As I studied deeper, I found several shortcomings in psychoanalysis. I began losing confidence. My belief in this therapy started diminishing. I felt that there were some drawbacks in the fundamental premises of psychoanalysis.

The first premise was that once a person becomes aware, his problem gets cured automatically — since the origin of his emotional problem is rooted in some repressed emotion in his unconscious mind. The job of a psychoanalyst is to make the client aware, that is to give him 'insight'. In psychoanalysis, it is assumed that the solution to a client's problem lies in giving this insight.

This assumption seemed incorrect to me. I found that many clients could not get rid of their problems in spite of this insight. This indicated that insight alone was inadequate for curing a problem.

I noticed this inadequacy especially while treating a client called Alex. He hated his boss, Philip, very much. He came to me to get over this feeling of hatred. While treating him, I noted that he had extreme hatred for his father in his unconscious mind. Since Philip resembled his father, he would remind Alex of his father and this made him hate Philip.

I made Alex aware of his insight, that the origin of his hatred for Philip was in his hatred for his father. But in spite of this, the intensity of his feeling had not reduced. Thus, even after becoming aware of the reason, Alex could not solve his problem.

Finally, in desperation, Alex said to me, 'Doctor, you are right. I do hate my father. I totally agree with you. But I am still unable to lessen my hatred for Philip even after so many months. Why is it so?'

After Alex's case, I became further distrustful of psychoanalysis. There were other clients with the same experience. All these cases were strengthening my opinion that psychoanalysis was not very effective in solving a problem.

Whenever a client asked me why he was not being cured, I would answer according to the psychoanalytical method, 'You are right. You have not improved because you have obtained your insight only superficially. You are yet to obtain deep insight. Till then we will continue with your analysis.

You will notice improvement when you will obtain deep insight.'

Although the answer I gave was in line with psychoanalysis, I was not fully convinced of it. Such an answer was a short-term escape from the truth. In psychoanalysis, there was no genuine answer to this question. This therapy could not go beyond making a client aware of his unconscious emotions. The client would feel better after giving vent to his feelings. But this did not bring about any improvement in his behaviour. Just making a client *feel* better was of no use. It was necessary to make him *get* better with some special efforts.

The other inadequacy that I found in psychoanalysis was that it lacked proactive intervention. I did not agree with waiting patiently for the client to respond.

While treating clients at my erstwhile LAMP, I had learnt that a psychologist has to be strongly active-directive during therapy. It saves time and is also beneficial for the client. At LAMP, I would not only give my clients knowledge about sex, but would also consciously dispute their wrong beliefs, and motivate them to act. I would give them assignments. I would teach them different ways of copulation to make their experience of sex more joyful. This definitely made them not only 'feel better' but also to 'get better' and improve their behaviour.

I also began feeling that it was unscientific to search for the roots of a client's problem in his or her childhood experiences alone. This concept totally denies the freedom a person has in his/her later life. I firmly believed that we can control our behaviour and we are capable of changing it any moment. Childhood experiences may have some effect on our lives. But it is foolish to believe that our entire personality is formed by our childhood experiences and cannot be absolutely changed later.

Was it really necessary to dig out one's childhood memories? I felt it was futile because this search did not cure the problem. Instead, if we try to find why it persisted for so long, it may, perhaps, help us find the right path. According to me, it would be more beneficial to discover a person's present attitude towards the past and not what happened in the past.

Another drawback of psychoanalysis was its unscientific approach in many concepts; for example, our unconscious mind. The concept of the unconscious mind is mysterious, fanciful and attractive; it impresses people immediately. But since there is no scientific proof for this concept, after a period, I found it difficult to make an analysis on its basis.

I was experiencing the effects of applying an unscientific concept like 'unconscious mind'. Even if psychoanalysts found that the origin of a person's problem lies in his repressed emotions, there is no provision to verify this objectively. This is because the concept of unconscious mind is, in itself, not scientific. As a result, every psychologist interpreted its meaning differently, according to his own thinking.

Had Alex consulted some other psychoanalyst, he would have, perhaps, found that the origin of his problem was in his hatred for his brother, instead of his father. Because of its unscientific basis, it is not possible to say which psychoanalyst was right.

Suppose Alex told the other psychoanalyst that he does not hate his brother and disagreed with this reasoning. Then, instead of searching for other possible causes, his psychoanalyst would have asserted, in line with his therapy, that, 'The truth I have found is absolutely right. Since your conscious mind is not aware of the hatred you have for your brother in your unconscious mind, you disagree with me.'

Disagreeing with the client, to force him to accept your view under the pretext of the unconscious mind, was totally incorrect, according to me. It is necessary to have the concurrence of the client about the cause of the problem. If he is not in agreement, the psychoanalyst has to look for other reasons. Such flexibility in approach is necessary for a psychoanalyst. This was missing in the therapy.

There were some more drawbacks in this therapy. I found that dream-analysis lacked objectivity. I did not experience these drawbacks all of a sudden. They had been striking my mind one after another over a long period. Staying within the framework of psychoanalysis, I tried to express my thoughts about through some research papers. *An Operational Reformulation of Some of the Basic Principles of Psychoanalysis* was the name of one such paper, which was published. In this paper, I had critically evaluated psychoanalysis. I had also expressed my opinion that psychoanalysts should lay more emphasis on writing and in giving therapy in a more scientific way.

But the response I received from the psychoanalysts was not to my expectation. Their dogmatic rigidity was impregnable. New York was the epicentre of psychoanalysts. To try to change or improve this therapy was a David versus Goliath fight against the established community of psychoanalysts. But for me it was necessary to break the barriers to go ahead.

Although psychoanalysis was very popular, I decided to discard its unscientific principles. This put me at peace. I decided to call myself a psychologist and not a psychoanalyst. Now I was free to treat my clients according to my independent thinking.

I was in search of a psychotherapy, one that was comprehensive and proactive; a psychotherapy that does not entertain any mysterious or fancy concepts; that gives importance to the present, not to the past; a psychotherapy that is scientific, rational and realistic; that does not stay contented just with the feel-good status of the client, but also makes him get better.

Outwardly, I worked as per my routine, but my mind was constantly occupied by one passion: A new psychotherapy.

***

'Hello. Could I speak to Dr. Albert Ellis?'

'Speaking.'

'Good Morning. This is Rhoda here, Rhoda Winter Russell. I seek an appointment with you for my younger sister, Sandra.'

'Please hold on, let me check my schedule. Who suggested my name?' I asked, as I checked my diary.

'I work as a receptionist at the Manhattan State Hospital. You had visited our hospital two years back. At that time you had delivered a lecture on psychological problems for the hospital staff. We all still remember that lecture. But I obtained your telephone number from Dr. Collin. He was full of praises for you. He told me repeatedly that you were the best psychologist in New York.'

'Thanks for your compliments. Could you meet me next Saturday at eight in the morning?' This was the earliest slot vacant in my diary.

'Perfectly alright. I will bring Sandra along. Could I know the address of the clinic, please?'

I gave her the address.

As I put the receiver back, I remembered my visit to the Manhattan State Hospital two years ago. It was Manhattan's biggest psychiatric hospital situated in Wood Ireland. I had visited the hospital for an annual inspection on behalf of the State Department of Institutes and Agencies. As usual, besides the routine inspection, I also gave a lecture on the nature of psychological problems and treatments before the entire staff, and cleared some of their common misunderstandings.

'The cause of our problems does not lie in the circumstances around us but in the attitude we bear towards those circumstances. Hence, it is advantageous to change our attitude.' I had elaborated on this point by citing an example. Dr. Collin was the chief of the psychiatry department at this hospital. We were still in touch and would often talk on the phone or meet to consult each other. I could not remember Rhoda at all.

We met on the day of the appointment. Rhoda was smart and attractive, with a shapely figure. She reported, along with Sandra, ten minutes before the scheduled time. Sandra was a victim of Obsessive Compulsive Disorder (OCD). She would constantly repeat certain actions, like washing hands unnecessarily, removing and wearing shoes again and again, keep turning lights on and off, opening and shutting a door frequently, or writing and instantly erasing that matter.

Instead of finding the root of this disorder in her childhood incidents, I tried to discover which attitude had provoked her to behave in this way. I was successful in doing so in a very short time. She was keen that her every action should be perfect and it was this attitude that dominated her behaviour.

A number of questions kept pestering her continuously. 'Have I washed my hands properly?', or while wearing shoes, 'Have I put them on properly?', or 'Have I pressed the right electric switch?', or 'Have I closed both the doors together?' Such insignificant thoughts disturbed her every moment. She would then repeat her actions until she was convinced that it was done perfectly.

I showed her that her thoughts could not stand any test of objectivity. I asked her to write the thoughts that occurred to her while she did a certain action, and taught her to counter that with a new thought at that moment.

I also taught her to question herself about her attitude towards perfection. No human being is perfect in this world. I told her not to be unfair to her own self by forcing such an inhuman demand. I trained her to accept herself along with her shortcomings.

In every session, Rhoda was present with Sandra, watching closely. Sandra soon improved and was not required to see me as frequently as before. I gave her some homework and asked her to report after a month. Rhoda was overwhelmed after the last session.

'Dr. Ellis, I have no words to express my gratitude. You have relieved not only Sandra but also our entire family from this problem.'

'That is my job, Rhoda. You can only say that I did my job satisfactorily,' I was candid in my reply.

Before leaving she said, 'Dr. Ellis, I have a request. I am very fond of dancing and I train at the Nikolais Dance Theatre Centre. An American Dance Festival is held every year in New York. Our Centre is hosting the festival this year for the first time. The festival is for six weeks. Well-known dancers from the country will participate in this festival. I am performing on the very first day, that is next Saturday. Will you please attend the programme?' She was genuinely earnest in her request.

I tried to tell her that my knowledge about dance was very poor and I did not know to dance either. But she insisted, 'Doctor, dance is also a form of language. You know the language of the mind. Dance is the language of our body. You do not need to have any thorough knowledge of dance to understand this language. I will be disappointed if you do not attend.'

The next week, she came home to give the invitation. Rhoda was probably around twenty-four years, much younger to me. Besides working as a receptionist at the hospital, she was also completing her graduation from the University of Wisconsin. While giving the invitation, she briefed me about her dance. 'Currently, there is a wave of modern dance in America. Alvin Nikolais and Hanya Home are the main promoters of this dance. They are not only dance-trainers but expert musicians and choreographers. I train under them. My dance is called Rock Dance. Acrobatic movement is the special feature of this dance.'

This information was, of course, new to me. I was not connected with dance even remotely. Rhoda was in a hurry and she left immediately, but not without reminding me to attend the show.

I did go for the show on Saturday. I did not know anybody in the audience. Before the show was about to begin, Rhoda came to meet me. She wore jazz shoes and a costume made of some synthetic elastic fibre. Her hair was pinned up with a matching fancy cap. She looked so different that I did not recognise her.

'Dr. Ellis, I am so happy to see you. Now I will definitely perform well.' Her tone was sincere.

I watched her dance with attention. Her footwork was excellent. She danced with ease. Her body was very elastic and agile. I was amazed to see her dance to a very fast beat. Her proficiency in dancing was so good, it was as if she was born to dance.

Rhoda danced extremely well without doubt. But I was not able to mentally involve myself in her dance. Her dance appeared like some form of exercise. It had the capacity to excite the viewer but it could not express different shades of an emotion. The fast pace of the dance and the accompanying music was definitely entertaining, but it was not able to touch my heart.

I was inclined towards classical music and dance. I preferred a form of art, which was capable of stirring up emotions, besides exciting the mind. I considered that art to be classical.

Rhoda and I began meeting frequently, and, within three months, we were married legally. Rhoda was very passionate about dance. She was dance personified. Because of the constant dancing, her body language had also become rhythmic. Sex became more interesting because of her agility. She also displayed extraordinary spontaneity in her sex-play. I had never before seen such ingenuous seductive moves in sex.

By the time I finished my last appointment, Rhoda would return home. Then she would start her practice. To avoid disturbing others by the loud music, she changed the windows of the living room to double-paned chambers. They were fitted with sound-proof honey-comb curtains. The floor carpet too was replaced by a thicker one. She danced to music with a frequency of 150 beats a minute. Its volume would become unbearable. I would shut my ears and lock myself in our bedroom.

'Step! Step! Kick! Settle! Settle!' She would count her steps as she practised.

I had trained myself to remain immune to external disturbances. So her practice did not disturb me. I would remain absorbed in my work.

But Rhoda could not remain indifferent to my aloofness. 'Albert, how can you stay unaffected by this music? Stop all this boring work. One should feel the urge to dance the moment this music is turned on. This dance is meant for a couple. Come on, I will teach you. It's not at all difficult. Start with the slower steps first. Then gradually increase the pace. In the beginning you must dance on your toes. Then take a circle and rest your foot down.'

'Come on Albert. Get up. Start!'

Rhoda's words began ringing something else in my mind. The idea of a new psychotherapy began dancing in my mind. In the beginning, thoughts would just creep into my mind. Gradually, while dancing with Rhoda, my thoughts would pour in, tune with my body and begin dancing rhythmically. My mind would remain focused only on my thoughts. They would tell me, 'Albert, get up. Pick up your pen. Start writing….'

Then, like an obsessed person, I would keep writing, oblivious to the surrounding world. My mind would keep dancing around several ideas. It would become difficult to leave the world of thoughts. I enjoyed the intoxication this world offered me.

One evening, Rhoda came home limping. Her dance partner accompanied her.

'Rhoda, what happened?' I was startled.

'I really don't know how it happened. All of a sudden, I slipped. My knee has been fractured.' She was in acute pain, unable to stand properly.

'Why didn't you call me immediately?' I asked in worry.

'Furmin, my dance partner, was with me at that time. Instead of wasting time, I felt it was more important to see the doctor first. Almost every day someone gets injured. So the centre has appointed a specialist doctor. He applied plaster and Furmin dropped me in his car.'

'How serious is the injury ?'

'Not much, but the plaster will be removed only after three weeks. Till then I cannot dance.' Rhoda looked depressed. The pain of not being able to dance was more than that of the injury.

She was home-bound for three weeks. She could hardly do any work, apart from looking after her own self.

'Albert, let's buy a TV. Everybody has a TV nowadays. I'm getting bored,' she would nag me every day.

Finally, I could not refuse any longer. One day I bought a TV.

'Albert, your books give me a headache. Please stop your reading and writing,' one day, she came up with this new complaint.

It was not possible to fulfil this desire of hers. Reading and writing was my life-force. It was my life's passion. This proposal was impossible to accept, even if it came from my wife.

After three weeks, the plaster was removed, and we both heaved a sigh of relief. Of course, Rhoda was happier. Although she was asked to go slow on dance, she had got back her mobility. That day we sat talking till late at night.

'Albert, these three weeks were terrible. First, because I was unable to dance, and second, because there is no one to talk to during the day. It was stifling, Albert. I cannot survive without friends.'

'But you had TV to watch.' I said.

'Yes. But, frankly speaking, I was getting bored. I would often feel like running away somewhere.'

'Is it?' I could not guess what was going in her mind.

'You know, I desperately wanted to see Macy's Thanksgiving Parade last Thursday. Those funny clowns, colourful balloons, my favourite cartoon characters. Oh, what fun. The parade was so near to us. It passed the Columbus Circle to go towards Broadway but I missed it. All of New York City gathers to have a glimpse of it, when it stops near Macy's flagship store. And guess who gave the dance performance there? The best troupe of New York. Sam Arnold's troupe. I could hear its music even here. I was dying to go there to see the dance. But, Albert, I am so surprised. Did you plug your ears? Didn't you hear the sound of the parade? How can you work in the midst of such loud noise? Tell me honestly, didn't you realise that the parade was passing us?'

I kept silent. I was really not aware of the parade. In fact, I was not aware of Thanksgiving Day itself. Now I realised why I had had very few clients last Thursday.

Perhaps my silence gave Rhoda my answer.

'Albert, how can you live without friends? Apart from your clients, you are not in touch with anybody else. You do not know anybody except Mom, Paul and Manny. Nothing matters to you. You are not at all aware of the world around you. Day and night, you are busy only in reading and writing. You are not interested in what happens in the world. There is a rumour of a Third World War by the Soviet Union. The Civil Rights Movement started by Martin Luther King is gathering strength. Leave aside all this. Do you know that Mr. Eisenhower of the Republican Party has won the Presidential election?'

I had lost interest in such news. I would read the newspapers, but my eyes would just scan the news; my brain not registering their significance.

'Albert, you talk to me, you move around in the house, you work; but I get the feeling that your mind is engaged elsewhere. Many a times even when we are at the climax, I can guess that deep down in your mind you are thinking about something else. Then everything that follows becomes a mechanical process. What is so important in your research? Sometimes, when I wake up at midnight I find you missing. Either you are reading or writing. You are surrounded by books and papers all the time. They are my enemies. I hate them, Albert, I just hate them!'

Tears flowed as she spoke. She began sobbing.

I could not bear her crying. I took her in my arms and comforted her for some time.

'Rhoda, I'm really sorry but I don't behave like this intentionally. Please forgive me if I have hurt you. But please understand, my new therapy is my life. It is the topmost priority in my life. You want to know about it? Listen. I am in search of a psychotherapy that can reach the root of a problem. I am spending all my nights in its pursuit. Rhoda, will you please understand me? Please, Rhoda! Rhoda....'

I saw that she was already fast asleep.

It was too late to catch sleep. I moved her aside and got up. I came to my writing-table and put on the lamp. I picked up the books to continue reading. But, that night, I could not apply my mind. I took my pen and writing pad. New thoughts were waiting to be penned. More followed. My pen flew without pause. The night passed in writing. It was early morning when I went to bed.

***

'Men are disturbed not by things, but by the views they take of them.' Epictetus, the great Greek thinker, had discovered this truth two thousand years ago, and now it had infused my mind fully. I realised that this was the life-philosophy that bonded with my psychotherapy.

Epictetus was a Roman slave who believed in Stoic's philosophy. His master was so impressed by his intelligence that he sent him to a famous teacher in Rome to learn Greek philosophy under him. Later, he was freed from slavery. But the Roman emperor felt that thinkers and philosophers were a threat to his throne, and so he expelled all of them, including Epictetus. Later, Epictetus settled in a small village in Greece and opened a school of philosophy. Although he had to lead a hard life, he spent his entire life teaching philosophy.

All the lectures given by Epictetus were compiled by his disciple Arian into eight volumes, called *Discourses*. Of these, four volumes were destroyed and the balance was abridged into one single volume called *Enchiridion*.

I had read this volume earlier. Now, I realised that his philosophy was closely linked to my theory. It was only now that my mind had become ready and capable of realising this connection.

Many of his quotes would linger in my mind. They opened a new door for my therapy practice.

'Events are impersonal and indifferent,' says Epictetus.

Events are not solely capable of creating emotions. If it was so, a particular incident should create the same feeling in all the people. But we do not see this happening because every person interprets an incident differently and evaluates it on the basis of this interpretation. This evaluation determines the feelings of that person.

For example, we say that a student committed suicide because he failed in his examination. If this were was correct, every failed student would have committed suicide. But this does not happen. This means that the reason for suicide is not failure, but the meaning given by that student to his failure.

Epictetus' philosophy is extremely important for psychotherapy. Every person has some beliefs rooted in his mind and it is with these beliefs that he interprets and evaluates the situation. It is important for a psychotherapist to find his evaluation of that event and his belief behind it, instead of concentrating only on that event. If this belief is self-destructive, the psychotherapist can inculcate a constructive belief in its place and help the client strengthen that constructive thinking.

Epictetus says, 'Understand what you can control and what you cannot.'

This statement is very important in psychotherapy. We cannot control every situation in our lives. Without understanding this reality, we insist on having control. This creates emotional barriers in the path to recovery. The psychotherapist should train the client to accept factors that are beyond control. Then he will find it easy to concentrate on those that can be controlled.

Epictetus says, 'Your will is always in your power'.

This statement appears simple at the outset, but it is very difficult to put into practice. People try to change their circumstances first, and get frustrated when they cannot. They forget that instead of wasting their efforts in this attempt, it is much easier to change themselves.

I have derived a new principle out of Epictetus' thinking. To change means to try to adopt a rational view towards ourselves, others, and towards the world in general. For example, if you have differences with your superiors at your job and it is not possible to change your job, then, by changing your attitude towards your superiors, you can lessen your suffering. If the psychotherapist helps the client imbibe such a rational attitude, it will help in getting rid of self-destructive emotions from the mind.

'Reason is supreme.'

This quote from Epictetus is like a lighthouse. The rational attitude I have suggested is based in reality. It is not easy to think rationally. The root cause of most of our suffering and agony is in our irrational thoughts, which are unscientific, illogical, and unrealistic. Therefore, if we inculcate the habit of rational thinking from childhood itself, it is possible to improve the collective mental health of society.

What a wide perspective Epictetus's philosophy has. It encompasses all aspects of human life. How similar are the thoughts expressed by ancient and modern philosophers, and those written by Epictetus. I am convinced that unless we uproot the destructive philosophy from a person's mind, we cannot cure him of his problem. For this, we have to change his thoughts, his emotions, and his behaviour. Only that therapy which can bring about this change will be useful for eradicating a problem.

So far, I could hold a few of these thought that I had formed after years of study and contemplation, but only in pieces. There were some missing links in these pieces. Now all these scattered parts were manifesting together before me in a homogenous form of a therapy! It was giving me a unique sense of contentment! For years, I had struggled internally to create a composite form! Now I could see this form appearing before me in a clear defined structure!

I realised something more. The seed of these thoughts had been in me since childhood. Without being conscious, I had been taking steps in a specific direction. I tasted success because I behaved in accordance with this direction. Therefore, I was able to give a concrete structure to my thoughts.

My new psychotherapy was based on two main principles. One of them is that emotions are mostly created by our thoughts, our imagination, and our life-philosophy. The second principle is that all these factors can be changed. And the best way to bring this change is to strike at the irrational life-philosophy forcefully, and make it more rational.

I discovered that if you adopt a rational life-philosophy, you can bring about healthy changes in a person's thoughts, emotions, and behaviour. I developed this philosophy from my research and from the various experiments with myself and my clients. The culmination of all this is the birth of my theory, using scientific and rational methods. Hence, I have named it Rational Therapy.

I am thrilled with my brainchild. I would dedicate my entire life for its growth. Yes! This would be the aim of my life. My mind and body are bursting with new energy. I do not feel any hunger, thirst, or fatigue.

I have discovered that the song of my life does not get created naturally. We have to create it ourselves. Today I can hear these notes clearly. Rational Therapy is what it's called.

***

August 31, 1956. I had been anxiously waiting for this day. A two-day annual convention of professional psychologists was being held at Chicago. It was organised by the American Psychological Association, the most prestigious organisation of professional psychologists in the United States. On the second day, I was going to read my paper. The title of my paper was *Rational Therapy*.

I was aware that a majority of psychologists would be disappointed with this title. But in order to introduce my psychotherapy to other professionals, I had to face their criticism. Frankly, I was not too worried about it. On the contrary, I was excited at this opportunity. My brain-child had become old enough to take its first step into the world.

I was thrilled when I stood on the dais. I announced the title of the paper and there was pin-drop silence in the auditorium. I knew my paper word-by-word. I had toiled hard over every word; it was the fruit of several years of labour. I had treated innumerable cases where I had used Rational Therapy. It was not just a research paper. It was a manifestation of my entire life's dedication and hard work.

'Rational Therapy is based on realistic thinking. Its aim is to cure emotional disturbance in a person. Emotional disturbance is not created by a situation or people around us but created mostly by ourselves. Our emotions—love, grief, happiness—are mainly dependent on the beliefs we adopt towards ourselves, others, and the world, and on our interpretation and evaluation of them. Just as we create our own disturbance, we can also unlearn the creation of this disturbance.

'Rational Therapy tells us that, to reduce emotional disturbance, we must first find which irrational belief is dominating our thoughts at the present. Then we have to attack this belief and replace it with rational belief. Since the origin of emotional disturbance is in our irrational thinking, we can spend our lives more happily and contentedly, if we make it a habit to think rationally.

'The importance of mental factors in emotional disturbances has been pointed out earlier by many thinkers. After making a thorough study of the views expressed by these scholars, I have constructed a theory - ABCDE, which explains how this emotional disturbance is created. This theory is the basic principle of Rational Therapy.

''A' is the event happening in one's life. 'B' is belief held towards this event. And 'C' is the consequence, which includes emotions and behaviour.

'If you go deeper, you will learn that the cause of emotions and behaviour is in 'B' and not in 'A'. This can be demonstrated by a simple example. Suppose John is travelling in a train. John is immaculately dressed. His shoes are well polished. He appears cheerful and fresh. As he alights from the train, a person who is in a hurry to climb the train, stamps John's foot very hard. John is angry as he is hurt, and he expresses his anger openly.

'In this case, 'A' is the event in which the man stamps John's foot and 'C' is John's anger, his open dissent over the man's action. From this information, we would normally deduce that John is angry because the man hurt him. This means that we think that the cause of 'C' is 'A'.

'Rational Therapy says that this is not true. 'Something' happens between 'A' and 'C', and it happens so fast that we are not even aware of it. This 'something' is the collection of thoughts that flash in John's mind within a fraction of a second. When the man stamped his foot, John probably thought, *what a careless person. How could he hurt someone in this way? Doesn't he have any manners or discipline? At least he could have apologised. How rude.....*

'In reality, John is hurt just for a few moments. But the thoughts that were generated at 'B' remain in his mind for a long time and keep him in a disturbed state. Now what gives rise to his anger is this belief that to hurt someone in this manner is a not only careless but unjust, too. No one must ever behave in this way.'

'If 'A' is going to cause 'C', everybody who gets trampled should be angry like John. But we do not see this happening. If it were James in place of John, he may perhaps have thought, '... there were so many passengers, but unfortunately it was I who got stamped. It always happens with me. Especially on the day on which I polish my shoes. It's useless polishing shoes....'. He will end up with self-pity. The belief hidden in his mind is that he is always a victim of unfortunate circumstances.

'Let's take a third example, of Jack. He may possibly think, '... Oh, it's just my foot. It's really difficult to manage oneself in such a crowd. Thankfully, I could at least save my glasses and my bag.....' and he would heave a sigh of relief. His attitude is: 'Whatever happened was okay; something worse could have happened.'

'This means that although the incident was the same, the reactions were different because of different beliefs; John becomes angry, James feels self-pity, and Jack is calm. This shows that even if the incident 'A' was same, 'B' was different in each case; consequently, 'C' was also different.

'There is a scientific basis to the statement that our emotions are mainly dependent on how we evaluate 'A'. Physiological psychologist Magda Arnold has shown in her research that not all thoughts create emotions. Only those thoughts that are based on evaluation are capable of creating emotions. Whether this emotion is healthy or unhealthy depends upon this evaluation. The theory of Rational Therapy is similar to this inference. Therefore, a psychotherapist following this therapy gives utmost importance to 'B'. Every person thinks according to his own belief, which he has nurtured. I have divided these beliefs into two classes: the rational and the irrational. Rational belief helps us achieve our goals and irrational belief prevents us from achieving them.

'Now, what causes these beliefs to develop in our minds?

'The first cause is that an inclination towards a specific belief is inborn in every person. The second is the learning we import from society around us, and the third is that our beliefs are our own creation.

'Many of the beliefs which are deeply-seated in our mind are those that we have accepted without testing scientifically and without thinking independently. Thus, we adhere to beliefs which are illogical and unrealistic. These are at the root of unhealthy emotions such as anger, anxiety, depression, self-pity and guilt. I call these *irrational* beliefs. I have found, during my long career as a psychotherapist, that this is the cause of emotional disturbance.

'In the course of my career, I found out many such irrational beliefs falling under the 'B' category. I have classified these irrational beliefs logically into three sub-categories. The first such sub-category encompasses irrational beliefs about one's own self. A person who has this belief thinks that 'I must be perfect in every aspect of life' and 'I must be appreciated by important people, otherwise it will prove that I am useless.' This belief creates inferiority complex, anxiety, and depression.

'The second such sub-category encompasses irrational beliefs towards others. A person who holds such beliefs, thinks that 'Others must behave kindly and justly to me'. He believes that those who do not behave in this way are worthless, that they deserve punishment and should be damned. This belief encourages enmity and anger.

'The third such sub-category encompasses irrational beliefs about the world. The belief here is that the world around *must* make their life easy; or else, everything is worthless. This belief gives rise to inertia and despondence.

'I have found a solution for mental disturbance and that is to bring about a change in these beliefs. In order to achieve this, the client is taught to identify and rigorously evaluate his irrational beliefs. This is the 'D' of Rational Therapy. When you scrutinise these irrational beliefs realistically, with perseverance, you arrive at the last and most important stage—'E'. At this stage, I help the client to grow a rational set of beliefs in place of his irrational beliefs. I teach the client to accept an effective philosophy of life. This marks the end of my ABCDE principle of Rational Therapy.

'Today, there is great chaos in the field of psychotherapy. There is a lack of coherence amongst the various existing therapies. Psychotherapy today broadly means just consulting or giving some professional advice. If we have to stop this, we have no other alternative but to incorporate scientific methods. Rational Therapy follows such scientific methods and, therefore, there is very little possibility of disagreement about 'B', once you know 'A' and 'C'.

'Rational Therapy tells us to search for the cause of emotional disturbance, mainly at 'B'. This facilitates a systematic diagnosis of the client's disturbance. It helps in identifying the irrational belief that has occupied his mind, and in eradicating it. To be able to implant rational belief in its place and encourage its growth is the special feature of Rational Therapy. It is my experience that the success rate of Rational Therapy is much higher than traditional psychotherapy. Therefore, I am confident that Rational Therapy has a great future.'

I returned to my seat with satisfaction. The new psychotherapy I had propounded was a shock to the conventional methods. I never expected to receive a red carpet welcome. I had prepared myself for the criticism that is faced by everyone who tries to break tradition. I was calm and composed. But I knew the reason behind my composure. When you are thoroughly convinced of a thought, you automatically get the strength to pursue it. This strength is so powerful, that it gives you the courage necessary to fight the system. I had waved my flag of rebellion. I was prepared to face its consequences.

In that peaceful state of mind, I remembered my favourite quote by Nietzsche, the great philosopher— 'He who has a *why* to live for, can bear with almost any *how*.'

***

11

'One last signature. That's all.' Mark Baker pointed to the last page of the document. Before signing, I went through the clause.

I, Albert Ellis, hereby apply for a legal divorce from my wife Rhoda Winter Russell in the court of law. I have fulfilled all the formalities necessary for the same....

'You don't have to wait very long to get a divorce these days. Give me a call after a month. You will get your papers,' said Mark.

'Thanks, Mark.' I said as I left his office.

I had kept myself free for this day. There were no appointments. I took the subway and got down at 59th Street. I came to Columbus Circle and took a seat on my favourite bench. I had found peace after a long time. My visits to this place had become very rare in recent days, especially after I married Rhoda.

The second chapter of my married life had just ended. But this time, even after applying for a divorce, I was calm. Was this divorce because of a weak relationship between us or was it because of my excessive involvement in work?

Our marriage lasted for two years. When did our relationship begin to sour? Was it from the days of Rhoda's fracture? Perhaps that was the beginning. But she had definitely begun to dislike my work from then onwards. Unknowingly, I too made some unpleasant comments on her dance a few times. Rhoda possibly took these comments as an insult.

Gradually, we became aware that we were drifting apart. Our professions were different. But that was not the reason for the growing distance. Encroachment on each other's space was the primary cause. The excitement in sex had also begun to diminish. The feeling of oneness had faded. Of late, spending time together would result in stress, instead of happiness. Subsequently, our sexual relations became mechanical—like a routine chore.

I was getting increasingly busier with my work. Rhoda's social life also had expanded considerably. She became fond of her new colleagues and friends and would frequently be away from home. I noticed her special affinity for Furmin nowadays. In his opinion, California was a better place than New York for modern dance. She was convinced that she had very good opportunities as a movement therapist in California, and began insisting on moving there.

My work was my highest priority. I was not ready to make any drastic change in my professional life in order to accommodate Rhoda. I was firm in my decision that I would not leave New York under any circumstance. In reality, this was just a pretext for our legal separation. We had already separated mentally. Somewhere deep into our hearts, we knew that some day we had to separate. Although we never had any serious argument on the issue of moving to California, how long could we carry on this strained relationship? But her decision of moving to California conveniently solved this question.

It was she who put before me the proposal of divorce. Of course, I did not refuse. I considered it immoral to have a relationship with a person against his or her wish. I agreed without any argument to the figure of alimony she claimed, although it was a somewhat unreasonable amount.

I knew the hardship I had to face when Dad had stopped paying alimony to Mom. Besides, I did not wish to drag the issue on grounds of money and waste energy, since the decision was already taken. We had taken this decision with mutual consent. We never had any heated arguments or fights. Something that was typical of our relationship was that we came close very fast and separated also equally fast!

As I returned home from Columbus Circle, a thought kept recurring. What were my exact feelings now? I noted that I had not collapsed in grief. In fact, I had recovered from the situation very quickly. I had not come to any exaggerated conclusions like 'all women are the same' or that 'I do not deserve any long-term relationship.' It had been wrong to marry Rhoda, that's all.

I also made another practical decision. Henceforth, even if I found a woman who was compatible, I would only live with her, I would not marry her. I had shelled out a hefty amount to pay Mark's fees. Additionally, Rhoda's alimony had almost emptied my coffers. I had to start from scratch once again.

Even though my needs were minimal, and I had a habit of living frugally, I was definitely unhappy because I had to spend my hard-earned money on alimony instead of my work. But it was worthless brooding over this loss. It was not going to help me reach my goal in any way. It was necessary to establish an institute to achieve my goal. An outline of a plan for such an institute was already taking shape in my mind.

Rhoda left, and once again I was driven to loneliness. I began analysing the event and my emotions according to my theory of Rational Psychotherapy. I felt that I should make the 'ABCDE' formula more clear. I now found that we do not simply add 'B' to the event 'A', but in fact multiply 'A' and 'B'. So it is actually $A \times B = C$. Because of multiplication, we are escalating the intensity of A to a disproportionate level. So even at C, the emotional disturbance gets unreasonably higher, and this sometimes results in self-destructive behaviour.

My first divorce had caused me severe emotional disturbance. But this time I had Rational Psychotherapy to help me. I could view this incident objectively without nursing any hard feelings for Rhoda. Where else could I find a better example of the practical use of Rational Psychotherapy?

***

The Institute for Rational Living in the Park Vendome Apartment was now two years old. The purpose of this institute was not commercial. I had registered it as a Non-Profit Organisation. For me, Rational Psychotherapy was an educational process. My aim was to guide people, to make their lives more happy and creative.

I wanted the institute to flourish but I was aware that my path was full of hardship.

I utilised every given opportunity to expand my work on Rational Psychotherapy. The paper I read at the Chicago Convention got published in the Journal of General Psychology. Subsequently, the number of invitations increased considerably; and along with it, so did the number of critics.

There was an onslaught of criticism from established psychologists and psychoanalysts. When I would begin to speak about my A-B-C formula, these eminent authorities from my fraternity would become vigilant. They would aggressively attack every statement I made: 'What do you mean by saying that you can understand human emotions in such an easy way? By some A-B-C formula? Is it so simple? ... And what about that unconscious, mysterious and hidden layer of the human mind? Human emotions are so complex and powerful. How can you associate emotions with thoughts? ... This is outrageous.'

Even Freud had to face severe criticism when he had put forth his psychoanalysis. His theory too was considered revolutionary and rebellious. But even those thoughts that are born out of a revolt, later become dogmatic. Therefore, on such occasions, I would fight back with the equal ferocity.

In their opinion, it was non-empathetic to tell someone that his beliefs are wrong. They felt that my therapy was very superficial and that it was incapable of dealing with deeper emotions. To counter this point I would say that my therapy evaluates life-philosophy, which is at the core of our personality. So it is deeper and more fundamental in nature.

Another reason for their wrath was the name Rational Psychotherapy. Some scholars connected the term 'rational' to the seventeenth-century philosophy of Rationalism, which had followers from Europe including Descartes, Spinoza, and Leibniz. This philosophy accepts the premise of 'a priori knowledge', which means knowledge that comes before experience. Hence, some scholars had the objection that a philosophy that supports such a premise cannot be scientific.

I honestly felt that I had made a mistake in calling my therapy rational. There was a vast difference in the meaning of the word as used by me and that interpreted by my opponents. The meaning I intended was 'reasonable' or 'sensible'. Because of this misinterpretation, I had to spend considerable time in the beginning of the lecture in clarification.

Another objection often raised said that: 'Rational Psychotherapy does not give importance to the emotional aspect of a problem as much as it gives to the cognitive aspect.' Some psychologists felt that Rational Psychotherapy meant helping a client become insensitive to emotions.

I took note of this objection seriously. Actually, our cognitive processes are so powerful, that they alone can bring about change in our emotions as well as in our behaviour. Our thoughts, emotions, and actions, are interrelated, interdependent, and set in reciprocally interactive processes. So, in our daily lives, our thoughts become our emotions and emotions become a part of our thinking. In my therapy, quite often I used cognitive, emotive and behavioural techniques. My interventions were very empathetic, as I would use plenty of humorous anecdotes and a variety of examples to reach the clients. Therefore, I totally disagreed with the objection that my psychotherapy ignored the emotions of a client.

The aim of my psychotherapy was not to get rid of all emotions. This is absolutely unnatural and unwanted. To experience an emotion is to be human. Rational Psychotherapy helps us experience healthy emotion. I had made a list of healthy and unhealthy emotions. The former includes concern, sadness, annoyance, regret, disappointment and frustration. The unhealthy emotions were anxiety, depression, anger, guilt, shame, and self-pity. I believed that healthy emotions take us towards our goals, while unhealthy emotions take us away from our goals.

So, when my therapy is viewed from all angles, the objection about ignoring emotions appears baseless. In fact, in my paper on Rational Psychotherapy, I had stated that thoughts, emotions and actions are not separate or disparate processes, but that they all significantly overlap and are rarely experienced in a pure state. Much of what we call emotion is nothing more or nothing less than a certain kind of thought. But emotions and behaviour significantly influence and affect thoughts, just as thoughts influence emotions and behaviour.

In spite of giving this explanation, the word 'rational' was perceived wrongly, as only 'cognitive'. Finally, I decided to change the name to Rational-Emotive Therapy, or RET in short. This change was intended to show that I gave equal importance to emotions and thoughts.

The opposition from my fellow psychologists did not dampen my enthusiasm. They were not able to make me retreat. It was my mission to keep RET alive through every possible resource, like lectures, seminars, conferences, research papers, and essays. The collective effect of all these efforts was that some eminent psychologists like Dr. Edward Sagarin and Dr. Robert Harper began extending active support to RET.

On one occasion, when Dr. Harper was giving a lecture, a psychologist from the audience stood up. He began shouting angrily, 'Dr. Harper, enough of all this bullshit. The field of psychology is hundred years old. It stands solid as a witness against RET and you still stubbornly profess RET? This is extremely annoying.'

Dr. Harper replied very calmly, 'Let us keep aside this hundred-year-old history for a moment. Before that, I want to ask you something. May I? From the tone of your words, I guess you are angry. Isn't it so?'

'Yes.' He agreed, although hesitating a bit.

Dr. Harper continued, 'Now allow me to tell you the exact cause of your anger. It is the talk you had with yourself before getting angry.'

'What talk did I have with myself?' He was baffled.

'You perhaps said, "This Dr. Harper is a fool. And his friend Ellis is a bigger fool. ... What nonsense are they talking about? Why should we tolerate them in a scientific conference?"'

Dr. Harper stopped for a moment and asked, 'Isn't this true?'

'Of course.' He instantly replied.

'This means that you are not angry because hundred-year-old psychology is against this theory. You are angry because of your thoughts.'

Dr. Harper continued, 'I can identify one more emotion from your changing pitch. That is "worry". Were you not worried before getting annoyed?'

'Yes. For a few moments I was worried.' He reluctantly admitted.

'Shall I tell you why you were worried?'

'Yes.'

'Because you said to yourself, "Should I speak? Will people agree with me? Will they laugh at me? If they laugh, will I not be considered to be a fool?" But still you chose to speak. Shall I tell you the reason?' Dr. Harper asked him again.

'Because you again had a self-talk: "Let people say anything. I cannot tolerate this anymore. Somebody has to teach this Harper a lesson". Because of this thought, anger overtook your worry.' Dr. Harper finished his analysis.

That psychologist had no other option than to accept this because he had really experienced those thoughts and feelings. Our emotions and behaviour—'C'—depend upon our thoughts—'B'; and when thoughts change, emotions and behaviour also change. This is the basic theory of RET. Dr. Harper proved the validity of RET with this live example, and gained popularity.

My pen had also become vigorously active along with my lectures. Soon, I published a book called *How to live with a Neurotic at Home and at Work*, which explained the basic principles of RET. This was my first book on the subject. After this book, many more were published. I received encouraging responses from scholars everywhere; all except for my essays on sex. Almost every such essay created a storm.

In fact the decade of 1960 was considered a revolutionary period for sex: the feminist movement, the Gay Rights movement, the spread of hippie culture, government approval for birth control pills—all such changes made the decade noteworthy. Although this period was popularly called the 'liberal sixties', the change in the attitude towards sex was limited only to a certain section of society. Common people still maintained the same conservative and orthodox views about sex. As a result, I kept receiving flak for my rebellious writings.

The editor of the Journal of Social Therapy requested me to write an essay on masturbation among prisoners. From my experience, I knew how poor the enthusiasm of the publishers was in publishing anything on this topic. I jumped at this opportunity and immediately sent it to him. But when I read the actual essay published in the journal, I was shocked. The most important part of the essay was the conclusion I had drawn towards the end. To my surprise, this conclusion was missing! I had stated: 'The jail authorities should not prohibit prisoners from masturbating, because that is the most natural way of expressing a sexual desire.'

To my surprise, this conclusion was missing. When psychologists themselves were finding difficulty in accepting my essay, how could I expect it from common people?

Thanks to my inflammatory opinions, most journals and magazines did not invite me to write—that is, except two publications. These were *The Independent* and *The Realist*. These two well-known magazines regularly published my essays on love, marriage, and sex. Obviously, every essay created a storm of controversies.

When my essay *A New Light on Masturbation* was published, I had to face severe criticism. In this essay, I had scientifically studied every view expressed on this subject. Masturbation does not harm a person, physically or mentally. This view had been already approved by psychologists. I went further and wrote, 'If a person masturbates without feeling guilty, then nothing is better than masturbation, since it is the easiest and the least harmful method. It is an act that relieves a person from his tensions.' This essay too added to my infamy but I continued to place my views before the world.

The book *The Civilized Couple's Guide to Extra-marital Adventures* once again raised a storm. This book was subjected to severe criticism that it was explosive enough to encourage such affairs and could spoil the society.

As my essays began getting published regularly in these publications, letters protesting against my language and content began raining in. The Governor of the State of Arkansas was so furious that he even banned me from entering this state.

Even though circumstances were so adverse, I was not disturbed. I had the choice of not getting disturbed, so these incidents did not affect my work. Apart from some sleep and daily chores, I worked the entire day, almost for sixteen hours continuously.

When I did feel mental fatigue, I would sing 'rational songs'. These were humorous songs composed by me. These songs had a vein of light humour and discussed the effects of having too serious an approach towards life. These songs served as an antidote to my gloomy feelings. I would also call them 'anti-depressing' or 'anti-panicking' songs.

I had chanced upon the idea of composing such rational songs during a conference held at Washington by the American Psychological Association. I was required to present a paper on 'Humour' at this conference. It was my hobby to select popular tunes and compose new songs using them. For this paper, I selected some popular but serious songs and presented them in such a way that it made everyone laugh heartily. Through these songs, my message was: 'Learn to laugh at yourself, not to take yourself so seriously and not to take life so seriously; develop a bit of irrelevance at times, so as to release your insane expectations of yourself, others and life.'

People appreciated these songs and there was a growing demand for it. The outcome of this was a book of songs called *A Garland of Rational Songs*. These songs later found a proud place on the walls of the Institute of Rational Living.

Whenever I felt gloomy, I would sing my favourite song, 'I'm Depressed, Depressed.' This song would tell me- 'In this world, there are much bigger hardships and hurdles. We unnecessarily make a big fuss of over small difficulties, and magnify them. Consequently, we ourselves become the cause of our frustration!'I had composed this song to the music of the album *The Band played on...* by Charles Ward. It went thus:

'When anything slightly goes wrong with my life,

I'm depressed, depressed!

Whenever I'm stricken with chicken shit strife,

I feel most depressed!

When life isn't fated to be consecrated,

I can't tolerate it at all!

When anything slightly goes wrong with my life,

I just bawl, bawl, and bawl!

***

12

'D r. Ellis, perhaps you may not recognise me. I am....'

'Just a minute...,' I gestured him to stop.

It was not necessary to stretch my memory very far. He was Edberg. He had been in therapy with me to increase his self-confidence.

'Edberg Lewis? If I remember correctly, you had come to me in the winter of 1957!'

'Dr. Ellis, you have an extraordinary memory. You remember me even after five years?'

'Thanks. What can I do for you?' I asked.

'Doctor, I have come especially to thank you. I can never forget the therapy I had with you. I was only a sales executive when I came. After five years, there was such an improvement in my performance that I have been promoted to the post of General Manager. I got the letter about my promotion just yesterday. I wanted to convey this news to you immediately. I perfectly remember what you had said to me—that one should not waste time in postponing something that they want to do very intensely. So I decided to see you today itself.'

'Congratulations. You have really made remarkable progress.' I was truly happy.

I was happy as well as surprised with the change I could see. I remembered our first meeting; his shy demeanour, lethargic gait, timid expressions, listless gaze. His frequent actions of wiping his face and pushing back his hair. ... There was no trace of any of these characteristics anymore. The change was dramatic. Now his face radiated confidence. His body language displayed the smartness fit for the post of General Manager.

He thanked me again and left. Even as I finished the day's work, Edberg's case kept coming back to my mind all through the day.

I had discarded the method of psychoanalysis and just begun applying RET when Edberg came to meet me. During those days I had modified RET. I began recording my sessions with the client. I would later listen to this recording over and over again. If I found any loose links in any of these sessions, I would make suitable changes in the next. Sometimes, if necessary, I would send these recorded tapes to my associate psychologists and use their suggestions.

Now, after meeting Edberg, I felt that I should go over his case again. I was extremely happy to see the result of RET, but, at the same time, I was also curious to find how my psychotherapy had brought about this noticeable change. I dug out those tapes and got ready to listen.

I remembered my first meeting with Edberg.

I had asked him to select a recent incident that disturbed him. He narrated an incident from the previous day. He had attended an important meeting at his office that day. Although he had many points to raise in the meeting, he had preferred to remain silent. He felt that he was not confident enough to speak, but later felt depressed since he had wasted the opportunity. In the following few days he remained disturbed. He was not able to work in the office properly. We decided mutually that the aim of the first session would be only to lessen his disturbed feeling.

'First session with Edberg Lewis'… I began the tape.

'So, you mean to say you are disturbed because you were unable to talk, although you had an opportunity and you had some points to make. Right?' I had asked Edberg.

'Yes.'

'Why were you unable to speak?'

'…. … …'

There was silence for some time. Perhaps he took a long breath.

'….That meeting was very important. I had five suggestions to make for improvements in my department. I had rehearsed these points several times. I had an opportunity to put forward my suggestions. I do not know the reason, but I did not speak.' His tone was dejected.

'It's okay. Can you tell me what happened exactly at the time that you remained quiet?'

'I get worried when I have to speak in a meeting,' he answered, in the same dull tone.

'Oh.... Does it mean that the meeting in which you have to speak is the reason for your worry?'

'Yes.'

'I am sure this is not the true reason behind your worry.' I told him firmly.

'What? Is there any other reason?' There was disbelief in his voice.

'We shall have to take a close look at this incident to know the true reason. We will call 'A' the meeting in which you had an opportunity to present your points. You remained silent. We shall call this 'C'. But you have done something between 'A' and 'C'. I was trying to bring Edberg on to the main point.'

'Who, me? I did nothing.' I could sense his shock at this.

'You did do something; but you did that in your mind. What did you do before you decided to stay silent? Try to remember once again.'

'Absolutely nothing.' He answered instantly.

'Are you sure? I guess you talked to yourself at that moment.' I said confidently.

'Oh, did I? ...I? ...I never said anything to myself.' I could feel the astonishment in his voice.

'Our self-talk happens so fast, at the speed of lightning, that we may not be aware of it every time. If you preferred to remain silent, it means you did have some self-talk.'

'....' There was silence for a few moments. Edberg seemed to be rethinking.

'But I..., I honestly tell you, I did not have any such talk.'

'Just try. Think it over again,' I was boosting him.

'...' There was silence again. This time it was much longer. Edberg was probably trying hard to remember.

'No, I really do not remember.'

'It's alright. We talk to ourselves so fast that it is not possible to remember everything.'

'So...what do we do now?' he stammered.

'Listen carefully. Now I will try to guess your self-talk logically. You said that "I must present the five points perfectly without making any mistake. If I cannot, I will be damned".'

'Yes. ...I did think that.'

'Now I will also tell you when these thoughts occurred. It was after the incident 'A', but before the worry you felt at 'C'. The stage at which these thoughts occurred is 'B'.'

'That means 'B' is between 'A' and 'C'.' Now Edberg seemed interested.

'Yes, and it is an important stage.'

'Now I know. The cause of my worry is not the meeting, but it is 'B', my thought about the meeting.' He quickly answered. He had understood what I said.

'Perfectly right. You have understood that the reason for your silence was not what happened at 'A', but the thoughts that flashed in your mind.' I said.

'Yes. Now it is clear to me that the thoughts at 'B' gave rise to my worry. But how to fight this worry?' He was now on the right track.

'For this, we will move to 'D'. At this stage, we will have to thoroughly examine your thoughts at 'B'. Are you ready?'

'Yes. Let's begin.'

'Now suppose there is a person who thinks he must be perfect in his speech and he is worthless if he is unable to do so. How will he fare in actual speech? Will he talk properly?'

'No. He will stay silent.'

'Why?'

'…Because he will feel that if he fails to talk perfectly, he will be proved worthless. So he will avoid such an embarrassing situation.' Edberg's answers were quick.

'Good. Now let us also examine your statement that, 'he must talk perfectly well or else he will be proved worthless'.'

'How do we do that?'

'I will show you. Have you come across anybody who has done his job in an absolutely perfect manner without committing a mistake even once?' I wanted to point out his unrealistic demand in insisting perfection.

With this question, Edberg seemed to be thinking. Again, there was silence for some moments.

'…No.' He appeared somewhat unsure about his answer.

'And suppose, in case a person does some work perfectly, can we say that he will do that work always perfectly?' I asked him.

'I don't understand. Can you please explain?' He seemed perplexed.

'Suppose a person plays a tennis match perfectly and wins. Can he play every match equally well each time and win?' I simplified my point.

'No, of course not. How can we expect this?'

'Why can't we expect this?' I asked.

He began thinking. After a while he said, 'There will always be some variation in his performance each time. How can it be the same every time?' I could see that he had understood my point.

'You are right. There is no universally accepted definition of perfection. And if we keep searching for one, we will never be able to do any work. If a work is done perfectly even once, it is difficult to achieve the same perfection each time. Isn't it?'

His silence was suggestive of his agreement. I further asked, 'Now you can decide for yourself, if your thought at 'B' was rational or not.'

'No, it was not rational. If I insist that I should present all my five suggestions perfectly, I will not be able to speak at all any time.'

'Yes, anything more…?' I wanted him to open up and talk.

'Also, it is not correct to think that I am worthless if I am unable to present my suggestions well.'

'Can you explain why?'

'I do so many things. How does it prove that I am a worthless person if I am unable to do one of them properly? It will only indicate that I am not a good speaker. But to conclude that I am totally a worthless person, will be an exaggeration. Therefore, this conclusion is an irrational conclusion.' Edberg was now on the right path.

'Very good. Now you have realised the discrepancy in your thoughts. Now tell me, what will be your self-talk, if you want to change your behaviour?' I was happy with his progress.

'I will say: I have prepared thoroughly. I have rehearsed my points well. If I get an opportunity, I will definitely make an attempt to present them in the meeting.' He said spiritedly.

'And, if at all…,' I took a pause .

'…I make mistake, if I stammer, if forget any point, nothing disastrous will happen. Nor will it prove that I am worthless.' He completed my sentence with the same exuberance.

'Can we say that we are successful in replacing your irrational thoughts with rational ones?'

'Of course.'

'This is point 'E', which you have reached; where your new thoughts are rational thoughts. At this stage, a person experiences a healthy, useful and effective perspective on life. Will this new perspective help you to achieve your goal?' I asked him in a neutral tone.

'Yes. This perspective shall definitely help me. It will motivate me to talk boldly, without insisting on perfection. I shall speak with confidence without feeling unworthy, even if my speech is imperfect,' he answered instantly.

'In spite of this, if you do make some mistake....'

'...I will not blame myself. On the contrary, I will ensure that I do not repeat the same mistakes again at the next meeting.' Edberg had learned an important lesson of life.

'Good. Now I will teach you a new technique, which will help you use of your rational beliefs at your next company meeting. You are now ready to learn this technique, I think,' I encouraged him.

'Of course, yes. I am eager to know what you intend to teach me next.'

'To begin with, close your eyes. Try to picture the meeting you recently attended,' I told him.

'Should I recollect the entire meeting exactly the way it happened?'

'Perfectly right. Raise your right hand when you start worrying.' I instructed.

'....' There was silence for a few moments. Perhaps Edberg had raised his hand. I heard myself speaking in a clear tone. I said, 'Good. How did you create worry in your mind?'

'I repeatedly uttered the same sentences in my mind.'

'Which sentences?'

'Those five points I had prepared....'

'Alright. Now retain the scene, but create confidence with the help of your imagination. Raise your right hand when you feel confident.'

'....' Again there was silence for some time. Edberg had perhaps raised his hand.

'Good. Now tell me, how did you create confidence within yourself?' There was satisfaction in my voice.

'It was very easy. I repeated the sentences we said at 'E'. That made me confident.' Edberg said animatedly.

'Excellent. Now open your eyes. Henceforth, before every meeting, you will rehearse these two scenes mentally.'

'That means, first create worry and then create confidence. Is that so?' Edberg asked.

'Absolutely correct. If you practise this regularly, you will gradually gain confidence....'

I put the tape recorder off. I had created an intellectual and emotional insight in Edberg's mind at our very first meeting. This insight was necessary to cultivate a rational approach in his mind. The technique I taught him at the end of the session was the emotive method used in RET. I remembered the subsequent meetings. I had tackled only one irrational belief at the first meeting. At the following meetings, I taught him to scrutinise other irrational beliefs arising out of the first one. I had also emphasised on implementing those thoughts, to which he agreed. I gave him homework assignments to make rational self-talk a habit. I closed my eyes and reviewed his case. I understood why there was a total change in Edberg's personality.

The therapy I gave Edberg was not just a therapy; it was a philosophy of life. The therapy had not only accessed the problem he faced at the meetings, but had also reached the root of his disturbance. The impact of the therapy had, therefore, stayed with him.

When I was young, I had arrived at a conclusion about changing a person's behaviour. Edberg's case strengthened this conclusion. Edberg changed only when I provoked him to make a stringent analysis of those beliefs that were deeply rooted in his mind. A person changes only when he changes his fundamental beliefs.

***

'You just heard an interview with the FBI Director, Mr. Edgar Hoover, by our channel representative. FBI is taking all efforts to unravel the mystery behind the assassination of President John F. Kennedy, which took place on November 22nd, 1963. Now stay tuned to hear more about his killer, Lee Harvey Oswald, from the NBC channel reporter, Thomas Campbell.'

I had been too busy in the past few months to watch TV. The assassination of President Kennedy had shocked the entire world. It was the key topic everywhere—on the streets, in shops and at subway stations. Subsequently, even Lee Oswald was murdered by some Jack Ruby within two days of the president's assassination. This led to frenzy amongst people.

'Hello everybody. This is Thomas Campbell of the NBC News Channel. We have just received some more information about 23 year old Lee Harvey Oswald. It says that Lee was an unsuccessful person. He was an average student at school. He was a staunch leftist. He wanted to surrender his American citizenship but he could not get asylum in the Soviet Union. He failed to hold on to every job he had. He was unsuccessful in every field of life. Perhaps this made him violent and....'

I put off the TV. My mind was diverted in a different direction. I did not wish to be distracted. While giving information about Oswald, Thomas Campbell had touched an important issue. Why does a person drive himself to depression if he is unsuccessful in life or if he fails to prove his merit in the world?

I had been thinking about this for many years. I had come across many clients who were emotionally disturbed due to failure. When I studied these cases, I noticed a fact that is ingrained in us from childhood. We presume that a person deserves worth only if he is efficient and successful in his career. One who is not successful is 'worthless'.

The premise that the value or worth of an individual is determined by his performance, efficiency and success, compels people to strive hard to succeed in life and prove themselves. But, in this process, one factor is overlooked. Success depends not only on one's efforts, but also on other circumstantial factors. These are beyond our control most of the time; also, these factors change constantly. Hence, it is impossible for anybody to be successful everywhere and throughout one's life.

When a person invests his individual value as a 'human' in a situation, it becomes dangerous. The thought that he 'must' succeed, takes hold of his mind. This compels him to adopt every possible means to achieve success. Eventually, he becomes incapable of tasting the joy of his own success. He lives under constant anxiety of losing this success. Ultimately, in spite of being successful, he remains agitated.

An unsuccessful person also gets infuriated, like his successful counterpart, because he measures his worth by the success he achieves. Therefore, he is unable to digest his failure, and thinks that he is worthless because he is unsuccessful. This enrages him and instigates him to extreme reaction.

Although I came to realise that persons like Oswald are angry with the world because of their failure, it made me subsequently contemplate on the human values in life.

I felt it was necessary for every person to have some stable value for himself. This value should be in-built and intrinsic. It should not change with external conditions. This value should remain constant in success or failure, through all the ups and downs of life. If he has such values, a person would not harm himself or get disturbed in the face of failure, and would not label himself as inefficient.

To my surprise, I found that modern psychology had not pursued the subject of 'human values'. Therefore, I had to take help from the philosophy of Existentialism. Dr. Charles Hulbeck, with whom I had been in psychoanalysis, was a strong advocate of existentialism. He had encouraged me to use this philosophy in psychotherapy. It was only because of him that I was inspired to study the philosophy of existentialism more deeply.

During my study of human values, many of my questions found answers in this philosophy. I had studied many existentialists like Soren Kierkegaard, Martin Heidegger, Friedrich Nietzsche, Martin Buber, and Jean-Paul Sartre. This helped me form firm beliefs about human values. I was also greatly impressed by views expressed by Paul Tillich in his book *The Courage to Be*.

These thinkers had said that a person has value because he exists and is alive. To exist on this earth is in itself very precious. To be successful or unsuccessful is a trait of that person. This trait does not determine his value as a human being.

I realised that if we teach a person, through psychotherapy, to believe that 'I am a good because I am alive and existing', he would learn to accept himself as a person of value, under any adverse circumstances. Then it is not necessary to depend on any external source for this self-acceptance.

This philosophy was helpful in treating emotional problems but, as I began using it, I was confronted with new problems.

Joseph, one my clients, was very intelligent. He raised an objection to this philosophy. He said, 'Dr. Ellis, you say that a person is a good because he exists. But what is the basis of this assumption? What if I say that, 'he is alive, therefore he is a bad person?''

This was true. I was not able to prove that the mere existence of a person endorses his goodness. I had to agree with Joseph.

But his question stirred my mind. After some hard thinking, I arrived at a conclusion. The concept of 'human value' per se is meaningless, if we consider the total personality of an individual. We cannot evaluate any personality in totality. In fact, it is illogical to decide whether a person is good or bad. We can determine whether his behaviour is good or bad. But it is unjust to label his total personality by some title; this presumes that he will behave in the same manner all his life, till his death. We do not take into consideration any possible change in his behaviour.

In other words, if a person's behaviour is found to be good on one occasion, it does not necessarily mean that he will be good forever. Similarly, if a person behaves badly on a single occasion, he cannot be labelled bad forever. We can evaluate a person's behaviour, but not him as a total person. My behaviour in various situations cumulatively makes me a total entity called 'I'. One specific instance of my behaviour does not decide my total personality.

To elaborate my view that a specific behaviour is distinct from a person's total personality, I took to writing. I expressed my views in the essay *Intellectual Fascism*, which attracted a lot of criticism.

Fascism believes that those who possess certain qualities are inherently superior to others. For example, fascists believe that white complexion, the Aryan race, and the males of the species, are superior by nature to dark complexion, Jewish people, and women, and that, therefore, they should enjoy special social and political privileges.

I expanded this concept and presented a new concept of 'Intellectual Fascism'! This concept was that it is fascistic to believe that all intelligent, cultured, talented, creative and successful people are naturally superior to foolish, uncultured, ordinary, non-creative, and unsuccessful people.

I knew several persons who were proud to be opponents of fascism. They were associated with trade unions or labour movements. But, surprisingly, whenever these persons came across people who displayed low intelligence, they would exclaim in great fury, 'The world will be much happier without such fools.'

Indirectly, they believed in fascism. It was this attitude that I called Intellectual Fascism. In my experience, a majority of liberal Americans spoke bitterly against fascism but were themselves perpetrators of Intellectual Fascism. They did not believe in racism or gender-inequality, but they believed that they were most superior where intelligence and culture was concerned.

I had fiercely attacked this attitude in my essay. I had shown that there is no evidence that says intelligent or cultured people are superior to those who are not. Every type of fascism is indirectly against the principle of equality. Therefore, this school of thought, which claims superiority on the basis of intelligence, talent and success, is nothing but a type of veiled fascism.

There were such strong reactions to my views that no publisher was willing to publish the essay. Of course, I was familiar with this situation. I finally managed to publish this essay, along with six others, in a book called *Suppressed: Seven Key Essays Publishers Dare Not Print*.

When I began expressing views on human values, one question was repeatedly asked: Was the ideology of Objectivism, as depicted by the famous American author and thinker Ayn Rand close to RET?

In some cases, yes. Regarding views about materialism, it was close, but it differed in an important area. Her ideology was based on self-esteem, whereas RET laid stress on self-acceptance.

According to Ayn Rand, a person who is intelligent, efficient, and who shows good performance in some field, can be called as a person of high value. In my opinion, it was irrational and unscientific to evaluate the entire personality of an individual. It is not necessary to prove oneself for self-acceptance. In fact, I went one step ahead. I rejected the concept of self-esteem totally. Self-esteem depends on performance, and performance may depend on external factors, which are beyond our control. It means self-esteem will have ups and downs according to external factors, and may cause emotional disturbance. This is acceptable in her ideology of Objectivism. But the source of self-acceptance is within one's self. It does not change or get affected due to external factors.

Although I differed with Ayn Rand on certain issues, I was quite in agreement with the eminent philosopher Prof. Robert Hartman. I had read his book *The Measurement of Value*, and some other papers. We exchanged our views through letters for a number of years. This correspondence gave shape to my concept of 'Unconditional Self-Acceptance'. But I did not restrict this concept to self-acceptance only. I widened its scope.

In my opinion, a person feels less disturbed when he accepts himself totally, along with his shortcomings, and his natural instincts. Many a time, we accept ourselves, but conditionally. For example, we are happy with ourselves only if we do a particular work in a specific manner. If we fail, we reprimand ourselves. Since we do not totally accept ourselves as we are, we create self-demoralising emotional disturbance in our minds.

Man is basically a fallible creature. He should forgive his own mistakes. How can we expect others to accept us if we do not accept ourselves? When we accept ourselves unconditionally, we can stay assured that there is at least one person on this earth who can take care of us—and that is we, ourselves. Similarly, we also learn to accept people and the world around us unconditionally.

I had concluded that by accepting ourselves, others, and the world unconditionally, we buy peace of mind. A person who does this not only displays empathy and tolerance, but he also faces the uncertainties of life bravely. He accepts his ignorance and his miscalculations with an open mind. He raises his frustration and tolerance levels towards the anomalies and ambiguities of life.

I had a strong urge to write on human values and on unconditional self-acceptance. Coincidentally, I received a letter from Prof. William Davis of the University of Tennessee. He was compiling a book to felicitate Prof. Robert Hartman. He requested me to write an essay for this book.

I was, of course, happy to accept his request. It was a great opportunity. What could be a better way to salute a contemporary thinker of the same school of thought? I sent him an essay titled *The Value of a Human Being: A Psychotherapeutic Appraisal.* Prof. Davis was full of admiration. He sent the essay to Prof. Hartman for his comments.

Prof. Hartman immediately sent me a letter in reply in which he said, 'Many concepts in this essay have not only enriched Psychology but have enriched Philosophy as such....' He further wrote, 'Your essay on human values is so comprehensive and all-encompassing, that you should be honoured with a Doctorate for this essay alone.'

This appreciation had come from a highly-revered scholar who had dedicated his entire life to the study of human values. I was overwhelmed. This was perhaps the most glorious and satisfying moment of my life.

***

13

'Institute for Rational -Emotive Therapy' … 'Chartered by the Regents of the University of the State of New York'.

As I closed the iron gates of the institute, I glanced back at the entrance. It was past evening but darkness had not set in. The name of the institute was glowing in the golden twilight. I looked at it with great contentment.

Feeling spirited, I began crossing 65th Street. I could see the huge gate of Central Park just across. The entrance was crowded with vehicles. I found my way through the maze and entered the park.

After a long time, I had set out for a stroll. The institute was now ten years old. The world had changed so much. Memories of the bygone years floated past as I relaxed in the cool greenery of the park.

I had started the Institute for Rational Living at Park Vendome, with the sole purpose of educating common people about mental health through RET. Later, I began organising workshops and lectures on other related subjects. too. I also began providing books, cassettes, and other study material on RET.

Gradually, the institute became well-known. I started receiving invitations from several institutions to give training in RET. To facilitate this training, I established the Institute for Advanced Study in Rational Psychotherapy. This was affiliated to the first institute. Various training programmes for psychologists, psychiatrists and professional social workers kept me and my associates very busy. I also started an RET centre for common people. Soon the space in Park Vendome became inadequate for the activities of these two institutes and I began the search for a bigger place.

In the course of this search, I landed at Upper East Manhattan for the first time. Its ambience amazed me. Large magnificent embassies of different countries and beautifully designed houses of 'the rich and the famous' adorned the area. So far, I had only heard the names, 'Lincoln Centre', 'Manhattan House', and 'Cosmopolitan Club'. But when I actually stood before them, I felt as if I was in a dream.

'This is the most prime locality, not only in New York, but in the entire country. The famous Town House which was sold for fifty million dollars is also located in this area. Dignitaries like Rockefeller, Roosevelt and Kennedy reside here,' the realtor informed me.

'Now we shall go to 65thStreet and 45th East Avenue. This is a transverse road with one-way traffic. It is always crowded with vehicles. Walk carefully,' he continued.

'This is the building we are going to see.' He pointed across the street.

What a majestic building it was! A six-storey mansion that could easily catch one's attention from a distance! It had huge halls on every floor; each with chandeliers in their ceilings. The corridors were large and spacious. The windows were tall and arched. I was very impressed.

'Such buildings are called Town Houses. These were earlier the residence of aristocrats. They would move from their country houses to these town houses during the season of cultural activities. These houses were fully equipped to cater to their luxurious lifestyle in those days.

'The one where we are now was once the residence of our 28th President, Mr. Woodrow Wilson. At present, it is the office of the Woodrow Wilson Foundation. This building is for sale as the foundation has purchased a new place in New Jersey.' I climbed stairs as I listened to him.

The sixth floor surpassed all imagination. It was very spacious, with a high ceiling. Beautifully designed arches and pillars gave a royal look to the place. I was just bowled over by its architecture.

This floor will be my new home. The institute would be run from the other floors, I thought. I finalised my plan immediately.

Acquiring such a property in a city like New York and in an elite area like Upper East Manhattan was like a dream come true. This dream could become a reality only because of my book *The Art and Science of Love*. Published by Lyle Stewart Books, it had become extremely popular and consistently ranked number one in the Bestseller list. Readers from all sections of society queued before bookshops to buy it. The royalty I received was a huge figure. It was only because of this windfall that I was able to purchase a property worth twenty-five thousand dollars at the age of fifty one.

I moved my residence to the sixth floor, which became my new address. The other five floors were converted into offices, lecture halls, meeting rooms, consulting rooms and conference rooms. I merged the two separate institutes into a single institute, the Institute for Rational-Emotive Therapy. I also obtained the certification from the State Board of Regents as a training institute.

In Park Vendome, I had been handling the entire administration of both the institutes alone. When we shifted to this new place, I appointed office staff. I was the Executive Director of the institute. Paul and Manny joined me as Administrative Consultants. On an average, we were generating revenues of around twenty thousand dollars by organising lectures and workshops, and from the sales of books and cassettes. I would retain a nominal amount for myself and donate the balance to the institute.

The horizon of RET was expanding fast. I conducted several new programmes. Seminars and workshops on different topics, and various training programmes, like Group-RET, Marathon-Group, and Encounter-Group, were held at the institute. Each of these was based on a different technique.

There was more emphasis on practical examples aspects at the workshops we held.

In Group-RET, we would demonstrate the role of social factors in the creation of irrational beliefs.

In the Marathon-Group sessions, we would give training in experiential learning for fourteen continuous hours.

In the Encounter-Group sessions, we would teach through RET, the use of our senses in experiencing an emotion.

Demand for RET began flooding in from all sections. Managers, counsellors, social workers, professionals, lawyers, doctors from all over the country started inviting us for RET. I started touring different parts of the country extensively.

I also started a journal called Rational Living. It was an opportunity for researchers to publish papers related to psychotherapy and comparative studies. Preference was given to research based on rational thinking. We got such a huge response to this journal that I had to appoint an editorial board to handle the workload.

I took a deep breath as I walked through the garden. The fresh air energised my mind and body. Even as I soaked myself in the fragrant air around, my thoughts were hovering only around the institute.

The satisfaction in witnessing an all-round development and the progress of RET was beyond words. I wanted to make RET a comprehensive therapy through my institute. The institute and Albert Ellis have become one. I do not exist without my institute. It is in every breath I take. The progress of the institute is my only passion.

I paused for a moment. I could see Sheep Meadow at a distance. It was a vast green expanse at the south of Central Park. Some old memories were aroused. Along with Paul and Manny, I would often come to this meadow for the Summer Festival. In those days, we would envy people who lived close to Central Park. I could never even dream about living in this area ever in my life. And today, here I was, at a stone's throw from Central Park. All this was possible only because of one book. Some years ago, I had to make frantic rounds to the publishers' offices to get my books published. Today, the earning from just one book had made me the proud owner of such a huge property. How did this happen? Why was this book so popular?

Almost all persons have some kind of problem in their sex-life. The available information generally is only as good as a dressing. It does not go to the root of the problem. Perhaps *The Art and Science of Love* fulfilled this need.

I had been treating problems in sex from the day I started LAMP. But back then, I had not classified sexual beliefs as rational and irrational. I could do this only with the help of RET. Sexual desire is primarily psychological; this was the conclusion I had explained with examples in the book. I had also discussed how we destroy our sex-life by rigidly holding on to many irrational beliefs about sex. In fact, I presented a list of rational beliefs I had come across while scrutinising irrational beliefs.

The first irrational belief in this list was: 'Sex-life should be private and should be treated with utmost secrecy.' I had observed the influence this belief had on the common man. Even couples, who are married in compliance with social customs, tend not to utter any word about their sex-life because of this belief.

A rational belief was that, although sex cannot be performed openly, it need not be hidden. Sex is a personal connection between partners. It is one of the ways of making each other happy.

The truth is that sexual relations, which are considered personal, private and secret, and are prohibited from being discussed openly, are in fact prevalent universally. But ironically, each partner treats it as his or her own secret and private matter. Also, there is great curiosity about sex universally, without exception. Hence, rationally, it is pointless to maintain extreme secrecy about sex-life.

The second irrational belief in the list was: 'To talk openly with your partner about sex or to express your desire, indicates promiscuity.' I had experienced how deep an impact this belief had made on society. I knew many couples who had sex in darkness at night and in silence, without uttering a single word.

The rational belief was that such sex was nothing less than a formality, executed mechanically. When spontaneity in your verbal and physical reactions is directly visible to your partner, the flavour of sex enhances to a great degree.

I had also pointed out in this book another irrational belief — that it is a 'must' for both the partners to experience orgasm at the same point. I had come across many couples who considered that their sexual relations had some shortcoming since both the partners could not climax simultaneously.

These couples would strive hard to achieve this state. If they failed, the partners either accused each other or agonised over it themselves, feeling guilty of incompetent. As a consequence, they would keep pining and deprive themselves from enjoying sex.

The range of sexual desires is so wide, that it is unrealistic to expect both the partners to experience sexual climax simultaneously. Such a demand is unnatural, since sexual desire varies from person to person. This was the rational approach offered by me in the book. Having different climaxes was not harmful to sex. It was just an indicator of the difference in identities. Instead of grieving over the issue, both partners should accept each other as early as possible and make their experience more enjoyable.

There is one more irrational belief held by many people. They believe that when one enjoys sex with a focus on 'perfect sex', it gives us utmost satisfaction.

Rationally speaking, this poses a hurdle in the way of joyful sex. This thought divides the mind into two parts. One part is engaged in sex and the other is engaged in keeping a vigil on whether it is perfect. This division makes us incapable of performing both of these activities properly. It also affects our involvement in sex. Constant evaluation spoils the fun. When there is no such irrational belief, we get fully involved in sex, without bothering about evaluation, and consequently derive utmost satisfaction.

Another irrational belief I had observed was that 'one is lacking something if he or she is not able to perform satisfactorily during sex-play'. I had come across several people who suffered from this inferiority complex to such a level that they showed very little interest in improving their skills.

A person's sex skills are a part of his personality. If he lacks this skill, we can say that he is likely to experience some disadvantages due to this inadequacy. If we think objectively, this is the only conclusion we can draw. A rational belief could be:

The thought that one lacks in his or her sexuality is not only an exaggeration, but also unjust.

I had also discussed one more irrational belief that was prevalent—the belief that sexual desires are purely physical and, therefore, we cannot change them.

A rational belief in this regard is that sexual desires are not purely physical, but they are psychological as well. If there is change in one's attitude towards sex, there can be a change in sexual desire also. Sexual desire varies from person to person. With some efforts, its intensity can definitely change to a certain extent. One can improve his sex-skills, and, by adopting a rational approach, he can enrich his sex-life.

In this book, I had also presented a thorough analysis of irrational beliefs. I attempted to train the reader scientifically to incorporate rational beliefs in place of his irrational ones. The book provides information on the physical and psychological aspects of coitus, the different ways of mental stimulation, and about different methods of enhancing sexual climax. I had also discussed sexual problems that are frequently faced in daily life and included a chapter on counselling to tackle these problems.

There are plenty of books available as a guide to a happy sexual life. These books give information about various methods of sex and sexual positions in detail. But my book told the reader about the psychological aspect of sex. Knowledge of different techniques of sex is the second step towards a happy sexual life, but to possess a rational belief about sex is the first.

We can enjoy our sex life by suitably using different techniques, only if we follow a rational approach. If our approach is irrational, we create several self-damning thoughts during sex. Only having knowledge does not help much in actual practice of these techniques. In my book, I had given a psychological analysis of sexual desires. This was written especially to create awareness about the mental processes of one's own mind and of one's partner. Perhaps it was this analysis that had lent uniqueness to this book and made it so popular.

I looked at the institute-building with great satisfaction. It made me forget the fatigue of my long walk and revived my cheerful mood. But there was also another reason for my cheerfulness.

I knew Jane was waiting for me. She had joined the institute as my secretary when I moved to this place. It is really difficult to recollect when and how she conquered my heart. Our companionship was perhaps the happiest period of my life. Excited with thoughts about her, I eagerly entered the building.

***

It was evening, around six-thirty; growing dark. Although it was warm inside because of the heater, the weather outside was cold. I was ready to proceed to the lecture hall. Every Friday was reserved for the Friday Night Workshop. I had started this workshop to solve problems in the day-to-day lives of common people. It was held from seven to nine. The day and time was specifically selected keeping in mind that working-class people had a holiday on weekends. A fee of just seven dollars was charged and any person could attend.

The other programmes run by the institute were shared between me and my associates. But the responsibility for this workshop was entirely mine. Later, this workshop became so popular, that people started enquiring if any institute called Friday Night Workshop was really in existence.

This workshop was interactive. Any participant could come voluntarily and discuss his problem before the audience. I would request the audience to participate in the discussion. Anybody from the audience could help him in finding a solution.

After this interaction, I would talk with the person. I would present his case in the ABCDE format. Many a time, suggestions from the audience would greatly differ from mine. Then there would be a discussion on which method was more useful. The difference between our methods would become clear in this discussion. With this live example, I would explain the shortcomings of their methods and how RET could be used.

During these two hours, I normally invited two participants onto the dais to present their respective problems. I would then hold two counselling demonstrations before the audience. In a short period of two hours, I would show how effectively one could use RET. I would record the demonstrations and give the recording to the participants immediately, as a gift.

In the beginning, this workshop was held in the fifth-floor lecture hall. Later, the crowd increased to such an extent, that we had to open the lecture hall on the fourth floor also. It became difficult to handle the ever- increasing crowd; soon, I fitted the halls with close-circuit TV systems.

The intercom buzzed just then.

'Sir, this is Michael from the registration counter. Today, we have an extraordinary rush for registration. Our two lecture-halls are already full to their capacity. I stopped enrolling new registrations at six-thirty itself, but still there are many more waiting. These people have come from faraway places in this cold weather with great expectations. Sir, what can be done?'

I thought quickly.

'Michael, listen. Open the balcony on the fourth floor. Arrange for chairs. There is a connection for the TV in this balcony too. Move the TV from the conference room to this balcony. It should be okay'.

'That's fine, sir. I will get this done immediately.' Michael seemed to be satisfied with the solution.

I proceeded to the hall. Michael had done his job. I began the workshop. Today, Kenneth and Steven's cases were to be discussed. I finished the two live counselling demonstrations within the scheduled time.

I wanted to abolish the misunderstandings held by people. Normally, people expect the counsellor to speak kindly with them. But in my workshop, they would realise within a short time that I did not spare words while attacking their irrational beliefs. Although I showed my concern for them, I would talk very bluntly and in a forthright manner, with very little sympathy.

I did this with a purpose. I wanted to teach the participants so that they would get rid of the irrational presumptions, suchas the belief that: - 'I am in distress, so the other person has to console me. He must hear me sympathetically. This is my grave necessity.' There is no need to show emotional dependence even on the counsellor. It is not necessary to be liked or disliked by the counsellor to solve one's problem.

My kind talk would make them think: 'Dr. Ellis likes me. That means I can accept myself without trivialising myself.' In order to accept themselves, they might feel a dire need for acceptance from the counsellor. Paradoxically, in the end, this would have resulted in encouraging their tendency for self-trivialisation.

I would teach the participants to accept themselves, irrespective of whether others accepted them or not. To learn this, it is not always necessary for others to behave kindly with them. I showed in this workshop that one can help in solving a problem without being particularly kind and sympathetic.

Just as I taught the participants not to bother with whether they were liked by Dr. Ellis, in the same way, I did not burden myself with the thought that they must like me. I would always warn myself that being liked or disliked by others does not prove my worth.

Due to my forthright and outspoken way, many people were scared of me, but the experience I had that day was far different.

The last fifteen minutes of the workshop were reserved for the question-answer session. When this was almost over, Kenneth raised his hand.

'Dr. Ellis, I do not have any question. I want to say something, if you will kindly allow me.'

'Of course, you may. Please feel free. I will be happy to know your views.'

'Dr. Ellis, before coming to you, I had consulted another psychotherapist. I sincerely liked him very much. But frankly speaking, even though I liked him, he was not much help in solving my problem. On the other hand, I do not have much affection for you, but your counselling has definitely helped me.'

I was really happy to receive this acknowledgement from him. I said, 'Mr. Kenneth, I am thankful for your honest appraisal. I do not want to be known as a kind-hearted counsellor. I would be glad if people find me helpful. It is my duty to help, not to love. The sole aim of this workshop is to teach you to solve your problems. I am very happy that you have understood this.' The workshop ended with my reply.

Immediately after the workshop, I rushed to my cabin. It was my habit of years to note down a review of the day's work on the same day. I became busy in writing the questions and answers, about the modifications needed in the therapy, but the intercom interrupted my thoughts. It was Jane on the other end.

'Al , did you have your sandwich?'

'Sandwich?' I could not imagine what sandwich she was referring to.

'I was sure you did not eat. Don't you remember what the doctors said? They have strictly warned you to eat every two hours. I knew you would forget this because of work. I had reminded you to eat even when you left for the workshop. But you didn't notice. Just look towards your right. You will find a plate with a sandwich. Did you? Now eat it immediately. It's already late.'

I looked to the right. A sandwich wrapped in foil was kept at a corner of the table.

'Jane, thanks. I will have it.' I was overwhelmed. Jane remembered every small detail about me.

'And yes. Don't sit there too long. Come upstairs fast. I am waiting for you.' She finished her instructions.

I was so busy that I had forgotten to eat. Eating at regular intervals was very important for my health. My diabetes was getting worse day by day. The doctors had to increase my insulin units. I would face extreme thirst and sip water throughout the day. This often made me lose my appetite. Besides, I had to go to the washroom very frequently.

It was necessary to eat every two hours and exercise regularly. I would go for a walk in Central Park during the summers, and in the winters I would exercise at home. But I was much undisciplined in my food habits. Whenever the situation became worse, I would fall into an insulin coma. Then they would carry me to the hospital as an emergency case. This would happen at least two to three times a year.

As I drew the plate of sandwich close, I saw the glass of grape juice next to it. I remembered what the doctors had told me.

'Dr. Ellis, you are suffering from a disease called hypoglycaemia. It develops in patients who have been insulin-dependent for a number of years. In this, the blood sugar level suddenly goes down so much that the patient can go into a coma. This is a very dangerous state. If the patient does not get sugar immediately, there are chances of permanent brain damage and even death. The first action that should be taken in such an emergency is to give the patient glucose or fruit juice immediately. You must always carry glucose with you. If you do not follow this, mind you, it can turn fatal.'

According to his instructions, I always carried a Glucagon Emergency Rescue Kit with me. But the sight of a glass of fruit juice wherever I went, was a mystery. Nowadays I saw glasses of fruit juice everywhere around me—on the lecture hall table, in the conference room corner, near the microphone during the workshop and, of course, in my cabin.

Then, it struck me. This must be Jane's idea. I was very sure.

'Al, I am so worried about you. I want to accompany you.' She would insist whenever I went on tour.

'No, Jane. So far I have managed all alone. I can take care of myself. If you come with me, I will become dependent on you. I won't be able to handle things in your absence. I must learn to be self-dependent,' I had explained firmly.

Thereafter, Jane never insisted on accompanying me, but perhaps it was she who had started this new idea. Even during the recent Los Angeles tour I had spotted fruit juice wherever I went. Definitely, this was Jane's business. Jane looked after all the correspondence related to my invitations from various institutions. She was no doubt concerned about me. But this was sheer harassment. I was not a child. In fact, I was extremely annoyed.

I decided to see her immediately.

'Jane! Jane!' I was almost screaming as I entered.

'Yes? What's the matter Al?' Jane came rushing from inside.

I was still holding the glass of grape juice in my hand. I talked furiously. I complained about the barrage of fruit juice she forced upon me.

'Jane, tell me the truth. Do you write about my health to the institutions I visit?' I asked her in a stern tone.

She was silent. She quietly went inside and brought the file in which the record of all the correspondence was kept. She handed over the file to me.

I browsed through the file. It consisted of information-leaflets, course-brochures, commercial terms and conditions and also a letter marked Very Important in bold letters. It said:'Dr. Albert Ellis has severe diabetes. One of its symptoms, 'Hypoglycaemia', can occur any time. His blood sugar level drastically lowers all of a sudden, and this can turn fatal. Hence we request your medical team to stay alert. All those places where Dr. Ellis is likely to be present should be equipped with grape or orange juice or glucose.

'He might repeat the same sentences or same jokes again and again. This is the first indication of his low sugar level. If you ask him, he will say he is alright. He may even get very angry. At this stage, it is extremely necessary to make him drink the juice, forcefully, if required. Or else there may be a danger to his life....'

I stared at her in amazement.

'Jane, was this necessary?' I asked her.

'Yes. I can't see you sick,' she said calmly.

'But I always have my rescue-kit with me.'

'Al, what is the use of simply carrying the kit with you? One has to be conscious enough to use it. Do you know what happens to you in that state? You become uncontrollable. You scream. You bite. You romp around crazily. You are unable to keep your balance. You shiver. You never smoke or drink, but in this state you create a ruckus like a drunkard. Suddenly you gather so much strength that I cannot handle you. Coincidentally, whenever this happens, I happen to be alone with you. Of course, you may not remember anything, because in that state you lose control over your brain.'

I was stunned. I knew everything about hypoglycaemia but this behaviour of mine was unknown to me.

'Jane, is this true? Do I create such chaos?' By now I had sobered down.

'Yes, Al. Every word is true.'

'What do you do then?' I asked miserably.

'When you start behaving erratically, I force you to have the juice. The moment it enters your body, like magic, you regain your senses. Al, don't be angry, even I keep a pack of juice in my purse. Look at this.' She opened her purse to show me.

I was ashamed. I became silent.

'What's wrong? Why are you so serious? Come on, Al. I'm always there with you. Don't be so worried.' She tried to restore normalcy.

'Jane, do you hate me when I behave this way?'

She looked deep into my eyes. In a cool and calm tone she said, 'Should I be honest? Then none of what you said.' There was a naughty twinkle in her eyes.

'Al, you may be a great psychologist to the world. But to me, you are my sweet little baby,' she said, as she embraced me and kissed passionately.

***

14

22ndFebruary, 1980

'Dear Jane,

The world knows you as Ms. Janet L. Wolf but to me you are just Jane. My beloved Jane. My dearest Jane. Jane, not Janet. A name short and sweet just the way you are. I began calling you Jane because my younger sister is also named Janet. I do not exactly recollect when 'Jane' entered my life and occupied my entire existence. I also do not recollect when this Jane transformed me, Albert Ellis, to just 'Al'. How easily you could make this change. Now everyone addresses me as Al.

Jane, do you remember? We have completed fifteen years of our companionship today. It is one of the most special days of my life. I had decided to gift you something in celebration. The streets are still overflowing with gifts meant for Valentine's Day. I made several rounds of the shops to select a good one for you. But none of them deserved you. I wanted to gift you something very exclusive. But the more I thought about you as I scanned them, the more worthless they appeared to me.

So, instead of some mundane gift, I decided to offer my heart itself through this letter. I am sure you will value it more than anything else. To be frank, I am not articulate like you in expressing love. You are skilful in this art. But now I am learning. This is the magic of your companionship.

Jane, we are so much in tune with each other. I can easily guess the way you will react when you read this letter. You are also perhaps equally confident about my reactions. I am very sure you will be touched. You will hug me tight, kiss me passionately and whisper, 'I love you Al. I love you so much.' Holding me, you will ask, 'You keep harping 'rational-rational' all the time. Tell me how did my rational Al mellow down today?'

In reply, I will press you close to my heart and say, 'Darling, RET is not only rational but also emotive. Don't you think you deserve this today? It's a special day for both of us.'

The days have flown by so fast. Our relationship is now fifteen years old. But even today the memory of every tender moment spent with you, is so fresh.

Jane, do you remember our first meeting? After moving to this place in Upper East Manhattan, the institute began flourishing at a fast pace. You had just joined as a secretary. I had interviewed you for this post. The impression you left after the interview was only that you were a 24-year-old tall, slim, attractive girl. You seemed to be intelligent and you also had some experience in publishing.

Apart from routine office work, we had hardly any interaction. Within a short period, you became well versed with the administrative work of the institute. You soon became interested in the various activities and began attending the lectures, seminars and workshops on RET.

I noticed that you attended all my lectures. Initially you were just another person in the audience to me. But you attended so regularly, that gradually I began checking your presence before beginning every lecture, and later, this became a habit. You would listen with rapt attention. Your eyes would remain glued upon me throughout the entire lecture. Your earnest desire to learn would be evident in your eyes. You seemed to treasure every word I spoke. This was definitely a unique experience.

There was never any direct communication between us but the expressions on your face spoke a thousand words. Those meaningful glances. That enigmatic smile. I could understand the play of emotions behind all this. Your unspoken dialogue would leave me perturbed. Slowly you created a special place in my heart. I began searching anxiously for you in the audience before every lecture. The exchange of glances when we would meet in the corridors, or your gaze which followed me everywhere, or the turmoil in your eyes if I was late…. I began registering mentally not only your presence but every expression of yours.

27th September. My 52nd birthday. Everybody at the institute wished me, except you. I had already seen a red rose on your table in the morning as I was entering my cabin. But the moment you saw me, you hurriedly pushed the flower inside the drawer and fumbled 'Good morning'. The hurry in hiding the rose, the pretence to cover this action, and the naivety in this flurry; it was amusing and gladdening. I could not but help smile secretly.

The day was busy as usual. It was evening. I began to wind up. But your rose had not yet reached me. Although I was occupied in work, the picture of your rose kept on popping in my mind throughout the day. I was about to leave for the day when there was a knock on my cabin door. I knew it could be none other than you. You entered the cabin meekly and stood before me without speaking for some time. Those few moments seemed like hours. Then, very softly, you wished me and gave me the rose. I was observing you. You tried to appear composed but I could feel your anxiety even in that slight touch of your hand. Your face was displaying a mix of modesty, shyness and control. I could easily guess what played in your mind at that moment.

Your wish was so simple. You wanted to wish me with a rose. But you were restless throughout the day. I could guess its reason. I was sure that you must have thought at least a hundred times during the day, over the selection of the right time and right place to present the flower to me. Perhaps you even came several times up to the cabin door but retreated without wishing me. Every time, at the last moment, you lost the courage you had mustered up for this action. Finally, you could manage to enter my cabin only when the office was about to close for the day.

I was sincerely moved by your demeanour. This experience was quite new to me. We did not exchange any words. There were no suggestive gestures. The interaction between us was very subtle. But your action hinted at something deeper.

The feeling was strange. I was not familiar with such an inscrutable and unspoken communication. Whenever I liked a woman, I would express my feelings without any inhibition. If

I had sexual desire for a woman, I would tell her so without mincing words. But further progress of that relationship depended on the consent of the woman. If she refused, I would honour her freedom of denial and end the relationship without getting disturbed. This was possible for me because I was never emotionally involved in such relationships. I never approved of any inhibitions in expressing feelings. In my opinion, such behaviour amounted to hiding true feelings behind a veil of fake decency.

As I thought more about your silent communication, I realised that you did not intend to hide your feelings. There was no secrecy, no inhibition, and no deliberation in your behaviour. There was absolutely no articulation. Actually, you were ignorant about your true feelings. This was exactly the reason for your naivety. But this naivety was very sweet. Your silent language had its own unique beauty. I was definitely new to such a language. But the underlying love in it had definitely excited me.

This love was so subdued. It was not coercive. It was not seductive either. But it pleased my mind and body. Jane, I wanted this mute dialogue between us to stay forever. Had you tried to verbalise it, it would have lost its flavour and suppressed its inherent spontaneity. It would have lost its delicacy. Jane, your simple gesture had won me over instantly.

Your rose was of great significance to me. After you had gone, I caressed it to feel its softness. Then I wore it carefully on my coat, near my heart. Even today, it stands very proudly in a vase on my writing table. Its petals have withered but it still has the capacity to enliven me.

Later on, we kept meeting frequently. These encounters were very casual and natural. It was never necessary to make any special attempt to arrange these meetings. I never touched you. I knew your mind was still not conditioned to move on to physical love. You were still bound by social pressures and by natural shyness. I did not want to mar the freshness of our relation by some highhandedness from my side.

Your naive demeanour had a distinct language of its own. Your reluctance, controlling your mind even when you were eager to go ahead; checking the true intention behind my actions; all these nuances were so captivating. You were not feigning indifference, it all happened very naturally. Perhaps this rendered a unique sweetness to your behaviour.

You were taking me through the realms of unspoken love and I wanted to show you the intricacies of sex. We were travellers towards the same destination, the total union of our identities. But on different paths. Gradually our paths merged and reached the destination—our live-in-companionship!

One fine morning, I sprained my leg. This incident led to the beginning our companionship in its true sense. I was virtually handicapped. It had become very painful to do daily activities. I desperately needed some help. Of course, I thought only of you. You too were anxiously waiting for my call. I was sure you would agree, but I was doubtful whether you understood the gravity of the implications of your answer. I did not want to keep you in the dark about my feelings, nor did I want to deceive you or take advantage of your young age.

22nd February! How can I ever forget that day! I remember every moment. It was George Washington Memorial Day, a public holiday. Our institute was closed. I took you to 'The Pierre' for dinner that evening. Since it was very close to the institute, we walked down the way. It was biting cold outside. The air was very chilly. But we were oblivious to everything at that time.

We entered The Pierre. Its magnificent ambience further lifted our mood. The restaurant had a grand lobby with black and white Italian marble flooring. The furniture was antique with a reddish tinge. Colourful flower arrangements were artistically placed all over. The atmosphere was very cheerful.

We went to the dining hall on the 21st floor. It was a circular hall with full glass windows. Large crystal chandeliers emitted soft yellow light. Huge murals on the walls between the arches gave a majestic look to the hall.

We selected a table in a corner near the window. From the window, amidst the twinkling lights of the city we could see the brightly illuminated Times Square, Lincoln Theatre Subway and the Theatre District. Soft piano music was being played and it gave a romantic charm to the atmosphere.

'Beautiful! Just beautiful! Al, I feel as if we are sitting in a huge glass crystal.' You were very excited.

I smiled in reply. Even I was somewhat excited.

'Al thanks for selecting this place.' You said.

'My pleasure.' I was really happy.

Inside it was warm and comfortable. We removed our overcoats, scarves, mittens and put them aside. Now I could behold your beauty to my heart's content. There were two swan-shaped candles on a side-table near you. Your face was glowing in the gentle light of those candles.

I was eager to kiss you. With great difficulty I controlled myself. I talked on various topics. I talked about marriage, about expectations from my life-partner, about companionship, about my views on sexual freedom.... It was an outpour waiting for a long time to be shared with you.

I told you, 'We will have a live-in-relationship. Its foundation will be our individual happiness. A relationship loses its charm when you try to fit it within some framework. Neither of us will be bound by marriage or by loyalty. We shall not force each other to remain loyal even in matters of sex. I believe that it is irrational to think that only one person in our entire life can be compatible with us. If either of us gets interested in someone else, we will be free to have a relationship with that person. If either of us feels that our relationship is not pleasurable, then that person has the right to exit. In such a situation I expect that each one of us will honour the freedom of the other person, without any bitterness.'

I was firm also on my decision of not having any children. I had dedicated my life to one single goal. My first priority was my work. RET was my child in a real sense. Bringing up children would have hampered my efforts in achieving my goal. Although children bring stability and strengthen life, it was harmful to a live-in-relationship. A woman gets more involved in child-rearing than a man. This involvement eventually becomes a hurdle in a live-in-relationship if one of the partners wishes to end the companionship. I sincerely wished that you should arrive at your decision without any emotional involvement or pressure. I wanted you to think independently. I wanted you to take the decision yourself without seeking any external help.

The most important factor in our relationship was our age difference. You were younger than me by 28 years. I was more than twice your age. I was of your father's age. I had been divorced twice. And you? You were new to a man's love, untouched, virgin, like a delicate flower not yet fully blossomed. If you wished, it was possible for you to find a socially compatible young partner. For me, the decision for live-in-companionship was easy but for you it was really very tough.

You listened to me very attentively. You were undisturbed but you grew quiet. The animated expressions on your face had disappeared. I still remember what you said. You said, 'Al, I said 'Yes' not because I have been carried away by your greatness, or without giving thought, or in haste and anxiety. I have taken this decision only after thinking very seriously. Whenever I ask myself about the expectations I have from my life-partner, I find that Al, it is only you who fulfils all those expectations.

'Al, our minds have become one. You know what I want to say even before I speak. You know my mind so well. You can put into words those feelings that are difficult for me to express. My thoughts, of which I am not sure myself, you can untangle them easily, one by one, before me. And when you do this, my belief that you have understood my mind gets vindicated. Al, when two hearts unite, external factors like age and marital status absolutely do not matter.

'About the compatibility factor; yes, I can certainly find a young man. But a question always occurs to me: who decides this compatibility? Age, status, money are issues of pragmatism. Who can check the compatibility of two minds even if there is compatibility on these issues?

'Yes. The decision about a live-in-relationship was really difficult. Some might call it sheer madness. Others might think that this is a rash decision, taken in haste. I am aware of this. But when I put aside all these social pressures and peep into my mind, I see only you, Al! Only you!

'Al, you have taken charge of my entire mind and body. It is much more difficult to reject my mind, than to make the decision of living with you. I have spent several restless nights without sleep before arriving at my decision. Frankly speaking, RET was of great help in the process of taking this decision.

'I do not care what others might say, but I know that this decision will hurt my Dad and Mamma. They love me so much. I really feel bad about that. But I have no option. So at present I want to hide this from them.

'I am also aware that it is more difficult to implement a decision after making it. I am already firm on my decision. But Al, if you support me, I will get the strength to face its consequences. Will you support me?'

Now it was my turn to get overwhelmed. I certainly fell short in recognising the greatness of your love. How easily you demonstrated before me, my concept of unconditional acceptance. You had accepted me totally as I was. Along with my faults. Along with my strengths and my shortcomings. You had shown courage in sacrificing the love of your parents too.

You were not aware, Jane, what a great gift you had given me. I knew your decision required extraordinary courage. I also knew that it required a strong mind, a tough mind.

And you proved that women did possess this strength!

Jane, I was seeking exactly this all my life. Like a mirage, it kept evading me. I had lost all hopes of receiving such unconditional love in life. But unexpectedly it appeared before me in your form. I was ecstatic. I could not hold myself.

I pulled you close, gently pressed my lips on yours and kissed you deeply. We had become one. My inner lava was now cooling. My writhing mind was calming down. A new life had begun to sprout within me.

You know whom I remembered while returning?

I remembered Prince Edward VIII, who was to be crowned as the King of the United Kingdom, in 1936. He was deeply in love with an American woman called Mrs. Wallis Simpson, who was waiting for her second divorce. Edward was admonished by the British people and also by the Church of England, because she was a two-time divorcee and also from a low lineage. He was harassed for choosing such a woman and was also pressurised with the threat that they would reject his claim to the throne. This love affair had created a constitutional crisis in Britain in those days.

It was suggested he should maintain her as his mistress after he was crowned as a king. This was a very practical solution. But Edward ruled out this suggestion with great determination. He was against insulting his love by keeping it secretive. He showed extraordinary courage in foregoing his kingship for the sake of his love and cleared the path for his younger brother Prince Albert, to become the emperor of the United Kingdom. Finally, he abdicated his monarchy after a short reign of 326 days.

The entire world was screaming and asking Edward, 'What have you seen in Wallis that you are ready to renounce the throne for her?' Truly, it is not possible to evaluate why he was infatuated with Wallis. Their love cannot be measured by conventional thinking. But definitely, it was far more intense and deeper than what one could perceive. It had challenged the rules of this insensitive world.

Edward had the capacity to pose before a challenge and to face its consequences. Those who lack this capacity, treat this as madness. But a sacrifice on this scale, for the sake of love, lends a significant meaning to this so called 'mad' action. In such a situation, questions—such as, 'why did they like each other, or what qualities made them fall in love'—are totally frivolous. This madness reaches such a height that such questions appear Lilliputian before them.

I still remember every word of Edward's speech when he was leaving Buckingham Palace after Prince Albert's crowning ceremony. In this speech, he said, 'You must believe me when I tell you that I have found it impossible to carry the heavy burden of responsibility and to discharge my duties as king as

I would wish to do without the help and support of the woman I love.

'And I want you to know that the decision I have made has been mine and mine alone. This was a thing I had to judge entirely for myself. The other person most nearly concerned has tried up to the last to persuade me to take a different course.

'I have made this the most serious decision of my life, only upon the single thought of what would, in the end, be best for all.'

I was not sure if I was as courageous as Edward, but I became sure that you definitely possessed that courage. As we returned from the dinner that day, only one feeling had occupied my mind—a genuine respect for you.

Thereafter, our life has been a beautiful celebration of love. Your company would enliven me. You had totally relinquished yourself to me. I had never experienced such intense love. I was amazed by your devotion. In love, when you also concentrate on your partner's happiness, love-making becomes the elixir of your life. It becomes the highest source of inspiration in life.

I was a seasoned player and you were a complete novice. You did not have any expertise in playing back to male advances. There was so much naiveté, so much tenderness in your responses. Your body would quiver with my slightest touch. The feel of your quivering body would set me on fire. I would open you up by different ways of love-making, and in reciprocation, you would uninhibitedly offer me your lissom body.

Our minds were in tune, our hearts had become one. So powerful was our oneness that it gave us the strength to draw each other together, irrespective of the obstacles of society, age or social status. The rapturous moments spent with you made me forget all the woes and worries of the outside world.

There are many gratifying moments that I vividly remember today. When we started living together on the sixth floor, you decided to change the interiors. You were very interested in interior decoration. You spent several hours deciding the wall paint, the type of furniture and coordinated drapery. Richard Moore, the architect appointed for this work, was also your find. I would always overhear your discussions with him.

'Richard, how about creating two levels in the bedroom?'

'This staircase is a bit narrow. Can you make a little wider?'

'I want a French door and plenty of windows for this balcony. The door should of full-length glass.'

You had asked him to revise his plans many times when they were not to your satisfaction.

'Richard, this is not a genuine parquet floor sample. It does not have that geometrical pattern typical of the true parquet. Also, the wood is not thick enough to last long. I am rejecting this sample. Please arrange for a new one.'

Your argument would continue while I would remain engrossed in my reading. I never understood your talk, but to see you moving around enthusiastically would give me immense pleasure.

You had varied interests in life. You were very involved in pursuing them. I had shut my doors to many such interests. I was obsessed with only one thought. My life-goal. My requirements were minimal. A shelter, some food and a bed. Interior decoration did not fit in my philosophy of life. While living a thrifty and frugal lifestyle, I had killed the artistic bent in me before it could mature. I had not nurtured my love for art deliberately. It would have distracted me from my goal.

Perhaps this was the reason I was referred to by many with adjectives like 'curt', 'arrogant', 'eccentric', 'mad', and 'stubborn'. I frequently used so-called 'indecent' words in my writing, and this had given rise to many scandals about me. I had faced every attack from society with determination and self-respect but at the cost of my softer self. I had totally forgotten to develop a taste for such small simple things of life.

Jane, I see this softer side of my personality, which I had buried deep down myself, revived in your form. I am so touched. I am always criticised by the world for my behaviour, but you have never mentioned it nor shown any disapproval any time. Like other women, you have never questioned me as to why I devote all my time to my work, or why I have still not purchased a car. Even by remaining silent, you have understood me entirely.

I do not seek any sympathy from you Jane. I have the strength to bear the consequences of my decisions. I only want you, your presence around me. After a tiring day when I relax in your arms, I feel so refreshed. My fatigue vanishes in a moment.

How colourful has our romance been these fifteen years. Arguments; debates; periods of silence after a huff. All these shades of love have made our relationship fascinating.

Do you remember? In the beginning, sometimes you would get annoyed with me. I would make promises of an outing in the evening. But the moment I would enter the office I would get transported into my world of RET. Like an obsessed man I would work the whole day. I would forget all the plans and promises given to you. And then when I would return home, oh…. With what fury you would receive me. You would calm down only after some amorous coaxing.

'Only you and you alone are responsible for my anger. For you, your work is more important than me.' You would burst out. Sometimes you almost cried when your temper rose too high.

'Jane, please cool down.' I would say. 'It is quite natural to get angry for a moment, when the reason is genuinely serious. But your anger has been simmering for a long time. It means that the reason is not external. It is because you have fanned your anger with some self-talk. Try to remember what you said to yourself before you became angry.' I would try to pacify you. But my words would only add fuel.

'Al, don't experiment your RET with me.' You would warn me in irritation.

After sometime you would calm down and confess, 'Al, I uttered almost a thousand sentences in my mind. Many more than I actually spoke. It is this self-talk at the root of our emotions, isn't it? Why don't we stop talking to ourselves, Al?'

Whenever I explained to you, the theory of RET would pour out from me with great force.

'Jane, very rarely are there instances when we do not talk to ourselves. Even if we decide to stop this talk, the thought that 'I am not talking to myself at the moment' does occur. So finally it again amounts to some self-talk. Do you know the number of words we speak to ourselves? Almost around 600 to 800 words a minute. We talk to ourselves very rapidly. We talk every moment. But not always at a conscious level. This talk goes on so incessantly that, although outwardly we are engaged in some activity, it is actually active at the bottom of our mind.

For example, right now, I am explaining and you are listening. But between these external actions of talking and listening, some self-talk is also going on.'

'Shall I tell you what that talk is ?' You said enthusiastically, 'Although, apparently, you are talking to me, in between you were saying, 'How much of my talk has she understood? Should I explain to her in some other way?' And although I was apparently listening to you, my self-talk was 'Does Al's talk has any substance? How much of his talk applies to me?''

I congratulated you and said, 'You have guessed my self-talk very accurately...except one. I also said 'You look more beautiful when you are angry. But should I be satisfied just watching my beautiful angry Madame. When can I enjoy her beauty?'

At this, there was a seductive blink in your eyes and the next moment we were lost in our own world in each other's arms. But Jane, I have noticed that of late, you have really sobered down.

Our day starts at six. I work in the office from nine in the morning up to eleven at night. Except for lunch and dinner breaks of half-an-hour each, I work non-stop. This has been my routine for several years. I reach the lecture hall exactly fifteen minutes before the lecture. Although you live with me, I never expected you to get up early and share my morning chores. But you did so.

'Jane, please don't pamper me like this. I will lose my habit of self-dependence.' I would grumble.

In reply, you gave me the same answer each time, 'You have to be a woman Al, to know the satisfaction of working for your beloved, to experience the pleasure in making him happy.'

Do you know Jane, how delightful it is to watch you working in the peace of early morning. I feel so fresh, so energetic. I feel so contented even to have you around. You know I like melodious symphonies. When I sit for my breakfast at the table you never forget to play my favourite albums on the tape-recorder. How blissful it is…. The morning freshness, my favourite music, and you around me, attending my small needs!

I am surprised that you know exactly what music I prefer. I cannot really explain why it never occurred to me to play music at breakfast all these years, until you entered my life!

You have an answer to this question also. 'To know this, you have to first know your own heart. You have to learn the language of your heart. I know this because I know your heart better than you.'

Then I lunge at you saying 'Show me your heart. Let me see it carefully so that I can also learn its language.' At this, you kiss me passionately and say, 'Al, I love you so much.'

I complement your kiss not with one but a shower of kisses. But honestly, Jane, there is no lust in this love-making. There is only peace. A sublime peace. Then I can work energetically the entire day. But Jane, every moment I am conscious that you are the fountainhead of my energy. I have dedicated most of my books to you after we started living together. It is a just a token of my love. In fact, it is not possible to convey how much I love you. It is only a way of expressing my love for you.

It is my daily routine to work at least for two hours after returning from office. When we started living together, you would sit beside me. You would read with great interest whatever I wrote. I realised, Jane, that you had not only become one with me, but also with my aspirations.

We would have long discussions. I would share with you new concepts of RET germinating in my mind. I would discuss with you every minute aspect in detail. How attentively you would hear me. I could see how engrossed you were, with your deep brown eyes focused on me and ears at full attention to my talk.

You would often relax in my arms or just spend hours cuddled up on my lap. We would enjoy reading together. This habit has continued till today. We have read so many books and articles together.

Jane, I really admire your capacity to grasp, your ability to understand. You have an inborn talent for writing, editing and management. This is the reason I elevated you from the post of secretary to that of Managing Director. You have, of course, justified my decision by managing the institute very efficiently.

But Jane, I wanted you to go ahead in life. You had not completed your graduation. You had never tried to explore your potential. Your life so far had been like a ship without a sail.

I told you, 'We ourselves have to shape our future. It is in our hands to set it loose or to keep a goal and give it a specific direction. This decision is ours.'

One day, quite casually I mentioned a quote, 'My life is not a wooden plank that floats in the ocean but it is a ship with radar.'

But it appeared that you took this quote very seriously. You later graduated in Bachelor of Arts from the University of Columbia. You went on progressing step by step. It was a prosperous period for both of us. We were ascending in our respective careers with each other's support. I had begun making a mark in RET and you were also climbing up a new step in education every passing year. Finally, you also achieved your goal of getting a Doctorate in Psychology from the University of New York. I was so happy, Jane. You took control of your life and did not allow it to wander aimlessly.

Now you work as a psychologist in our own institute. Jane, I am so proud of your spectacular success. It was my wish that you use your knowledge and proficiency for the cause of women. You had fulfilled all the requirements needed by a professional psychologist. You had already acquired the necessary knowledge for this profession. The most important quality you had was your gentle and warm personality. You could easily win a person's heart. I had observed many women sharing their thoughts with you at the institute.

As usual, you agreed to this proposal. 1975 was declared by the government as International Year of Women. On this occasion, we started Consciousness Raising Groups for women in our institute. This is purely your baby. You have undertaken the entire responsibility of this programme. You plan the course and you also make modifications from time to time.

In this course, you help women regain their self-consciousness. You encourage them to reinvent themselves. You motivate them to revive their potential, which has been suppressed for years by culture, upbringing and social norms. You also ask them to find if their beliefs and values of life were truly formed by themselves, or if they were formed out of social pressures. You train them to abandon their irrational beliefs. Through RET, you help them break the chains of unrealistic restrictions in sex, as well as those imposed by society.

After every course, we have a discussion. You get to witness how women keep burdening themselves day after day, with self-downing thoughts. These thoughts are created by some unpleasant trivial incidents happening in their daily lives. One such common belief was that if one was not able to return home before her husband to receive him, she failed in her duty as a wife. This belief is proved by women who attend the course. As the clock turns six, most of them get fidgety and lose interest in the course. They soon get disturbed by a feeling of guilt that they are getting late.

The intensity of self-damning thoughts, because of social restrictions, is more in women than among men. Consequently, the intensity and the range of irrational beliefs are also larger in women than among men. Therefore, I am aware that your work is more difficult than mine. You also write on problems faced specifically by women. Your manuscript of a forthcoming book is in its final stage of completion. You are an active supporter of the feminist movement. You keenly follow women-centric activities and your knowledge in this subject is worth boasting about. Jane. How busy you have become with such multifarious activities. Your work is really commendable. It further adds to my pride in you.

One of the sensitive issues of our companionship is sexual freedom. We have accepted our individual rights to sexual freedom. We have an unwritten contract between us that we will not question each other about our personal lives, or about our other relationships.

Before you entered my life, I was in relationships with many other women. I continued with some of them even after we began living together. But honestly I no longer found these relationships pleasurable after your entry into my life. In each one of them, I see you Jane. When they touch me, I remember your touch. You have filled my entire existence, Jane. Be it Karyl, Gertrude, Rhoda, or any other woman in my life; the genre of our relationship is far different. You are not only my companion but you are also my darling, my sweetheart, my inspiration. You are the source of my happiness. I find that I have begun to lose interest in other women. But to insist that the same should happen with you is an irrational demand and I am conscious of it.

You are not an introvert like me. You have a large social circle. I know that there are more young men than women in this circle. You are in the prime of your youth, like a flower in full bloom. I am sure you must be arousing your young male friends. It is quite natural to feel an urge to experience different ways of male physicality, after tasting it in the first relationship. I absolutely do not have any objection. In fact, I believe that there is nothing objectionable in it.

But Jane, to be honest, my mind agrees to this thought but not my heart. You have accepted my relationships very easily but I am unable to accept yours with the same ease. Unlike you, for me it is very difficult to accept you unconditionally.

In all my relationships so far, I was never disturbed by the relationships these women had with other men. But you have proved to be an exception. Does deep love suffer from the curse of possessiveness? My heart suffers silently in pain, when you go out specially dressed up, or when you return in a cheerful mood, or when your male friends drop you home. Jane, do you know how agitated I am? I lose sleep with images of you romancing with them dancing before my eyes. I have to make great effort to calm myself. You are only mine, Jane. I cannot share you with anybody else. My soul craves for you. I keep warning myself that my demand that you should belong only to me, is an irrational thought. I have to repeat this warning again and again to keep a rein on my thoughts.

In spite of these efforts, I lose my balance. My mind goes out of control. I go crazy. I assault you like a beast. Like an obsessed person I want to wipe out from your body impressions left behind by your other suitors. Nothing matters at that moment; whether these men are real or imaginary. But you understand me so well… even the emotions behind my animal-like behaviour. Finally, I just collapse in your arms when I am exhausted mentally. But you are capable of understanding even this state. Your compassion is incomparable. When this spate of outburst subsides, you hold me close and keep patting me. You perfectly understand the 'human' in me Jane. I am so grateful to you.

In our relationship, there is no place for any misunderstanding or any ill-feeling. Let any calamity befall us. Let there be any criticism. We can fight back if we are together. Like a phoenix, we can rise again from ashes. We will reach new heights. Such heights from where controversies, criticism, calamities, everything will appear irrelevant, meaningless.'

For a while, I stopped writing. Several thoughts had crowded my mind. It became difficult to express all of them in words. I began speaking in my mind.

Jane, I earnestly wished to give you this letter today. But I realise now that I feel something more about you, which I cannot put into words. Its essence is lost when I try to write. I understood the reason behind this difficulty. Such an innermost feeling, which is unspoken, which is mute, inexpressible in words, which has to be only understood and experienced, cannot be arrested in some lifeless words. Such an attempt will give this feeling only a cosmetic beauty.

What you say is true. The ability to speak from the heart is genuinely your territory! I should not have spent time trespassing here. I have already bought a rose as beautiful and sweet as you. I feel, instead of a letter, I should now present this rose to you, the way you had offered one to me fifteen years ago!

But you know where the fun lies? I, Albert Ellis, who stands undaunted in any situation, am exactly in the same state of mind you were, fifteen years back! Even I have thought at least over a hundred times about the right place to keep the flower. Should it be your bed or the table? I too have reached the bedroom door several times and returned back. But now I am running out of time and inanimate objects like the bed or table do not deserve this honour. So I have decided to present it to you exactly the same way you had presented to me…right into your hand!

I am anxiously waiting for you to finish your work. My hands are quivering with the thought of presenting the rose to you. But I am calm. I am sure you understand my predicament. I am also sure you will understand the intensity of my anxiety, my passion, my longing…the same intensity you had fifteen years ago! Jane, I am eagerly waiting for you to hug me, to kiss me, and to hear from you, 'Al, dearest, I love you so much!'

***

15

The calendar showed 1st August. The date took me ten years back in the time machine. In 1971, on this very day, I had started a unique project, a school for the mental health of children.

Jane and I would discuss various issues. One of them would often recur—the mental health of children. We had already begun writing extensively on this topic. I had also published a book named *How to Prevent Your Child from Becoming a Neurotic Adult*, with the help of Jane and Sandra Moseley.

I had analysed problems that children commonly face and indicated how some irrational beliefs gave rise to these problems. I would offer guidance to parents about the rational beliefs they could encourage their children to inculcate. I would also demonstrate, with examples, that it was necessary even for the parents to change their irrational beliefs.

Most of my clients were adults. Over the years, their irrational beliefs had grown stubborn. Eradication of these beliefs would generally turn out to be a difficult task. It was my opinion that from a young age itself people should be trained in rational thinking before these beliefs became very rigid. I was confident that this would help them lead a better life from childhood itself. One can get education for various professions but there is no scientific education available for maintaining sound mental health. Therefore, there was great necessity for this. I did not have the unrealistic expectation that after such training a child would never face disturbance in his or her life. But I was confident that he or she would be able to face any crisis later with minimum disturbance.

There is a common perception that children do not have enough maturity, and that they largely live in a world of fantasy. It is therefore difficult to teach them to think rationally. But, it is my view that it is easier to change irrational beliefs at a young age than at the adult stage. As we grow, the irrational beliefs nurtured during our childhood gradually become an integral part of our life-philosophy. Hence, it is easier to uproot these beliefs in childhood, before they are allowed to grow stronger. Children can learn rational thinking easily, once you show them how irrational thinking leads to problems in life.

To implement my ideas, some special efforts were needed. There was one more reason behind this thought. Violence among schools kids had become a serious issue. A high-school shooting had recently taken place in Olean. A boy called Anthony Barbaro had shot a school employee and random passers-by, and injured many others in a violent spree. Such incidents among youngsters were growing day by day. Children were now victims of serious psychological problems from a very young age. Anthony later committed suicide in jail as he was unable to recover from his disturbed state of mind.

This incident made me firmer in my decision to educate children in mental health.

This thought haunted me day and night.

'Al, we can provide this education through a school. Why don't you open such a school yourself?' Jane suggested, while we were discussing this incident one day.

It was a very good proposal. I pursued the idea. After some time, I opened a private primary school in the institute. I called it The Living School.

The main aim of this school was to prevent the escalation of psychological problems in children. The courses followed the prevalent American school curriculum, with supplementary education on mental health. I did not feel the necessity of teaching mental health as a separate subject. I was keen on teaching it in an informal way along with other subjects.

Generally, when a school is established with the purpose of promoting a political, religious, social, or communal ideology, the students get brainwashed in that ideology. Therefore, as a policy, I decided to avoid any ideology, even if it was rational. My emphasis was on motivating a child to think independently about what constituted as rational and irrational. Therefore, I ensured that the education in my school was entirely informal in nature.

The school provided education up to the eighth grade. It was open to all and not just children with psychological problems; nor was it restricted to middle-class children or white Americans. In fact, I also announced many scholarships to encourage underprivileged children.

With the help of my associates, I prepared a curriculum on the subject of mental health. The purpose of this curriculum was to make the children aware of the irrational beliefs that give birth to destructive thoughts. The course material selected was aimed at training children in rational principles. It was carefully structured to make a child accept himself along with his faults and shortcomings, while making him more amicable and confident in life.

There were many fairy tales, stories, and skits in this course. Fantasy plays a great role in the thought process of a child. Therefore, we did not omit traditional fairy tales and fantasy stories, but modified them slightly so as to teach rational thinking through them.

Cinderella's story was a very good example of this. In the original tale, when Cinderella is in difficulty, a fairy appears and helps her. This story is no doubt entertaining, but there is a possibility of it impressing some irrational thoughts on the children.

The first of these thoughts is: 'We should always depend on others for help because we are incapable of solving the problem on our own.'

The second thought is: 'Whenever we face a problem, even if we do not make any effort, some mysterious power comes to our rescue.'

The third thought is: 'Our problems vanish naturally, like magic.'

Without changing the outline of the story, we made a revision. In our story, Cinderella faced her problem without taking help from the fairy.

A similar example was that of a story named *The Open Boot*. In this, two siblings travel in a flying boot to a world of fantasy, where all the trees, leaves, flowers, birds and animals in nature are able to speak. In our version of this story, the children were shown to learn to distinguish between useful feelings and disturbing feelings, from their talks with nature.

We included many poems that helped in rational thinking. I was especially fond of the poem 'The Little Engine that Could'. In this poem a little engine climbs a tall mountain humming, 'I think I can', 'I think I can.' This poem gave a message that 'Do not underestimate yourself. Do not think that you are weak.'

The skits in the curriculum demonstrated how our thoughts and our own self-talk affect our emotions and behaviour. We also made colouring books with pictures based on rational principles, and comic books with RETMan as the superhero. It was a pictorial story depicting how the RETMan helps the children in their difficulties.

There were some work-books in this course, which consisted of questionnaires. These asked questions that made the children realise how far their views about themselves, others, and the world were right, or whether they had wrongly presumed that their views were right. There were puzzles based on problems faced by children in day-to-day life. It trained them to study all by themselves and to find which way of solving the puzzle was more useful to them. We had also devised some tests to check whether the children had created new irrational beliefs in place of the old ones, and which of their irrational beliefs had grown stubborn.

After preparing the curriculum, the question that arose before us was: Who should teach this? I formed a committee to make this decision. This committee decided that our school teachers should incorporate the subject of mental health in their regular teaching course. The other subjects were the same as those taught in the regular schools of New York. We had already appointed trained teachers for these subjects. Since these teachers were in touch with students constantly, this was a better option. Also, our main intention was to teach the subject of mental health very informally, and not separately as a special subject. So obviously, school teachers were the ideal choice.

We trained the school teachers in RET. There was a stipulated condition that the teachers should use RET at least on one person independently, before they start actual teaching. I also told them from time to time, what improvements they needed in themselves. I gave demonstrations to show how the children's problems could be handled.

From the very first day of the school, we took the students' parents into confidence. At the time of admission itself, we would provide information about the subject and how we planned to teach the subject. Every month, we held workshops for parents, where attendance was compulsory. In this workshop, we would scrutinise the problems faced by them in maintaining the mental hygiene of the children, and give guidance about the supplementary education they could give them at home. We also provided necessary material and self-help books. Parents were given free admission to lectures and workshops arranged by the institute. We also offered expert guidance on how to tackle their individual problems. The idea behind all this was to create an active and unified effort from teachers and parents together to make this novel project successful.

The real test was when the school actually commenced, and we began experiencing difficulties in the administration every day. In spite of this, we ensured that the children were not affected. It was challenging to guide the children properly during such situations. We had trained the teachers to give lessons in mental health, not by routine stereotypical methods, but in an interesting and creative way. To our satisfaction, the teachers were performing their duty very efficiently.

It so happened one day that a number of students in a particular class obtained very low grades in a subject. As a result, some of these students began crying, some started arguing with the concerned teacher, while others just got irritable. The teacher explained to the students, with the help of pictures, the difference between 'getting poor grades' and considering themselves 'poor students'. He explained that one could say that his performance in the test was poor but it was wrong to label oneself a poor student. He also told them that by such wrong labelling, one gets caught in a web of unhealthy feelings like anger and self-damning, and harms oneself.

Another teacher observed that a girl would always sit alone in class looking sad. On investigation, the teacher found out that her classmates teased and scorned her, calling her ugly and shabby. She would be hurt by their behaviour and keep sulking. The teacher decided to conduct an experiment in her class.

During science class, the teacher brought a bucket of water and a sponge. He asked the children if they knew what happened when one dips a sponge in water. 'It will soak in the water,' the children answered. The teacher explained how, sometimes, humans also behave like a sponge. When we hear what others say about us, we soak those words in, just like a sponge, without checking their veracity—and totally believe what they say.

A sponge is a non-living object. Therefore, it soaks. But we humans have a choice: Whether to soak in the words completely like a sponge, or not. Soaking in is similar to accepting what others say, without examining the truth. This is harmful. He gave the children an important lesson to be remembered throughout their lives—'Don't soak it up.'

Another case was of a girl who would get upset if she was unable to understand a lesson. She would immediately throw tantrums like tearing books or throwing pencils. Her teacher taught her to identify her irrational beliefs and to ask herself questions like: 'How right is it to say that I am incapable of doing a task, even before trying it?' 'Is there any rule that prohibits us from doing anything that is difficult?' 'Is it correct to damn ourselves in totality, if we cannot do a certain work perfectly?' With the help of these questions, she was taught to examine her irrational thoughts and replace them with rational ones.

Further, with the help of the children, the teacher made two masks with faces painted on them, as if they were speaking. One face said, 'This task is very difficult for me. I cannot do this ever in my life.' The emotions expressed by this mask were: Anger, frustration, depression. The other face said, 'This is very difficult.

But even if I am not able to it right now, it is not an impossible task. I will try to make some extra efforts.' The expressions on this face were that of satisfaction and enthusiasm.

The teacher asked her to keep these masks at her desk. She was taught to change her irrational thoughts with the help of the masks whenever she felt depressed.

Once a boy was very disturbed, when he failed in mathematics. During counselling, the teacher showed him that his disturbance was not due to having failed in that subject, but because of some irrational belief in his mind.

This belief essentially was: 'I should not have failed in mathematics. This is very horrible. This proves that I am simply worthless.'

The teacher taught the boy to ask some questions of himself: 'Where is the truth behind my belief that I should never fail in mathematics? Why is it so awful if I fail? How does it prove that I am worthless if I fail only in mathematics?'

The boy was given homework that trained his mind to overcome failure without self-downing thoughts. He was encouraged to appear for other tests in mathematics. This made him realise that failing in an examination may cause some pain, but it is not dreadful. His inability to pass an examination was only a shortcoming. It did not make him totally worthless.

We also devised games to play in class. The children were given a booklet that had pictures of two boys fighting over a ball. The first boy was shown to be snatching the ball from the other, and saying, 'It is my turn. I want the ball.' The space near the picture of the second boy was left blank. The children were asked to imagine themselves in his place and write an answer for him.

After filling the answers, the booklets were redistributed randomly. The children got booklets that had been filled by someone else. They would then realise that each one thought differently and gave a different answer. This made them understand that events do not create our emotions. Our self-talk originates from our beliefs. This game helped in impressing rational thinking on their minds.

We also created a game called Fact Detective. The teacher would write down a difficult situation on the board. Students were asked to make a list of thoughts that would occur to them in that situation. Like a detective, they were told to search for a correct answer, and to find which of their assumptions were not supported by facts. The child who could do this the best was declared a winner.

In our routine life, we easily adopt many ideas without verifying them, and, consequently, invite mental disturbance. We wished to emphasise this fact upon the children through this game.

Children misbehave not only in school but also at playgrounds, during excursions, or visits to museums, or other such places of interest. On such occasions, the teachers would bring to their notice the misconduct and motivate them to improve themselves. Sometimes, a few children would behave rebelliously. They would not cooperate during counselling sessions. We trained the teachers to handle such situations tactfully. It was necessary to make the children aware of the irrational approach behind their behaviour, and how this approach was harmful to them. The teachers were trained to guide children in learning the rational approach.

As a result, the teachers learnt to take control of such situations without getting disturbed. I was achieving my purpose of training children to think rationally through common incidents occurring in their daily lifelives. I was successful to some degree in inculcating in children a rational philosophy of life that was not limited to solving only a specific problem. We observed a noticeable improvement in the children's mental health. This change was more conspicuous in the older children.

A few results were surprising. Some children below six years of age had benefitted considerably. These children were too young to understand the scientific meaning of mental health, but they could easily imbibe the belief that it was advantageous to follow a rational philosophy of life. It was clear from this result that RET is extremely useful to children in the age group between six and twelve. Besides, for this endeavour, we had created a variety of study materials for the school and this, too, was one of its side-benefits.

Soon, The Living School was known for its scientific education in mental health. But we began facing other problems, which grew very difficult to manage. I had not started this school for monetary gains. I was not charging hefty fees. My only aim was improving the mental health of children. I had neither advertised about my school, nor had I sought help from government or private sources. I had founded the school entirely on my own strength.

The salaries of the teachers were paid according to government rules. I was incurring heavy expenditure in teaching, holding workshops, and making study material on the subject. I was charging nominal fees. Under these circumstances, I had great difficulty in meeting the budget of school expenses. After a period of five years, the total accumulated loss was worth around a million dollars.

It was a monumental task to convince parents about the importance of mental health and to encourage them to send their wards to my school. Parents were more fascinated by the facilities of dance, music or sports provided by other schools. I was unsuccessful in drawing a sizeable number of students, and the number started dwindling with every passing year. Finally, it became so financially non-viable, that I had to take the unfortunate and sad decision of closing down the school.

Although it appeared like a failure, there was a flipside to the venture, too. Many senior psychologists acknowledged that The Living School was definitely a novel experiment in education.

Many ex-students would come to meet or write to us to convey how their school education had helped them in life. This can be also considered as a proof of our success!

Two of the teachers wrote books on teaching methods for the subject of mental health in schools. Some schools in the United States were inspired to begin courses in mental health based on these books. As a result, there was consistent demand for the material that had been specially created for this course. Some schools even requested help from us to train their teachers in RET. This was also one of the positive features, if one took an overall view of the venture, ignoring monetary gain or loss.

The memories of The Living School are, therefore, not unwelcome to me. In fact, for the first time, a psychologist had been innovative enough to open a school especially for mental health. This reality was the biggest fruit of the efforts I made for The Living School.

***

16

The phone had been ringing continuously that day. Jane was exhausted answering all the calls. The American Psychological Association had declared that it would honour me for my work as a professional psychologist with a lifetime-achievement award.

'Another award means another flood of calls. Al, I think we should have a separate telephone connection to attend the congratulatory calls. And we should change this shelf too. We need a bigger one to place your awards.' Jane would lovingly grumble while rearranging the awards on the shelf.

Later that night, there was a call from Paul.

'Congratulations, Albert. I was sure you would be free to talk only at night. I have stopped keeping count of the calls I have made to congratulate you.' He was very happy. 'Albert, it is impossible for the world to ignore your work. These honours are proof of your greatness. You are offered these awards without any lobbying. I am so proud that you are my elder brother.' I was really embarrassed to hear Paul praising me so lavishly.

I knew he was speaking his heart. I was overwhelmed by his words. I recollected our childhood when Paul was a rowdy, mischievous boy. These days, he was no longer the stout healthy person of his youth.

'How are you keeping Paul?' I was deeply worried about his disintegrating health.

'Thanks, Albert. I'm okay. Everyone has to face problems of ageing. Albert, I have one last wish! I welcome death any moment, but I do not want to get bedridden. But alas! One can only wish! Nothing is in our control!' His words had a tinge of depression.

I knew the reason. Manny had expired from a cardiac arrest just two months back. Paul had not yet recovered from that shock. I felt sad to hear the usually exuberant Paul talking in such a dispirited tone. I earnestly wanted to have a long chat with him.

'Paul....'

'Come on, Grandpa. Play with me.' Jeff, Paul's grandson, was perhaps pulling him.

Our conversation was interrupted.

'Jeff has come to stay with us for a week. His schedule is very erratic. His day starts at night. But one thing is certain. He makes me forget everything.'

'Grandpa...,' Jeff seemed to be still hanging around Paul.

'Albert, it's not possible to talk when Jeff is around. I'll call you later. Goodnight.' Paul disconnected the call in a hurry.

As I kept the receiver down I remembered Mom. The reality that she was no more in this world became sharper.

Had she been there today, she would have definitely called to congratulate him. I tried to remember the last time she had called.

It was during the famous survey of 1982, taken in order to decide the most influential psychologist of the twentieth century. Around 800 psychologists from the United States and Canada had participated in this survey. From the ten finalists, Carl Rogers, myself and Sigmund Freud were selected in the first, second and third places.

Mom had called me immediately. I was busy in the office.

'Albert, even when you were a kid, I would always say that one day my little Albert is going to become a great person. Do you remember your favourite lullaby?'

'Yes Mom. Perfectly well.' I did remember every note of it.

'Mom, do you still sing?' I was curious.

'No, dear. Nowadays I cannot sing that well. I can't hold my breath for long, as before. But I am happy that I can still enjoy listening to music. I am a good listener now. Thanks to my health. At least I am able to hear your voice on the telephone.'

At that moment the intercom buzzed. It was Michael enquiring why I was late for my lecture. I had broken my discipline of reaching the hall fifteen minutes before. Mom probably overheard this conversation.

'Albert, it's okay. You seem to be busy. We will talk sometime later. Look after yourself. Take care.' She ended the call.

Within a few days of this call, Mom passed away. She had lived a long life of 93 years. Even on her deathbed, she had a serene smile on her face.

Paul, Manny and Mom. Many memories stirred up. How I longed for my family. There was a vacuum in my life without them. This would happen very often, nowadays. Perhaps it was my age that made me so emotional. I closed my eyes.

At such times, Jane's soothing words would ring in my mind. 'I understand your feelings. But Al, you still have so much work to do. I know you can never be happy with just a simple long life. For you, working ceaselessly till the end is most important. I am sure your wish will be fulfilled. You will live a long life, working till the last moment.'

"Jane thanks! Your words are really very inspiring!"

With great effort, I shrugged off my lethargy and once again concentrated on writing. I was co-writing *Optimal Ageing: Get over getting older*, along with Emmett Velten.

I intended to propound that old age is not the problem, but attitude towards old age is. I wanted to discuss beliefs and the myths about old age. For example, one of the myths is that sexual urge diminishes with age. Sexual desire is not age-dependent. It is both physical and psychological in nature. It can be intense even in old age. I wanted to explain this with examples. With the help of RET, I had formulated twenty rules to face old-age problems.

More than forty years had passed since I began my psychotherapy. It had spread its wings in various fields such as sex-therapy, marital-therapy and family-therapy. It was found to be useful in many professions—like teaching, medical care, social work, human resource management, and even in the corporate sector. Today, it has become inevitable to include RET wherever psychotherapy is taught.

My institute, which was founded in New York, had spread worldwide by now. We had affiliates in Canada, Argentina, Germany, France, England, Romania, Italy, Israel, and Australia. In Switzerland, The European Institute for Rational Living was growing very fast. I was touring the world extensively for lectures and conferences.

My work was increasingly being acknowledged by more institutions in the field of psychology and sexology. When a list of research papers from 1957 to 1982 was published, my work was quoted the highest number of times. No sooner this was declared, honours and awards began pouring. I was invited to be on the editorial boards of many psychology journals. I was also given recognition as 'Diplomate' by the American Board of Professional Psychologists. It gave me great satisfaction to see RET making its mark in the entire world.

In a span of forty years, I had made many significant changes in RET. I had introduced many active-directive behavioural techniques, along with cognitive and emotive ones. To highlight this transformation, I changed the name from 'RET' to the more all-inclusive name: Rational–Emotive Behaviour Therapy or REBT in short.

Consequently, I had to change the name of the institute to Institute for Rational–Emotive Behaviour Therapy. But soon, many institutions bearing similar names began mushrooming all over. These institutions were not affiliated to ours in any way, and as a result, there was confusion everywhere. I was again compelled to change the name of the institute to a much longer one—the Albert Ellis Institute for Rational–Emotive Behaviour Therapy. But this proved too cumbersome to use, and once again I changed it to Albert Ellis Institute. Finally, this concluded the chapter of changing names.

The journal *Rational Living* published by the institute also underwent similar changes in name. In the end, it donned the name of '*Journal of Rational–Emotive and Cognitive Behavior Therapy*.

I faced substantial criticism for changing the names of the therapy, the institute, and the journal several times. I would answer this saying,

'I do not want any stagnation in my therapy, which was formulated forty years ago. A therapy can develop only if it is synchronised with change in thoughts and with new research that takes place over time. It is quite natural for this theory, which was postulated forty years ago, to lack in certain aspects, which could also be incomplete in nature. But to refuse to accept this possibility and to oppose change in name will only indicate rigidity of thought. Our thinking should be flexible enough to accept changes with time. Then we can objectively assess the criticism and make suitable changes in the theory.'

With this flexibility, I included many new thoughts in REBT.

I had earlier stated the theory that religion had a detrimental effect on mental well-being. In my essay titled 'The Case against Religion—A Psychologist's View', I had refuted religion. But, at the same time, I did not support a society that follows no code of ethics. On the contrary, I had demonstrated with examples, how irrational it was to link religion with morality. The foundation of religion was based on belief in a divine or supernatural power. For a religious person, god is the most supreme authority in life. Therefore, he treats his own life as secondary. According to me, religion is nothing but masochistic self-sacrifice and dependence. Religion and self-reliance are exactly opposite terms. Religion makes a man emotionally dependent and is harmful for the mental health of a person-this was the conclusion I had drawn at the end of this essay.

But once it was found after a lot of research, that religion does help in preserving good mental health, I revised my earlier view. It was not religious belief that was harmful to mental health, but absolutistic religiosity.

By absolute religiosity, I mean belief that is very rigid, staunch, and inflexible. My conclusion was: The absolutist belief that a particular religion was most superior, or the demand that every person should follow a particular religion, was harmful to mental health.

Not only religion, but an absolutist belief in any ideology is harmful and this applies to atheism too. To believe that one can become emotionally independent only by following atheism is a dogmatic ideology. Once you accept this, you lose the flexibility to think of other views. In that case, even atheism can be blind, staunch and rigid, and hence harmful to mental health.

Thus, my final conclusion was that our beliefs about religion or atheism are not harmful by themselves, but our attitude towards these beliefs can be. If our attitude is stubborn and inflexible, it will definitely affect our mental health adversely. Conversely, if our attitude is rational, it will not cause hindrance in our work.

Personally, I was an atheist, and being thus was never an obstruction in my therapy. In order to prove that REBT can successfully be applied to religious persons as well, I started writing a book titled *Counselling Psychotherapy with Religious Persons: A Rational Emotive Behaviour Approach*, in association with two religious psychologists, Stevan Nielsen and Brad Johnson.

I had also changed myself considerably in these forty years. I had almost stopped worrying. I was convinced that *we* create our own worries, not the external circumstances. I had applied REBT to myself and had accepted myself as a human being.

But in comparison to other emotions, it was in dealing with anger that I still had to make an extra effort. I was still short-tempered and would get instantly furious over any disagreement or injustice. At such times, I would immediately diagnose which of my deeply-rooted beliefs had caused the anger. I found that I demanded that people should behave in a particular way. It was irrational to expect that no one should ever behave with me in an unjust and wrong manner.

I would immediately warn myself that my anger was not created by other people. At the most, they could provoke my anger. But this anger was primarily created by me. I would ask myself whether there was any evidence to support my demand that others should behave according to my wishes. Soon, I would realise that there was no evidence to support my wish.

It was an irrational demand. As a result, I would cool down in a short time.

In most interviews, one question was always asked: 'Dr. Ellis, which events in your life made you so rational?'

I would simply laugh and say, 'That something should happen in life to make you rational is itself irrational. See how deep-rooted your idea is, that to bring about a change in your life, you need an incident to happen. Incidents always keep on happening in one's life. What is more important is how you interpret that incident. Since childhood, I have been carefully analysing all the events in my life and those of the people around me. I have realised that changing wrong attitudes is entirely in our control. I strived hard to change my irrational attitudes. Perhaps this has contributed in making me rational.'

Harris Scott, journalist of the famous magazine *The New Way* had recently visited the institute to interview me. Towards the end of the interview, he said, 'Dr. Ellis, we have heard so much about your passion to work. For the benefit of our readers, please tell us the secret of your zest. How do you work so incessantly?'

I called for the record book from the institute office. I did not want him to believe just my words. I wanted to give him evidence.

I showed him the previous year's record of work done in the institute. In all, I had conducted 3,015 half-hour counselling sessions and 709 one-hour sessions that year; delivered a total of 62 lectures, held five group training programmes every week and imparted nine-hour deep-dive REBT training sessions to 12 fellows in total. Besides this, there was a long list of books, essays, reviews and research papers I had written, which were not recorded in that record-book.

Harris was so shocked that he forgot to ask the next question. I said, 'Probably, your next question is how I manage all this?' He just nodded.

I told him, 'Three factors contribute towards my ceaseless working. The first of these is that I have an inborn tendency to work untiringly. You may say that it is in my genes. Second, I have complete passion for things that interest me. And the third is that I have an extraordinary frustration-tolerance capacity. The last quality, that supersedes the first three, is the habit of working perseveringly. This habit I have consciously inculcated. I firmly believe that to change ourselves is entirely within our control. Also, the freedom to choose a habit is also ours.'

While leaving, Harris said, 'Dr. Ellis, you are literally following the motto on the wall: 'Work. Work. Work. Practice. Practice. Practice.' I had read it when I began the interview, but I learned its true meaning only now, while taking your leave.'

***

The past six months had been very hectic. The entire nation was shattered with the 9/11 incident. The Twin Towers, which were so iconic of New York, were destroyed in a terrorist attack. Around 300 persons had lost their lives. More serious was the condition of those who had survived this attack.

The next day, I held an emergency meeting with all the officials in the institute. We passed a unanimous resolution to provide free counselling services, or Pro-Bono Crisis Counselling Service.

We conducted this on the ground floor of the institute building and there were long queues from the first day itself. Most of them suffered from Post Traumatic Stress Disorder (PTSD), panic attacks, and anxiety disorders. Everyone at the institute was busy day and night, conducting individual and group therapies.

During these six months, the workload had almost doubled. It was very satisfying to see that REBT was proving useful to society. But along with this happiness, there was also a sadness that was eroding my spirits. One after another, all the members from my family had left the world. After Mom and Manny, Janet and Paul too had ended their journey. With my health failing day by day, I could look only at Jane for solace.

Old age was leaving its footprints on every part of my body. Every now and then, new health problems would pose new challenges. Diabetes was a permanent companion. Gradually, all my internal organs were getting affected.

My eyes have been weak since childhood. Despite wearing very thick glasses, I was now unable to bear the stress of reading for a long time. It had become necessary to rest the eyes intermittently while reading. I had consulted several doctors for this problem but it appeared that there was no medical remedy. So I had accepted it and had found a way to make it bearable. I would close my eyes and spend the resting period in contemplation.

Of late, this problem had aggravated. I was unable to read or look consistently at a person for more than fifteen to twenty minutes. A pricking pain would begin, as though fine sand grains had lodged in the eyes. It became necessary to rest the eyes for a longer time.

As I tried to find more ways of resting my eyes, I realised that there were many instances during the day, for which it was not necessary to keep the eyes open. It was not necessary to look at the client during therapy. It was more important to hear. Sometimes, looking at a person can hamper attentive hearing. So, I began closing eyes during the therapy sessions.

I experienced that I was able to better concentrate on speaking when I closed eyes. I could use pauses, exclamations, tone, during the dialogue more effectively. In psychotherapy, the concept of 'listening with the third ear' plays a very important role in understanding the life-philosophy of a person. I made full use of this concept in my therapy sessions. I took care, by every possible means, to ensure that my reading and writing was not curtailed because of weakening eyesight. As a result, I got more time for introspection.

Along with eyesight, my hearing too gradually began showing symptoms of impairment. I noticed this when I crossed seventy. Subsequently, two hearing aids found places of honour on my ears. I had to keep adjusting their positions according to the level and intensity of a client's voice. In spite of this constant adjustment, I had to request the client intermittently to repeat his or her words. This would interrupt the therapy frequently.

I would often get irritated with myself. But I had trained myself to accept every situation as it is, so the situation never became serious. To add to all this, the ENT specialist had already given a warning that my hearing capacity would deteriorate further with age. Therefore, I had to gather all my mental strength to prepare for a more difficult future. Of course, it was only because of REBT that I could manage to derive this strength.

My diabetes had taken hold of my work and food schedule, too. To keep my sugar level normal and to avoid insulin shock, I had to eat small amounts of food twelve times a day. Most food items were prohibited, and many times, I ended up eating peanut butter sandwiches almost day and night.

Several times in a day, I was pricked for blood samples. I could not escape the restrictions a diabetic patient needed to follow. In order to maintain a stable health condition and weight, I had to exercise daily without fail. Regular visits to the ENT specialist, the urologist, orthopaedist, skin specialist, and other medical experts, were necessary. After a while, even my feet and mouth were affected by diabetes. Additionally, visits to the dentist and a general physician were also included in this list of medical experts.

As if all this was not sufficient, my kidneys began making their presence felt. My bladder would get full very fast but urine would pass very slowly. I would take a long time to fully relieve myself. So, I began to urinate in a seated position instead of standing. But I never wasted even this time. I would use it to read something.

I treated all these health problems as new challenges. I had firmly ingrained a rational approach in my mind that this was inevitable in old age. In order to achieve this, I asked myself some questions which checked the rationality of my thoughts: 'What supports my thinking that I should not get sick with age, and if at all I fall sick, that my sickness should be of a mild nature? Am I a special human being or do I possess any divine power?'

I convinced myself that there was no basis to my expectation that I should not have health problems. Such an attitude would have hampered the medical treatment I was given. It could give rise to self-damning thoughts. It was within my power to reject those thoughts. I told myself repeatedly that there was a solution even to a very difficult situation. It was simply necessary to search for it with perseverance.

Without showing any self-pity, I accepted my illnesses and concentrated on the core problem. I started exploring different methods to lessen pain. I began writing about the various experiments I made on myself. I wrote an article on how to overcome sickness with the help of REBT. I had also enlisted a number of psychological techniques to live a happy and creative life, even with poor health.

To add to my health woes, there was some discontent brewing in the institute. Ironically, some of my colleagues who were appointed by me on the Board of Directors started conniving against me. They began a campaign to malign me. Indirectly, they were asking why I hadn't retired yet.

My work was my life. Had I stopped working, I would have been dead long ago. My identity had become one with that of the institute. I had dedicated every moment, every penny of my life to it. I was donating the entire income generated from the sale of my books, cassettes, lectures, workshops, which was to the tune of millions of dollars, to the institute. Although I was now the president, I was drawing only $12,000 annually.

This salary was far lesser than that earned by an average American. It was very difficult to manage the ever increasing expenses in a city like New York, and more so in the Manhattan area. But I had very clear ideas about my lifestyle. I could not afford any luxuries on this salary, but I could definitely meet the expenses required for my basic necessities. I could have easily demanded a fat salary, since it was my own institute; but this would have amounted to a betrayal of my life-philosophy.

Spreading REBT was the sole aim of my life. I was loyal to this aim all throughout my life. I never intended to become a millionaire. I could have easily exploited my position in the institute and created wealth. But such an intention would have distracted me from my goal. Therefore, I had knowingly refused to take extra remuneration. I wished to be remembered for my work and not as a millionaire! I was enjoying only two perquisites: my house on the sixth floor and my medical expenses.

My lowly remuneration was also a cause for discontent amongst the other directors of the institute. It indirectly put a limitation on their salaries. They could not demand a salary higher than the president's. In the past, I had refused to give them a raise many times. My institute was founded to spread REBT, not to become rich. They were, of course, free to resign and to try other avenues of making money.

As a result of my outspokenness, pressure started building around me, asking me to resign. Some miscreants at the institute were exploiting this issue for their own personal gain. But I was definitely not going to succumb to the pressure. The decision of resignation was in my hands.

I firmly believed in the fundamental tenet of REBT that however bad the circumstances were, we can decide how to respond to them. I decided to fight this situation with a balanced mind and viewed the problem objectively. I strictly avoided resorting to groupism or false propaganda. This was never in my nature. I believed in spending my energy on work instead of on such petty issues.

The efficiency I showed even at the age of eighty-eight was a fitting reply to all the criticism against me. Even at this age, I was giving individual therapy to eighty persons and group therapy to forty—in all a hundred and twenty persons every week! Without getting affected or without giving any excuses on health grounds, I was still working with the same enthusiasm.

Dr. Kurnikov, a psychologist from Argentina, had completed a fellowship under me. Afterwards, he wrote me a letter which was quite evocative:

'Dear Dr. Albert Ellis,

........The training I underwent as a fellow under your guidance is the most memorable period of my life. I joined the institute just after 9/11 when there was a great rush of people at the institute for psychotherapy. It was really amazing to see you working ceaselessly without resting even for a moment.

Many a time, persons get addicted to work after working hard for such a long time. But I have observed in you an extraordinary quality: you refuse to become a slave to not only any external situation or individual, but also of your own habits.

Before joining the institute, I had heard many rumours about you. I had heard that you never take leave, that you do not attend any entertainment programmes, you are averse to a good lifestyle, and that you were disinterested in social functions.... I had expected you to be a dry, boring, uninteresting dull old man.

But when I met you, I realised that while the information was right, my speculation of you was wrong. You have forsaken several pleasures of life but still lived life to its fullest. I learned this only in your company. The training I received from you in REBT was training in life-philosophy, not only in psychotherapy.

You have taught us to live spiritedly and zealously. You are a never-ending source of energy, inspiration and positivity for us.

I wish others also benefit from this source and make their life meaningful. I hope the victims of the unfortunate 9/11 incident get strength to recover from their grief and start a new life once again.

Thanking you,

Yours sincerely,

Dr. Kurnikov'

I regard this spontaneous letter to be far more valuable than any of the awards I have received.

***

17

It was six in the morning. I threw the blanket away in a hurry and tried to get up from the bed. But instead, a wave of pain drove through my entire body right up to the brain. I groaned loudly. A nurse instantly came running.

'Sir, please take care. You have to do everything very patiently, very slowly. It has just been two days since you have returned from the hospital. You had an intestinal surgery. It is a very risky operation. You have to be extremely careful. The more you follow the doctor's instructions, the earlier you will feel better.' She gave me an injection and some medicine while talking, and made my bed.

'Thanks, Mrs. Tailor.' I said, immediately collecting myself. 'I will of course obey the doctors. But I have been asked to take rest only physically. I am allowed to talk and I can hear properly. Do you mind if I lie in bed and conduct a lecture without exerting myself?' I was anxious to return to my routine.

Her eyes popped up in astonishment.' Sir, you are not allowed to walk up to the seminar hall.' She reminded me.

'Mrs. Tailor, the question of walking does not arise at all. My students will come to this room and I will deliver my lecture from this room, from my bed. My bedroom will be temporarily a seminar room.'

Amazed at my suggestion, the nurse just looked at me wide-eyed as if speechless! I took her silence as consent and instantly dispatched some instructions.

I had left my students' training half-way when I was at the hospital. As soon as I returned home, I told Debbie that I wished to complete the course. Debbie was undergoing a fellowship in the institute. She also supervised the other trainees.

This lecture on the topic of Anxiety was one of the most memorable lectures of my life. I forgot all my pain in those two hours.

'Situations do not make us weak. Our irrational belief towards situations makes us weak.' Without taking a single pause, I kept speaking. Words poured out naturally. Throughout my life I had refused to kneel down before any hardship. Bad health had turned me into a disabled person. But every drop of my blood bore a rational attitude towards life. It had conquered even this disability, and its concrete evidence was this lecture.

After the lecture, the trainees thanked me and left. I took my medicines and quietly lay down. I was physically exhausted but there was no mental fatigue. In fact, after staying dormant for two months, my brain was re-energized with the lecture.

I got up in excitement forgetting my condition, and immediately screamed in extreme pain. 'Jane... Jane!' I kept on moaning. I did not know if it was due to physical pain or due to Jane's memory.

The night she left had been the darkest night of my life. I had begun to notice, that off late Jane had become subdued. She was no more the lively, vivacious Jane I knew. Many a times I would find her brooding. But I had never imagined that this would finally end in our separation. Jane gave a full stop to our companionship very unexpectedly.

We had been sitting in the living room under the soft light of the chandeliers. But her face was not beaming as it did thirty-seven years back, when we were seated in the candlelight of The Pierre. She looked devastated. There was no glow. May be she had not slept for several nights. Dark rings encircled her otherwise sparkling eyes. She had probably cried a lot.

'Al, for the past few months, not months, you may say years, I have been thinking very seriously about what exactly I want in life. Do I want my independent identity? Or is it you that all I want? Till recently this question did not occur to me because my only priority was you, Al. But gradually I began feeling that I was merely your shadow. I had no existence without you. Am I worthless without you? After a long, agonising analysis of my thoughts, I realised that I was not worthless. I had made myself worthless.

'I have my own identity but it is being overshadowed by your personality. I am never introduced as Dr. Janet Wolf, but always as your companion Ms. Janet. I have developed a habit of depending on you for all my decisions. I feel this dependence is harming my individual identity. It is restricting my growth. It cannot grow under your shadow Al.

'In fact, it is more difficult for me, rather than you, to sever our relationship after thirty-seven long years. REBT is your first priority. But for me, it was only you Al, only you. You were my life. There was no first or second priority in my life. You had occupied my entire living. Your world was my world. But now I have awakened. I need to break this cocoon and set myself free. It is no doubt extremely painful to leave you. But I have to pay this price if I want to establish my identity as Dr. Janet Wolf. I am convinced of my decision.

'It was you Al, who encouraged me to create my own identity. You lit the spark in me. You provoked me to explore myself. Al, you have given me so much. But I want to find my path myself, alone, without any help, without depending on anybody. I want to fly independently. I do not think about the height I may reach. But that will be my own achievement. I can never forget the gratitude I owe you. You have given me the strength to fly. But I have to leave you to experience this independence. I have no option. Al, I was never attracted by your wealth or fame, not even when I decided to live with you. Honestly, even now I do not want anything from you.

'Although I am leaving you, Al, I still love you with the same intensity. I have decided to work as a professional psychologist. I have bought a small place with my savings. We shall meet whenever you find time. Good bye, Al!' Jane was overwhelmed. She placed her new address and telephone number on the side table.

There was anguish on her face. She was unable to speak further. She picked up her bags and left without turning back even once. Perhaps she was scared that her involvement in me might compel her to reverse her decision.

I was aghast, looking at her helplessly. Her every sentence had sliced my heart. A huge turmoil arose in my mind. Jane's entry into my life, our companionship of thirty-seven years, and now this adieu. Was it so easy, so simple to accept? My entire world was being churned in and out. A storm was raging furiously within me.

I did not question her decision at any point. I understood the significance of her decision. It was not an impulsive decision. She was not annoyed or displeased with me, nor had we quarrelled over any issue. It was a firm resolution, made thoughtfully with full awareness. I could never force her to stay with me against her wish. The foundation of our companionship was self-contentment. A companionship with a breach in its foundation was meaningless.

I had no prejudice, no bitterness either. Enmity was of course a forbidden word. She had shown extraordinary courage in living with me. It was impossible to measure her worth in my life. Her contribution to my life could never be affected or lose value because of her decision. I respected her decision. My best wishes would be with her, wherever she went and whatever decision she took.

I also knew that it was not a pleasant decision for her. She must have definitely suffered deeply. She must have felt equally miserable. It was definitely a torturous decision! But I lacked the ability she had shown in gathering strength at this critical moment. On the threshold of ninety, with a diseased body, I was unable to bear this stroke from Jane. Like a wounded bird, I collapsed.

My home on the sixth floor now wore a gloomy look. Barren…
Desolate… Bare walls stared at me from all sides. Totally wrecked,
like an insane man, I moved around the house…lifeless without
Jane. The large staircase that Jane had designed, the upper and
lower levels in the bedroom, the balcony with a French door, the
parquetted floor…every niche and corner reminded me of her. She
was everywhere but nowhere.

My heart bled with her memories. This window… I had
first embraced her passionately at this window! The bathroom
shower… It carried memories of so many romantic moments!
Each piece of art was a witness to our intense love.

Tears trickled down. No more of Jane chirping around the
house following me! No more of her sweet talk! No more of her
touch of love and affection! Everything was over! I had steered my
life through so many storms, but never did I cry so unabashedly.
Today, there was nobody to comfort me, to hug me, to hold me
close to the heart and kiss me! No one to call me 'Al' lovingly
anymore!

Slowly, I realised the big enormous vacuum-my loneliness!
An infinite black hole about to suck me in! I was drawn deep
inside that dark void. I began suffocating, sweating profusely. My
entire body shivered…

After some time I regained self-control. I told myself: No
emotion was capable of overpowering me, without my consent.
I am responsible for my emotions. I can control my emotions,
rather I must control them. Or else I will suffocate to death. I have
to act strong. I have to support myself. No one in this world can
help me. I have to help myself.

With great determination, I took control over my mind. It was not sufficient to just understand or feel the need for self-control. Some definite action was needed to overcome the grief of loneliness. I first figured out the irrational belief that was at the root of my loneliness. It was the belief that I was in dire need of Jane's company; that without Jane I was weak. To eradicate this belief, I made a strict examination of my thoughts about Jane. I classified them into different categories, such as 'exaggerated', 'irrational', 'realistic' and 'rational'. I tried to uproot the irrational thoughts and plant rational ones in their place. I thought of more severe calamities that could befall me and compared them with the existing situation. Every incident has its advantages and disadvantages. I was concentrating only on the disadvantages. There could be some advantages to the present situation also. I searched for them and wrote them down.

Gradually I recovered from the trauma. My daily routine resumed as before. But our bond was very strong. I could not snap it easily. Jane was everywhere! I saw her in every woman I came across. I would keep talking as if she was beside me. I would sit at the dining table, waiting for her to play my favourite music. At night, in bed, I would often turn around to kiss her.

Every piece of furniture reminded me of her. The bed, table, chairs, sofas, every item was associated with Jane. Her memories nibbled at my mind and body every moment. Finally one day, I determined to get out of this state. I realizsed that one day if I do not make any attempt to resurrect myself, I would drown myself in her memories, never to rise again!

I studied my cognitive process in peace, and decided to first strike at my habit of associating everything with Jane. I forced my mind to visualise situations without Jane. I imagined myself as a man who accepted situations smilingly without any grudges, who was busy making the world happy even in a pathetic condition. It was not possible for me to forget Jane totally, but I was successful, to a great extent, in living normally once again.

I had resolved not to let my professional life get affected by my personal problems. I began a study of other theories to make REBT more comprehensive. I began taking interest in Oriental and Eastern philosophies, especially Buddhism, and found some remarkable similarities between REBT and Buddhism. Both theories propagate unconditional acceptance of life. This prompted me to make a comparative study of the two philosophies. Once again, I resumed my work of writing and psychotherapy, sixteen hours a day.

This routine continued till the 31st of May. On that Friday morning, I had an attack of severe stomachache and diarrhoea. I did not pay serious attention to it and spent the day as usual. But there was no sign of the problem subsiding even by Saturday. In addition, I began vomiting. I lost all energy. I intended to finish the fellowship training but I was totally indisposed. I called Debbie.

Debbie was a forty-year-old Australian psychologist, who had formerly undertaken fellowship training at the institute. Debbie saw my condition and called the doctors. But, unfortunately, it was pouring since Friday night and the rains continued to lash the city. People were repeatedly warned to stay indoors.

It became difficult for the doctors to reach me. The telephone lines also failed. I spent the day miserably. Finally, the doctor managed to see me on Sunday. My blood sugar level had increased considerably. He advised Debbie to have me hospitalised immediately.

Debbie quickly arranged for an ambulance and had me admitted in The New York Hospital. After some time, it was observed that my stools had turned dark. Soon I began passing blood. After a number of investigations, CAT scans, and X-rays, it was decided to operate and remove the large intestine as I was running a great risk of fatal damage to the intestine. Surgery was most necessary. I gave my consent for the operation, which was successful.

I knew that, in the meantime, various rumours about my health could spread. I called Debbie into the Intensive Care Unit, two days after the surgery. She interviewed me according to my instructions, and distributed interview amongst my colleagues, friends and well-wishers. With this, I was able to prevent any misinformation about my health being spread.

I had to undergo a series of medical tests even after the operation. Finally, I was discharged on the 23rd of July, almost two months after the operation. But there were severe side-effects to the medicines I had to take in the hospital. I was still not able to get rid of problems in breathing and digestion. My ninetieth birthday arrived soon after. I received greetings from President Bush, former president Bill Clinton, and HH Dalai Lama. This goodwill of my well-wishers was my wealth and my lifetime's achievement.

What did I feel while suffering from such a serious illness? My approach towards my illness was realistic and rational. I was fully aware that this surgery was very critical. I could lose my life any moment. It was a test of my own theory, which I had to pass successfully.

I knew that faith in God, consolation, help and support from others- all this could reduce the intensity of pain and hardship. In fact, all this can give comfort to your mind. But I did not want such intoxication. I wanted to fight the situation rationally. It is not easy to face death without any support. It requires immense courage. I displayed this courage and tided over the danger. But I was conscious of reality. I was aware that I could not be lucky every time.

Death was circling around me. Not only health, other calamities could also attack me any moment. I had prepared myself to face them. In the course of the surgery, I came across many people, doctors and nurses, who enriched my knowledge about life. I wished my life to continue in this manner till my last breath.

Debbie had asked me a question during the interview: 'What will you request your fans and well-wishers to do for you?'

I had replied, 'Those who wish to see me happy may do only one thing. They should live life rationally. I will be glad if they remember that in every difficult situation they are in control of their thoughts. The more the number of people who adopt a rational life-philosophy, the happier I will be.'

***

18

Date?

…24….

Day?

…Tuesday….

Month?

…On the top right side corner? Yes….July!

Year?

Oh no. These letters are too small. Is it 2007? Probably, yes.

The table-calendar is right in front of me but the letters and figures appear blurred. Who kept it here? Debbie or the nurse? Where am I? In the hospital? Or at home? Or in the rehabilitation centre? ….. My eyes have become too heavy. Hmm…I am at home on my bed. My body has become so stiff. As if I am chained to my bed. Even if I try to move an inch, waves of acute pain pass though the entire body. Perhaps one by one, all the organs are taking my leave.

Since last night, I am having great difficulty in speaking. None of my organs, except my brain, are cooperating. But my brain is still active. In fact, my thoughts are running like a caged wild animal set loose. Free! Independent! More energetic than ever! As if my brain has sucked the energy from the other organs. But I will not try to rein in my thoughts. I will not reject them. I have only my thoughts to give me company.

How long have I been bed-ridden? I guess at least a year. To be accurate, since May last year. In fact, my health became more complicated after the intestinal surgery. Gradually, occasional visits to the hospital and rehabilitation centre began getting more frequent. But in spite of these difficulties I tried to keep my routine as normal as before.

Last year, on 29th March, I had conducted a workshop for two hours for some trainees from Belgium, from the hospital bed itself. Perhaps that was the last workshop I held. After that I became critically ill, first with pneumonia and later with a heart-attack. I had no choice but to be bed-ridden. Nevertheless, I consider myself one among those fortunate persons who almost meet death with great pomp and still manage to return.

I can see my awards and honours crowded on the shelf. Honestly, I was never interested in these awards. When your work becomes larger than yourself, you do not need any influence or recommendation for an honour. Awards automatically come searching for you. But the glamour of an award is very short-lived. I was always conscious of this. After a period, the world neither remembers the person nor the award.

Therefore, I value my writing more than the awards. Our work rarely becomes junk when we put it into words. It has the power to carry forward the legacy of your thoughts. Even death cannot halt this process. The worth of a literary work cannot be really measured.

What is my contribution so far? Books—more than 75. Research papers—above 800. Essays—around 400. Audio and video cassettes—more than 200. This is my wealth. To me, it is definitely more valuable than any award!

Benjamin Franklin said: If you do not want to be forgotten as soon as you are dead, either write things worth reading, or do things worth writing about.

How true his words are! I was never scared of death. Whilst dodging it for these 4–5 years, I had given a deep thought to the subject of death. On one occasion, when I had just recovered from some critical illness, a journalist had asked me sarcastically, 'How do you feel about being bedridden after being habituated to working sixteen hours a day without taking any rest?' I had instantly replied, 'That one cannot work if bedridden, is in itself is an irrational thought. Yes, one may be incapable of working physically, but nothing can prohibit him from working mentally.'

I had made this statement very honestly. For a long time I had wished to write a book on theories of personality. Even in this situation, I managed to fulfil this wish with help from Mike Abrams and Lidia Abrams. Even at this moment I am thinking over the A-B-C formula and planning to re-formulate it.

....

... ...But I cannot understand what exactly is happening with me nowadays. There is no continuity in my thoughts. All my memories have awakened and are running helter-skelter.

Thoughts and memories intermingle randomly. A confusing mix-up. No. I have lost my link again. ...I feel so drowsy.... What are these foggy images moving before me?

Bunches of colourful flowers....Thick, green, shaded trails. ...Vast expanses of lawns....Bushes shaped as animals....Where have I seen all this? Familiar yet strange. ...I need to stretch my memory....Yes. I got it. That's the Botanical Garden.

When did I last visit the garden? On the 29th of October. But that was two years ago. Yes. Now it's getting clearer. I had been to the garden when my old trusted colleagues had stabbed me in the back. That day I had stayed there for a long time, silently venting my anguish to myself.

My associates had made the first move. In my absence, they passed a resolution at the board meeting that henceforth the institute shall not allow any medical expenditure for Dr. Ellis. But I remained unshaken. I did not bow down to them. I did not beg. I had never sought any help even when I started the institute, neither from the government nor from private donors!

The institute stood on the foundation of my efforts and my work. I had not prostrated before anybody even in those struggling days. And now, even though I am bedridden and diseased, I will never go around with a begging bowl. I am capable of paying medical bills from my savings. When the savings get over, I will willingly embrace death. I still have that courage.

They tried to malign me with various malicious accusations. But I fought back each of them. Along with me, Debbie was also drawn into this infighting. But she could not bear the mudslinging. She insisted that I should marry her so that she would be treated with dignity by everybody. Then I decided to take a serious step. I married Debbie at the age of ninety-one. She was the only person whom I could trust.

'Ellis has gone crazy.' 'Ellis is insane.' Such were the scandals spread about me. They amused me. I was never sane in the eyes of the world. My entire life was unconventional. Defiant in every action! A case of complete madness! I was glorified as long as this madness was profitable to them. Now that I was old, diseased, physically inactive, they began conspiring to throw me out.

But such madness is rare! This madness is firmly built on a foundation of integrity, tenacity, confidence and sacrifice of all materialistic pleasures. Therefore, it has given me a unique strength to withstand every attack from society.

I have countered innumerable assaults so far. I had been conducting 'Friday Night Workshops' for forty-five years. Since I was holding them single-handedly, this was treated as a personal activity and I was barred from holding them in the institute. In fact, this workshop was the life-force of the institute. It had a noble intention of providing instant psychotherapy to the common man at an affordable cost. Although I handled these workshops alone, I was depositing the entire money generated from these workshops in the institute funds, without retaining a single penny for myself. How could it be treated as my personal activity?

They tried to sabotage this workshop. But I would never let that happen. They could refuse me the institute premises at the most. But nobody could prohibit me from holding the workshop elsewhere. I resumed the workshop in a rented place far away from

Manhattan. Debbie was a great help in making this arrangement. Besides fielding questions, she also acted as an interlocutor to offload my work. We even started teaching the theory of REBT together.

And then came the master-stroke from my enemies! When I was in critical health condition, completely disabled, I was suddenly ousted from my presidentship. There also an attempt to drive me out from my house. Now it became a fight for my existence. It no longer remained an issue about only injustice. It was sheer cowardice! Had they shown the courage to fight my position by an equivalent level of work, I would have perhaps resigned from my post spontaneously.

I had toiled all my life for the institute. Every brick was built on the sweat of my hard work. How could they drive me, the founder of the institute, out in such an insulting manner?

I was totally shattered when I came to know that the mastermind behind this conspiracy was the same person whom I had considered my right hand. It was a cruel shock to know that he, to whom I proudly referred as the heir to my work, my confidant, was the key planner. It was a wound that could never heal.

With a bleeding heart I had reached the Botanical Garden next day. I had bared my heart to this garden many times earlier too. I entered but I was shocked. Nothing seemed familiar. In fifty years, the garden had transformed totally. It was difficult to believe that this was the same Botanical Garden I had known fifty years ago. Glaring bright lights, colourful flower bushes, bushes shaped into animal forms. A complete makeover, but entirely artificial. Decorated, eye-catching, shining, but devoid of natural beauty. Trees cut to different shapes looked attractive, had lost the beauty of a natural flourish. The colourful flowers looked pleasing but the planned colour-scheme did not have the subtle appeal of a naturally grown coloured bush.

I was saddened further. It was this artificiality, this falsehood I had opposed all my life. So far, I saw only people who wore artificial masks, but now even the garden appeared to wear such false masks. I felt like tearing these masks one by one. But I realised that to wear a mask you need a face, a true face. Can something, which had lost its true face, understand my suffering?

I began reminding myself to gather strength one more time. I wanted the world to do no injustice to me. But reality was different. I convinced myself that even without demanding a just behaviour or a change in behaviour, I could still find some way out. I reminded myself of a quote from Epictetus: 'There are certain things which you can control and certain things which you cannot.' To change others was beyond my control but I had the freedom to do one thing—to fight lawfully without degrading myself.

While returning from the garden, I made a decision. I had to fight. I was deprived of my legal rights. But now the battle would be fought in the court of law, not on an individual level. Perhaps this was a longer route to justice, it might test my patience; but this was the only way that was consistent with my life's philosophy. It was the only peaceful way of fighting. I calmed down. I fought my case in court till the end faithfully, with utmost perseverance. Finally, one day, the Supreme Court announced its verdict:

'The resolution passed by the Board of Directors of the institute, vide which Dr. Albert Ellis was dismissed, is based on prejudice and conspiracy. The court orders to treat this resolution as null and void with immediate effect. The court also orders the Board of Directors to reinstate Dr. Ellis to his post as President and give him back the possession of his residence on the sixth floor of the institute building with immediate effect.'

I won the case in court but even today some activities are being carried out against me. I started the institute to spread REBT, but now numerous other psychotherapies have made an entry in the courses conducted by the institute. When the institute began losing its special identity for which I had struggled day and night, I could not stay silent. I had no option but to protest against the institute publicly. As a result, I was served a legal notice whereby I was told that 'Albert Ellis' was a trademark of the institute, hence I could not use this name. But this situation finally compelled me to leave the institute.

It was tormenting to witness my life-goal getting destroyed by others. This phase of my life was the acid-test of REBT. Day by day, circumstances were becoming more and more severe. But showing extraordinary courage I kept on defying these attempts each time.

When I look back in retrospection, I see some things clearly. It is true that my colleagues deceived me but it is equally true that I allowed them to deceive me. I cannot refute this. I must examine my behaviour once again.

For me, the institute was everything. I had become one with the institute. But this attitude was self-damaging. I had become oblivious to reality. The moment I converted my work into an institute, I had lost my personal right over the institute. Had I realised this earlier, I would have retired at a proper stage, without insisting on working till the end.

My behaviour was perhaps ideal. I worked dedicatedly for the institute, without making any compromises. But it was definitely irrational not only to expect but also to demand such ideal behaviour from my colleagues. I failed to realise that they were ordinary human beings and would always behave as humans.

As I count my last days, I am aware that I do not have time to learn from these mistakes but I can accept responsibility for my emotions. Therefore, I have decided to forget all my enmity and anger for my fellow colleagues permanently.... Oh...I feel so peaceful after this decision.

I was never helpless, even today I am not. Through the medium of the internet all my fans, my followers, psychologists, professionals and well-wishers have come to the rescue of REBT and myself. Many websites, fan-clubs, discussion-forums have been created in my honour. There has been a flood of emails, phone-calls and letters. It is really overwhelming to experience such love from people, especially given the background of the dirty politics that is being played within the institute.

Whenever I am requested for a message I say, 'My life is my message. I act as I speak. I dedicated my entire life to REBT and I believed in rationality all my life. How can my message be any different from my life?'

When I am asked about the future of REBT, I tell them, 'Although spreading REBT is my life's goal, 'Albert Ellis' is not synonymous with REBT. REBT is much larger than me, rather larger than any individual. And if this is true, it is better if the growth of this therapy does not depend on me. I have sown the seed, how large the tree grows depends upon well-wishers like you!'

....

... ...Who's that? There's someone here. I can hear some footsteps...

But these footsteps are very familiar. Why do I suddenly feel so energetic?

... ...Oh... I have to make great effort to open my eyes. ...Is it you Jane?

...Jane! I am so happy to see you! How beautiful you look in this soft light!

You know, my mind kept assuring me. I knew you would come to see me.....

....Jane, I want to know about you. I want to thank you.... But my words are stuck! I am so helpless!

I see some music albums in your hands. But Jane, I am unable to listen. You are silent. I know you understand everything. ... Jane, your mere presence has given me so much energy!

... ...

... ...Don't leave Jane! ...I can see your eyes are flooded! You are holding my hand. You are saying something very softly! ...

Jane, I can't hear you but I can still read your lips accurately. I know what you said. You said,'Al, I love you, I love you so much....See, death is loitering around me.... But Jane, you know, right now I want to call death and shout, 'Come. This is the right moment. Take me away!'

But death is so elusive! As usual, it fools me and keeps inching away farther and farther! ...Within my closed eyes I see only some golden light!

... ...

I am feeling drowsy. ...My eyelids have become heavy! ....

...What noise is this? ....

Who's fighting? ...Oh. ...Paul and Janet.....

Please don't fight ... at least for a day! But today I am unable to speak these words! Should I ask Manny to intervene? Why were you always so resentful of each other? What was the grudge that made you, Paul, avoid Janet's funeral? How could a blood relation turn so weak?

Blood relationships or other relationships, are they so fragile? Why do relationships crack so easily? Why do we nurture them? Why do we keep a false hope to see them bloom? Only to realise one day that this bloom was artificial? To find that these relationships never had firm roots? We are all alone in this world. This is the ultimate truth. We have to search for the relationship we have with ourselves. Therefore, I kept on insisting to trust your own self, to train our minds to become independent, to learn to be self-dependent in life to save ourselfves in difficulties!

Paul, we both have changed so much! When we were small, you were a rebel and I always took the conventional path. But when and how did we reverse our directions? As adults, I became a rebel and you trod the customary path. I refused to get stereotyped and followed REBT all my life, and you became a family-man, bound by social inhibitions. You never revealed to the world that you were a Jew. You were scared of racism. Once we begin to feel insecure about something we begin to get scared of everything. What a nice, secure, conventional life you lived! I cared tuppence for any type of security! The word 'security' never existed in my vocabulary! I went ahead breaking the chain of social inhibition at every step.

You and Manny would attend meetings held at the institute, but we always had brief formal talks. I never offered you any special treatment as my brother or friend. But believe me, there were some moments when I earnestly felt like hugging you. Later, after a period, I realised that our paths not only were different, they were just opposites. Paul, childhood is so sweet. There is no set route. No inhibitions. All the highs and lows of life are shared so innocently.

But when we discover our independent ways of life, everything changes. We create our own separate worlds. Definitions of happiness and grief change in this new world. This is inevitable. But yet the bond between two of us was strong. Till your last moment, you would regularly call me every fortnight. Your concern would touch my heart. Your death has snatched away the only connection I had with our family. How sorrowful I was when I heard about your demise. How unfortunate it is to witness the death of one's younger sibling!

... ...

I see a hazy image before my drowsy eyes. Is it you, Dad?

Dad! ....

I saw you last when we met to resolve the matter of our failed business partnership. I took a decision that time to do everything in life alone, on my own strength, even without taking any help from you and Mom. Our relation broke forever after that meeting. You never tried to connect with us later. You left the world at the age of eighty. I had come to know that you were doing good business in insurance in your old age. All of us had totally forgotten you. Why are your memories so effervescent today? All that I had buried is rising up.....

...Dad, do you remember the small-pox epidemic? It was some four to five years after you separated from us. Many citizens had died due to the disease. It was contagious. The sheriff had ordered to move all the patients outside the city.

I was in school that day. Annual exams had come close. Suddenly, you came to school to see me. You told me that Paul had contracted the disease and Mom was preparing to move along with him somewhere outside the city. You talked to me for quite some time that day.

'Albert, you are a clever boy. You will lose one year of your schooling, if you go with your Mom. I want your school progress to remain unaffected.'

You took me to the Empire Hotel in Broadway. You perhaps had some flourishing business that time. You had already reserved a luxury room in that hotel for me. You gave me $50 for a week's expenses and you left. This was an unexpected lottery for me. That whole month I enjoyed my freedom to the fullest. I saw one movie a day, a total of thirty movies in all! I also wrote a few poems and tried my hand at singing them in my own musical compositions!

At that age I did not realise the significance of your action. But your words 'Albert, do well' drenched in affection, whenever you saw me leaving for my examination, are still ringing in my ears. Dad, I still long to hear your voice! But even today I cannot comprehend your aloofness when I was being hospitalised so often in my childhood; or the reason you stopped giving alimony to Mom. How should I link your carefree attitude with the concern you showed towards my education?

Dad, now when death is only a few steps away, I realise that the fact that you cared for us is also true—as true as the fact that you neglected us. It's perfectly human to have such contradictions. When I reflect back I ask myself: Did I attach more significance to your neglect than that to the care you had for us? Was I partial to you in deleting you from my life? Why did I nurse a grudge about you all my life?

See the irony, Dad… To realise your humanness, I had to search for you in the broken pieces of my memory. As I see my reflection in these pieces, I realise that I failed in understanding you fully! Dad, we never had a heart-to-heart talk! There was an invisible barrier between us. Now, today, when I am lying on my deathbed, I want to cross this barrier. But the reality is that you are not there on the other side to welcome me and this reality is tearing me apart…

'The second most influential psychologist of the twentieth century' has failed to understand the humanness of his father!

This feeling will always nag me. But I do not treat this as a failure of the psychologist in me. I consider this incapacity 'my humanness'. Dad, will you please understand the human in me?

… … … … …

I can hear somebody singing.....

....That's Mom! Are you putting me to bed? You would always sing while putting me to bed when I was small! I never forgot your singing Mom! Please sing that lullaby one more time! It had words that went 'One day my baby will grow very big and make me proud'. Do you remember that song? It was your favourite. How soon I would go to sleep after listening to this song in your sweet voice!

Mom, your little baby has grown really big! Are you proud of me today? Or are you dejected because I did not dedicate to you even a single book out of my seventy-five books? But Mom, shall I tell you something? To dedicate a book to somebody is not a small action. In my opinion, it has a much more serious implication.

Some relationships in life do not fit in a conventional mould. These relationships are so complex, so potent, that they cannot be confined within the definition of the word 'relationship'. I have dedicated my books only to such relationships. To dedicate a book to you as a duty, just because you happened to be my mother, was not consistent with my principles. I never believed in such shallowness. Mom, will you be proud that your son defied such hypocrisy and lived a very truthful life?

I do not know what you really feel about me! But I am sure you can never get angry with me for not dedicating any book to you! That was never your nature. You never held any grudge for long. You lived a happy life without nursing resentment against anybody. You faced death with a smile. I want that courage of yours Mom!…Mom, please sing that song for me for the last time. Mom…..

… … … … …

I feel so weak…..

… … … … …

…I cannot breathe. I am getting sucked deep somewhere. I am being pulled towards an unknown void. But the journey is so peaceful. …My mind is totally free of emotions! Calm… Light… Beyond any feeling! … … …

I hear a voice. It seems to be an echo of my thoughts. As death is fast approaching, this voice seems to get louder and louder, as if to make its presence known.

It says, 'Human thoughts have the power to overcome every difficulty. It is this power that makes a human being special.'

Let this voice resound in the whole world! …It has the strength to change humanity!... My life will be fulfilled if it is useful to the world! …This voice should grow louder, stronger every day. This is my last wish!…I earnestly request my well-wishers in this world to fulfill my last wish! That will be the greatest tribute to me and my work!

_____ *** _____ *** _____ *** _____*** _____ ***_____

Appendix

A brief summary of Dr. Albert Ellis' work (1913- 2007)
Awards and Honours received

- 'Humanist of the Year' award by American Humanist Association.
- 'Distinguished Psychologist in Marital and Family Therapy' award by Academy of Psychology.
- 'Distinguished Practitioner' award by , American Association of Sex Educators, Counselors and Therapists.
- 'Distinguished Professional Contributions to Knowledge' award by American Psychological Association.
- 'Professional Development' award by Association for Counseling and Development.
- 'Outstanding Clinical Contributions' award by Association for the Advancement of Behaviour Therapy.
- Ranked as Second-Most Influential Psychotherapist in the survey conducted by American Psychologists and Counselors and honored as Most Influential Psychotherapist in the survey conducted by Canadian Clinical Psychologists.
- 'Townsend Harris Medal 'conferred by Alumni Association of City College of New York for his significant contribution in the field of Psychology.

- 'The Joseph Zubin' award by The American Psychopathological Association.
- 'Medal of Sexology' award by American Academy of Clinical Sexologists.
- Honored as 'Certified Sex Therapist' by American Association of Sex Educators Counselors and Therapists.
- Honored as Fellow of National Academy of Practice in Psychology.
- Awarded 'Certificate of Proficiency' for prominent work done for addicts by American Psychological Association College of Professional Psychology.
- Acknowledged as 'Diplomate in Clinical Psychology' by the American Board of Professional Psychology.
- Acknowledged as 'Diplomate in Clinical Hypnosis' by the American Board of Psychological Hypnosis.
- Acknowledged as 'Diplomate' by the American Board of Medical Psychotherapists.
- Acknowledged as 'Diplomate' by the American Board of Sexology.

Esteemed positions held by Dr. Albert Ellis President
* Albert Ellis Institute
* Division of Consulting Psychology of American Psychological Association
* Society for Scientific study of Sex

Fellow
* American Psychological Association* Society for Scientific Study of Sex * American Association of Marriage and Family Therapists*American Orthopsychiatric

Association*American Sociological Association* American Association of Applied Anthropology* American Association for the Advancement of Science

Consulting and Associate Editor
- Journal of Marriage and The Family
- The Journal of Marital and Family Therapy
- The International Journal of Sexology
- Existential Psychiatry
- The Journal of Individual Psychology
- The Journal of Contemporary Psychotherapy
- Cognitive Therapy and Research
- The Journal of Sex Research
- Voices : The Art and Science of Psychotherapy
- Psychological Reports
- The Journal of Rational-Emotive and Cognitive-Behaviour Therapy
- Journal of Child and Adolescent Psychotherapy
- Psychotherapy in Private Practice
- Journal of Psychology and Human Sexuality
- International Journal of Eclectic and Integrative Psychotherapy

Adjunct Professor of Psychology
- Rutgers University
- United States International University
- Pittsburgh State University , Kansas

Consultant in Clinical Psychology
- New York City Board of Education and To the Veterans Administration

Chief Psychologist
- Albert Ellis Institute
- New Jersey State Diagnostic Centre
- New Jersey Department of Institutions and Agencies

Published Work by Dr. Albert Ellis

- Around 800 Research papers in professional journals
- Around 400 essays on topics related to Psychology, Society and Sex
- More than 75 books written or edited by him

Before his demise, he was writing a book 'Theories of Personality: Critical Perspective' with Mike Abram and Lidia Abram as Co-authors. This was his last book which got published after his death.

List of some selected books written or co-authored or edited by Dr. Albert Ellis:
- Sex without Guilt
- How to live with a 'Neurotic'?
- The Art of Science and Love
- Reason & Emotion in Psychotherapy
- Executive Leadership: A Rational Approach
- Humanistic Psychotherapy: The Rational-Emotive Approach
- A Guide to Personal Happiness
- Rational-Emotive Approaches to the problems of Childhood
- Overcoming Resistance
- Rational-Emotive Therapy with Alcoholics and Substance Abuse

- How to stubbornly refuse to make yourself miserable about anything-yes, anything.
- The Essential Albert Ellis
- A Guide to Rational Living
- The Practice of Rational Emotive Behaviour Therapy
- Stress Counseling: A Rational Emotive Behaviour Therapy Approach
- Rational Emotive Behaviour Therapy: A Therapist Guide
- How to control your anxiety before it controls you
- The Albert Ellis Reader

Brief Profile of the Author

Dr. Anjali Joshi is a practicing counseling psychologist. She holds a Master's degree in Counseling psychology, M.Phil in Geriatric counselling, and Ph.D. in REBT psychotherapy. Presently, she is an Associate Professor in the Human Resources Department of a renowned Management Institute in Mumbai.

She has spent 20 years working in the field of education. She provides honorary services as a 'Consulting Psychologist' to many institutions. Having delivered several lectures and conducted workshops in organisations of repute, she also conducts personal and group counselling programs, employee training programs corporate training programs and weekend workshops on effective self-management.

She was awarded the 'Young Doctoral Fellowship' by the Indian Council of Social Science Research (ICSSR),Ministry of Human Resource Development,New Delhi, for her doctoral work. She is a recipient of several awards such as 'Best Academic Perormance','Best Mentor', 'Outstanding Achievement', 'Best Literature' by Maharashtra Foundation amongst them. She is on the Editorial & Advisory Board of a reputed international journal of Organisational Behaviour. She writes both, fiction & non-fiction and has 4 books & 90 articles and research papers to her credit.

Mrs. Meenal Kelkar: Translator and writer of '**I am Albert Ellis**'

She is a Chemical Engineer by profession and possesses a varied experience in fields ranging from entrepreneurship to consultancy. But apart from her actual profession, she has been an avid reader of Marathi as well as English literature. Marathi is her mother tongue while English was the medium of education since school.

Internet opened new avenues to individuals. It enabled her to explore her writing potential which had got side-lined during her professional career and hence remained dormant. She has been an active blogger on various platforms offered by the new electronic media. Her topics of interest range from health and nutrition to fiction. Although this novel is her first book to be published, she has other forthcoming works lined up.